Fly Fishing the Yellowstone River

Fly Fishing the
YELLOWSTONE
River

An Angler's Guide

Rod Walinchus & Tom Travis

Illustrations by Rod Walinchus
Photographs by Tom Travis and Rod Walinchus

PRUETT

PRUETT PUBLISHING COMPANY
BOULDER, COLORADO

Printed in the United States
10 9 8 7 6 5 4 3 2 1

Library of Congress Cataloging-in-Publication Data

Walinchus, Rod, 1946–
    Fly fishing the Yellowstone River : an angler's guide / Rod
Walinchus and Tom Travis.
        p.   cm.
    Includes index.
    ISBN 0-87108-861-4 (pbk.)
    1. Trout fishing—Yellowstone River. 2. Fly fishing—Yellowstone
River. I. Travis, Tom, 1950–   . II. Title
SH688.U6W35   1995
799.1'1'097863—dc20   95-44417
                                                                CIP

Cover and book design by Jody Chapel, Cover to Cover Design
Illustrations by Rod Walinchus
Photographs by Tom Travis and Rod Walinchus
Cover photograph by Barry Beck and Kathy Beck

Contents

Acknowledgements

We would like to thank the following people for their assistance and support throughout this project: Bob Wiltshire, Montana Department of Fish, Wildlife and Parks; Dan Carty, Yellowstone National Park fisheries biologist; Thurston Dotson, Montana Department of Fish, Wildlife and Parks; Wayne Black, Montana Department of Fish, Wildlife and Parks.

We would also like to thank the folks at the Montana State Library and at the state historical archives for their kind assistance. To all the unnamed fishermen we have talked to and shared part of the river with, we say thank you.

Finally, we would like to acknowledge our wives for their love, support, and endurance throughout this project.

Rod is now an old hand at the book-writing business, this being his second. Therefore, I, Tom, wish to thank Rod for his friendship and help as he led this novice through the drill. I also wish to thank Paul Gates for his moral support and friendship throughout the course of this endeavor. Finally, I wish to thank Jim Pruett, our publisher, for his understanding, belief, and patience while dealing with a greenhorn.

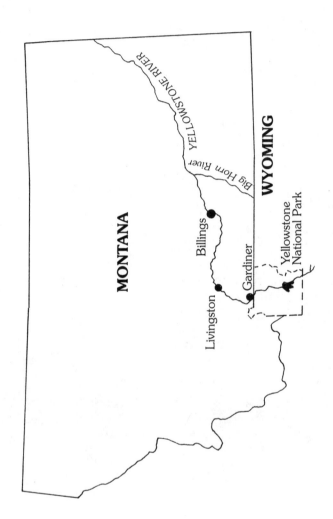

Area Map

Introduction

"I've known rivers: I've known rivers ancient as the world and older than the flow of human blood in human veins . . . " So wrote Langston Hughes in *The Negro Speaks of Rivers* (1926). The eternal coursing of water from headwaters to sea pulses with life and life-giving qualities and exists because of a grander scheme of things than mere mortals can comprehend. Ancient civilizations have personified them, paid homage to them, and used their water to sustain life. Modern cultures prey on them: the industrialist uses them without concern for their purity; the engineer alters them to suit human needs; cities take water from them and put back refuse; irrigators drain them; and we all take from them. Rivers have served mankind since first was mankind. It's in our nature to use whatever resource is vital to our survival. But our definition of survival has changed with the passing of generations, and so has our use of rivers. We no longer value them for the spiritual qualities or the food they offered or the transportation they provided. We look to them now for the water they carry: for drinking, power, and to support our agricultural and industrial needs. Rivers have become servants of man, a cruel master, and have suffered because of him. Yet some continue to flow despite man's intrusion, alterations, and abuse, and some even remain close to their natural state—or at least sections of them do. The Yellowstone River is one. Sure, it has had its share of abuses and threats and will, no doubt, continue to be threatened. But we as sportsmen and conservationists are taking the necessary steps to insure its survival, and in doing so insure ours.

1

The Yellowstone River is still the longest free-flowing undammed waterway in the lower forty-eight states. Its long, 678-mile, course begins in the high country of a pristine wilderness in the northwestern mountains of Wyoming and flows first north then east, to meet the Missouri near Williston, North Dakota. Most of this magnificent river flows through the state of Montana except the first 112 miles, which are part of Wyoming, and about 15 miles belonging to North Dakota. About 110 miles flow through Yellowstone National Park and the protection it offers. It would be hard to imagine what would have become of this river without the park and the conservation regulations that govern it.

There are three general river sections, each with different characteristics. The first is the upper river from the headwaters to about the Big Timber area. Here the river is a mountainous brawling body of water and an ideal cold-water fishery. The second section is a transitional section where changes appear in the landscape, water character, and fish species. The last is a prairie river that has become a warm-water fishery as it flows to the Missouri.

The Yellowstone River has had many names. The Crow Indians called it the Elk River, for obvious reasons. The Mandan and Hidatsa Indians called it *Mee, Ah-zhah,* "Stone Creek," and *Mi-tsi-a-da-z,* "Rock Yellow River." Later, the very early French explorers named it *Roche Jaune,* "Yellow Rock," as early as 1795, and eventually it became known as the Yellowstone River. The mighty river is floatable throughout most of its length, with the exception of the park waters. It does have some Class III white-water sections, other rapids, and quite a few diversion dams, especially in the lower reaches, that pose a threat to floaters. The average water flows at 3,717 cubic feet per second (cfs) throughout the year. Of course, the flows differ from year to year and season to season. The highest recorded flow was in 1974, when it reached 36,300 cfs, and the lowest flow occurred in 1989, when it dropped to 540 cfs. Average temperatures for the river on a seasonal basis are thirty-four degrees Fahrenheit in January, fifty degrees in April, sixty-nine degrees in July, and forty-eight degrees during October.

This river is for the most part, and at least in the scope of this book, a cold-water fishery, with its trout the most important species.

As such, many parts of the river are protected by special regulations that differ from the general state fishing regulations. Because Yellowstone National Park has its own set of protective regulations that are different from the state of Montana, before fishing any section of the river it is wise to become familiar with the general and specific regulations.

Reaching the river is generally not a problem along the Yellowstone. Different agencies have designated access sites that are available to the general public, and some of them are excellent facilities. Unlike many other western states, the state of Montana—and thus its citizens—owns the river bottoms. An angler may have legal access to the high-water mark along the Yellowstone as long as he enters the river legitimately—one may not cross private land without the permission of the landowner to reach the river. This rule seems to work well, because an angler that gets on the river at an official access point may work his way up or down river to fish without worrying about trespassing as long as he stays on the shoreline. A floating angler can effectively anchor his boat so he may be able to fish particular water and not fret about breaking the law. Some of the local landowners with holdings abutting a public access may have some problems with inconsiderate fishermen, but the landowners usually aren't a major problem. With the many access points along the river there is very little need to trespass.

As we work our way down the Yellowstone, we will encounter a variety of fish species that become more diverse the farther we go. Our focus in this book is on different trout species, but some of the other species are worth noting. The upper river has cutthroat, rainbow, brown, a rare brook trout, whitefish, and a variety of baitfish. The Yellowstone cutthroat and the mountain whitefish are the only gamefish native to Montana; the other species have been introduced over the years. The middle section of river has all the above-listed fish with the addition of burbot, goldeye, and additional bait- and nongame-fish, while the lower section holds walleye, sauger, catfish, pike, sturgeon, paddlefish, and others. The brown trout is found in nearly all sections of the river with the exception of the very upper portion in the park.

Heraclitus wrote, "You could not step twice into the same river; for other waters are ever flowing on to you." And in the late 1100s, Kamo no Chomei penned, "The flow of the river is ceaseless and its waters are never the same. The bubbles that float in the pools now vanishing, now forming, are not of long duration." The Yellowstone is such a river, and more so than many—it is an ever-changing river, one of constant transformation. It changes from year to year, season to season, day to day, and even hour to hour. It is never the same river and the water is never the same. This is one of the longest free-flowing rivers in the world and by its very nature a river in a constant state of change. Of course the water is always moving, flowing downstream, so there is always new water in any given spot and thus the poetic inferences, but that is not all that is variable. The other variables are what make this river so tricky to fish and so difficult for many to master, if mastery can ever be achieved.

The water temperatures fluctuate over the course of each year, each season and each day. These fluctuations can trigger feeding responses in the trout or they can turn off the drive to feed. Early in the year, when temperatures are cold, any warming trend might turn the fish on, and an angler could have a good day. Yet the next day the temperature may not rise enough to trigger the fish, and the angler will walk away from the river wondering what he did wrong. The same goes for water levels: they not only vary from season to season but often from day to day. Usually one can count on the river rising slightly or dropping slightly over the course of a day's fishing.

One of the variables that has a really noticeable effect on the fishing is the turbidity of the river. Very often a storm will roil the water far upstream of where we might want to fish, but the water is still clear in our area; however, we have one of those days where the fish just won't cooperate and the fishing is poor. They seem to sense a slug of mud or turbidity coming and go off their feed. The same happens as the water is clearing—it may be clear enough for us to fish, but the trout seem to need a transitional period to reacclimate themselves to the clear water before they begin feeding heavily again.

The many variables that make the river "never the same" make it difficult for an occasionally visiting angler to get an accurate read of the river. A wild river with wild trout in a constant state of change may explain those days when nothing seems to be happening and you can't seem to buy a trout. The next day may have conditions that appear to be the same or similar, yet every fish in the river has a death wish. We see it so often when we get to fish, and especially on guided trips—one day is great and the next is so-so. It is difficult to understand all these variables, and it takes a great deal of time on the river to get a sense of what the river will offer up on any given day.

Another of the variables that often is ignored or not noticed is insect activity. Hatches come and go on this large river without a great many anglers aware of their existence. We constantly hear that the way to fish a river as large as the Yellowstone is with big, general, attractor-style flies, either dry or wet. Yet much of what occurs in the form of insect activity is small and at times downright tiny. Yes, the fish do feed on the small stuff, and very often at the expense of an angler's large offering. There is a wide variety of insects that call the Yellowstone home, and at certain times of the season a wide variety of insects hatching. In much of the river it can be extremely difficult to see riseforms of feeding trout unless they are of the splashy or show-off type. A trout delicately sipping insects off the surface of broken water is tough to see even if you're looking for it. So much of the feeding activity can go unnoticed, unless you know it *should* be happening.

Some of the hatches are relatively localized, so an angler floating and covering water may fish his way past a hatch before he realizes there is one. Insects get forced to limited areas of the river by current and wind. If an angler isn't in one of those areas, the hatch could also go unnoticed. Combine these two situations and one can see how easy it is to miss a good fishing opportunity. Add to this mixture a "masking hatch," the kind when two or more insects of different sizes hatch at the same time in the same area. We, as anglers, may notice the larger insect, but the trout may key on the smaller bugs. Then stir in a complex hatch where many different insects are hatching at the same time, and to this recipe throw in a dash of individual preference by the fish. To make it even more interesting, add the fact that some of the fish may be keyed in to a specific stage of a specific hatch of a specific insect. Once you get all that worked out in your mind, add in that the temperature of the river might change or the water levels fluctuate and the weather's about to change. It's a wonder any of us can actually catch a trout.

Of course, while all this is going on, a fisherman can float down the river totally oblivious to it all and cast a #12 Royal Trude and still catch a few fish. This happens so often that many fishermen swear it's the only way to fish the river; unfortunately, so do some of the guides. It's one thing to go out and *catch* a few trout, it's another to *fish* for them. The angler who wants to maximize his time on the water and actually take an active part in what is happening should observe what's occurring around him, scope out the action, and make informed decisions about how to fish and what to fish with. This is a sport where a little knowledge goes a long way—our intent in this book is to at least make you aware of what is happening on the river in a given season so that you can make informed decisions about the what, how, where, and why of fishing here. No two people can completely relate the particulars of a river as large and as complex as the Yellowstone, and we don't pretend to be the last word—many of you will no doubt be more familiar with certain stretches or certain hatches than we are, but that is not the point. What we intend within these pages is to offer information about most of the river so that you, the angler, may discover aspects that you might not be familiar with—be that a specific insect, a specific section of water, or a different technique—in hopes that it may improve your day on the water.

The Yellowstone River is a special fishery, as special as any in the world, and for this reason alone should be afforded all the respect and protection our society can muster. Anglers from all over the world come here to fish its waters, so rich in western angling history. Men like Joe Brooks and Dan Bailey, among others of similar note, have waded the same waters as you and I and fished for the same trout. These are men who actively sought to protect this fishery, and much of what we have today is, in part, due to their efforts. Joe

Brooks left a great deal of money in his will to the local chapter of Trout Unlimited, to be used for the continuing protection of the river he so loved. He, and men like him, are responsible for the days we are fortunate to spend enjoying the fruits this river has to offer.

They lived through times when the fishing wasn't what it is today. They have witnessed arsenic poisoning, loss of insect species, threats in the form of dams, and other abuses of the past. They have also witnessed the good of the river and had the foresight to fight for it and change the attitudes that would do it harm. This was not always so in the past. Take the Earl of Dunraven, for whom Dunraven Pass in the park was named, as an example. In 1874 he wrote that fishing the Yellowstone was the finest sport he ever encountered. He considered himself a conservationist who criticized market hunters and fishers, but he advocated the preservation of wild areas for the unregulated pleasures of "true" sportsmen. This is the same man who purchased the land that now comprises Rocky Mountain National Park in Colorado, worked it until all the game and fish were depleted, then sold it. Then take in the account of General William Strong, who was also a "conservationist" and sportsman of his time. He and his party, over a period of thirteen days caught and killed 3,489 trout ranging in size from two and a half to four pounds and wrote that " . . . all had extraordinary luck, so that the pile of trout brought into camp was enormous." At that rate it didn't take long for the numbers of trout in the river to decline. These are but a few of the typical conservationists' attitudes of the past.

We can be thankful that attitudes are changing—they have come a very long way since those bygone days, and it has taken a long time to reach where we stand today. We now have state agencies that manage our rivers and do a good job, even though they are bureaucracies and have all the problems associated with bureaucratic administration. We also have organizations that take responsibility as protectors of our rivers. We have individual conservationists, unlike those of the past, who look over the shoulders of the state and local agencies. More important, we have individuals who take a personal interest in, and act as stewards of, our waterways. All combine in an effort to insure we retain what we have, and maybe even improve upon what exists. Yet the Yellowstone and other rivers are continually under siege from those who would take from the resource, our heritage, and our freedom to enjoy what belongs to us all.

It is our responsibility, as fishermen, to take an active role, no matter how small, in conserving a resource as valuable as the Yellowstone River. Aldo Leopold wrote in the foreword to *A Sand County Almanac* (1949), "We abuse land because we regard it as a commodity belonging to us. When we see land as a community to which we belong, we may begin to use it with love and respect." As fishermen, we all belong to the community of the rivers. We are all one and should love, respect, and protect that community with the fervor and ferocity with which we would protect our homes and families.

1

The History of the River as a Fishery

Two major events have determined how the Yellowstone River became the fishery it is today. The first is a natural phenomenon, the colonization of cutthroat trout east of the Continental Divide in the Yellowstone River headwaters. The second is the result of human intervention, through the introduction of non-native fish and the transportation of native fish. These events shaped and are still forming the fishery we have today.

Trout, specifically the cutthroat trout, are relatively recent residents of the Yellowstone River, recent in terms of geological time. Between six thousand and seven thousand years ago the cutthroat, a fish found only on the Pacific or western side of the Continental Divide, found its way to the Snake River south of Yellowstone Park via retreating glaciers. Eventually it worked its way to the headwaters of many of the streams and also into an area known as Two Ocean Pass and into North Two Ocean Creek. Here the creek breaks into two distinct branches—Atlantic Creek and Pacific Creek—each named for the ocean toward which it flows. Atlantic Creek flows east of the Continental Divide toward the Atlantic Ocean, and Pacific Creek flows west of the Divide toward the Pacific Ocean. Here the cutthroat was able to cross the Divide and work its way down to the Yellowstone River, where it is now a native species—the Yellowstone cutthroat. Over the years it worked its way downstream to as far as where the Tongue River meets the Yellowstone in eastern Montana, some five hundred or so miles from the headwaters section.

Historically, the Yellowstone cutthroat (*Oncorhynchus clarki bouvieri,* formerly called *Salmo clarki bouvieri*) was the only trout species in the river. This changed with the arrival of white settlers to the area. Although Native Americans inhabited the land long before the first white man appeared, it wasn't until the white man came that the complexion of the fish populations began to change. As white settlers began populating the area, they brought specific preferences as to what kinds of fish they liked to catch with them. People migrating from the East were familiar with brook and brown trout, so they naturally sought to bring these fish into the area. People coming from the West were familiar with rainbow trout, and they brought specimens to the Yellowstone.

Railroads were the single most important factor in bringing non-native trout species to the West, because they were the most effective means of transporting fish. Treks by horse and wagon trains were long, arduous, and not very practical for transporting fish. The railroads made it feasible to take fish over long distances.

No one in that day and age thought about the environmental impacts of introducing non-native fish species. Even the agencies that were responsible for planting fish in the river knew very little about what they were actually doing. It wasn't until recently that the Yellowstone fishery was studied and common-sense scientific management became a reality. Although the river is still not without problems and threats, the custodians of this resource are doing whatever they can to protect it for the future.

White men came to the Yellowstone River as early as 1742, when Pierre and Louis Verendyre were en route to the Pacific. In 1805, Francois Antoine Larocque traveled around the Yellowstone in what is now the Billings, Montana, area. By this time the Shoshone tribe was displaced by the Crow Nation, and Larocque was sent by the Northwest Fur Company into the Yellowstone Basin to meet with the Indians and teach them how to trap and care for the pelts. One year later, in 1806, the Lewis and Clark expeditions explored the river by land and water. They were the first expedition to make a record of Montana's fishes. James Stuart explored the east-west axis of the upper Yellowstone area in 1863. Interestingly, in his travels he stayed near what is now Big Timber, Montana, and he apparently fished, for his records show that "fishing, however, was still good; anyone who would take grasshoppers for bait and go fishing could catch an abundance of whitefish . . ." It was assumed that the river was devoid of trout at that time. Today one can use a grasshopper imitation and still catch whitefish at this location (remember, if this does happen, it's history repeating itself).

In 1859, Captain Raynolds covered the upper Yellowstone River area from the mouth of the Big Horn overland in a southerly direction. In 1860, Lieutenant Maynadier, a member of the Raynolds party, reentered the area from the south at the Clark's Fork River and traveled westward to meet with Raynolds at a rendezvous at the Three Forks. He then returned to the Yellowstone River to retrace Clark's route. The upper Yellowstone basin is the site of the first U.S. national park, created by an act of Congress in 1872. This was a result of an 1871 exploration by Dr. Ferdinand V. Hayden, a geologist. He had accompanied Captain Raynold's expedition in 1860, which failed to reach the Yellowstone Plateau. The Washburne-Doane Expedition of 1870 up the Yellowstone River was given official credit for the discovery of what is now Yellowstone National Park.

Around this time, gold was discovered in the Emigrant Gulch area, bringing with it the masses seeking their fortunes. Skirmishes between these settlers and the Natives of the area were common. Soon after the Battle of the Little Big Horn, most of the Indian tribes were relocated, and more white men entered the area. By now the southern herd of buffalo, once over four million head, were gone, and the northern herd, about one and a half million, was to be destroyed by the guns of the white hide hunters. With the buffalo gone, the Indians were faced with starvation. This event created a cattle market as the federal government contracted with cattle ranchers to supply beef to the Indians. Cattle numbers increased, helped along by several unusually rainy years. Drought years followed, starting in 1884, and by the spring of 1887 the cattle industry was nearly wiped out. In the years that followed, year-round use of the range was replaced with farm-based livestock operations. The growing and harvesting of forage for winter feed opened the way for the livestock industry to develop into a stable and lasting economy, as it is today. This factor resulted in many small ranches springing up throughout the Yellowstone Basin, many of which today remain in the same families who started them.

With farm-based livestock came the need to irrigate, and the resulting eventual decline of cutthroat trout. As farmers, miners, and ranchers settled along the river, population centers soon followed in the form of towns. Billings, Columbus, Huntley, Big Timber, Livingston, and Gardiner sprang up along the river in Montana. Although the river was the first major route of travel, especially along the Yellowstone's east-west axis, that usage was short-lived. Captain Raynolds wrote in 1860, " . . . the broad valley of the Yellowstone affords peculiar facilities for a railroad, and it is, moreover, the most direct route to the important region about Three Forks." The early 1880s saw the coming of the railroad as a means of transporting people and goods to the settlements. Livingston, founded in 1881, became one of the more important cities because of the rich gold diggings at Emigrant, and it grew with the coming of the railroad in 1883. Here the river turns south toward Yellowstone National Park and the town of Gardiner, and a railroad once followed its course to the original entrance to the park.

Not all the land near the river was suitable for farming, but dryland farming had developed with techniques of irrigation. As World War I occurred, high prices forced many large landowners to break up their holdings into smaller units. The Great Depression of the 1930s and several severe drought years created havoc among farmers as they sought ways of economically getting water to their crops and livestock. They began diverting water out of the tributaries of the Yellowstone, making it difficult for the native cutthroat to maintain its populations. The spawning streams were dewatered, and the cutthroat populations fell. As mining activities, agriculture, and a growing timber industry flourished, the river became threatened, and we are, to this day, still facing these threats.

As people moved into the area, an interest in fish was immediately apparent, first as a means of supplementing diet and eventually

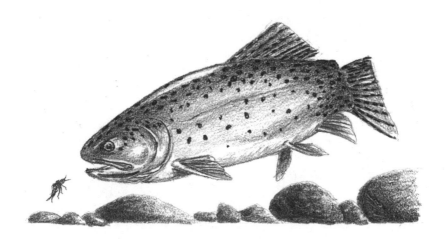

as recreation. With these people came an inherent need to mess with Mother Nature; of course, no one had the foresight or knowledge to understand that that was what they were doing. The Yellowstone River, to them, was a resource to be used, and in many cases abused. These settlers were of diverse cultural and ethnic backgrounds, and they all brought their preferences and prejudices with them. To them, it immediately became apparent that some of the waters could host other species of fish than the native cutthroat and whitefish, species that they were more familiar with and believed should be placed in the watershed. So, stocking programs, both official and nonofficial, were soon implemented.

Yellowstone National Park received its first transplant in 1881, when Col. P. W. Norris and his men, after catching a number of spawning cutthroats for their tables, decided to transplant some of them into areas that " . . . are destitute of them." This philosophy was apparent in words written in 1891 by Capt. F. A. Boutelle, the park superintendent: "In passing through the Park I noticed with surprise the barrenness of most of the water in the Park. . . . there are hundreds of miles of fine streams as any in existence without a fish of any kind . . . I hope . . . to see all these waters so stocked that the pleasure-seeker in the Park can enjoy fine fishing within a few rods of any hotel or camp." With this statement came official stocking programs of non-native fish. The expansion of these fishes within the park was a result of man's assistance, even though, in many cases, this assistance was not officially sanctioned, resulting in fish populations of unknown origin. There was a practice of supplying fry to certain park concessionaires and outfitters, who occasionally planted other than officially sanctioned waters with various species of fish. Even today there may yet be some nonofficial assistance by individuals, as the recent discovery of lake trout in Yellowstone Lake would lead one to believe.

These fish introductions were viewed by anglers as fortuitous because it gave them more fish and different species to fish for. For the people who are officially charged with managing, preserving, and restoring the native ecosystems in the park, these introductions were not so fortuitous. The non-native species have displaced, in many cases, the native species, and in all cases these introductions altered the native ecosystems. Five non-native fish species have been introduced into the park over the years and have survived to this day: brown trout, rainbow trout, brook trout, lake trout, and lake chub (the lake chub was one of those nonofficial plants). There are twelve species native to the park, and they are: Montana grayling, three or more subspecies of cutthroat trout, mountain whitefish, three species of sucker, four species of minnow, and the mottled sculpin. One result of introductions is the cutbow, a hybrid of matings between the cutthroat and rainbow trouts. This species is half-native and half-non-native.

Fortunately, some introductions were unsuccessful, as were early attempts at establishing Atlantic salmon, rainbow trout, and mountain whitefish in Yellowstone Lake. There were even attempts at establishing black bass populations in other sections of the park. One of the oddities of early stocking in the park was the possibility of "contamination establishment," or another species being mixed in with the species intended for planting. This may explain how brown trout became a self-sustaining population as early as 1919 in Duck Lake. Earlier, in 1908, Atlantic salmon were planted there, and it is possible that the fry were actually brown trout or were at least contaminated with brown trout. Some other odd species have been found in the park that may be a result of contamination: fish such as the yellow perch, for example.

The first fishes from outside the park were planted in 1889, when brook trout were introduced to assorted waters. The following year brought the Loch Leven brown trout and the lake trout to Lewis and Shoshone Lakes—these proved to be highly successful plants, and their populations survive to this day. Later, rainbow and brown trout were planted in the lower sections of the Yellowstone River.

The stocking programs in the park have undergone many changes in philosophy over the years in evolving to the current attempt to preserve and restore native ecosystems. The 1920s and 1930s saw annual plantings for put, grow, and take purposes, especially along the most heavily fished water. At the same time, in 1936, a formal policy was established that significantly altered the fishery's activities. The policy stated that non-natives shall not be stocked into waters containing native fish; propagation of native species for stocking shall not be encouraged; distribution of non-natives shall not be expanded; no artificial lake or stream improvements shall be made; introduction of non-native aquatic food organisms shall not be made; and selected water shall be left barren of fish. This policy was a significant change in philosophy, but it did not change the practice of put, grow, and take maintenance stockings along many roadside and accessible streams and rivers. There were also many unauthorized and "secret" plantings in selected water, and the early 1940s saw the stocking of catchable-size trout for put-and-take fishing.

Nineteen fifty-six saw another significant change in the philosophies of park and fisheries management as they looked to natural reproduction of wild populations of fish and a reduction in creel limits. The last of the put, grow, and take and put-and-take plantings and new introductions into fishless water took place in 1955. After that time, any plantings of fish were limited to the restoration of native species and for the preservation of distinctive subspecies.

Although the hatchery at Yellowstone Lake was the source of many transplants around the park, there were other hatcheries that supplied fish over the years. One of the earliest was the federal hatchery at Bozeman, but the Emigrant hatchery also supplied fish to the park, as the Big Timber hatchery probably did. These hatcheries are an important element to the planting of non-native species outside the park. Although inside the park, for the most part, stocking programs were regulated and officially sanctioned, things aren't so clear-cut and official outside the park. Much of the stocking came from calls for fish by private landowners, clubs, dude ranches, and similar groups. Apparently, anyone who felt they needed fish in their section of river or tributary received fish.

The Emigrant hatchery was a primary source of fish for the upper river, and the Big Timber hatchery supplied fish to the lower river. The Bozeman hatchery also added fish to the river, and there was a satellite hatchery in Red Lodge, but its primary function was to supply the high-mountain lakes and streams. These hatcheries did supply whoever wanted fish with non-native species. Prior to the 1940s, hatcheries were management tools and had the authority to stock the river. Before the Montana Department of Fish, Wildlife and Parks became the sole managing agent for the rivers, the local game warden was charged, as part of his job, to make sure that stocking took place wherever he deemed necessary. He was allowed to do this without necessarily getting authorization from the state; it was simply part of what he did on a daily basis as part of his job.

The department of fish and wildlife had a railroad car they called "the fishcar," which transported cans of fish for stocking. Since the railroad followed the river, in most places it wasn't a big deal to stop and dump fish. In fact, this was a common occurrence in the 1930s and 1940s. In old hatchery logbooks it is apparent that the Park County Rod and Gun Club wielded a fair amount of clout, because a good number of the calls for stocking came from this group. Local clubs were relatively powerful in the early half of this century and responsible for a good deal of what is now in the river. Dude ranches and private ranches were also deemed powerful, as some old records indicate: in 1926, 13,200 four-inch cutthroats were stocked at Armstrong Spring Creek. At the same time, cutthroats were stocked in the main river because the Park County Rod and Gun Club requested them, and Pine Creek was also stocked with cutthroats because of a call from the Ox Yoke and OTO dude ranches. In 1933, Armstrong's Slough was stocked with 10,000 brook trout, and later in the same year 60,500 two-inch steelhead trout. As we go through the years we find calls for steelhead, rainbows, Loch Leven brown trout, and brook trout for the tributary streams and the main river by all kinds of groups. There was even a call to stock Dailey Lake with 248,000 sockeye salmon. It would be a fair statement to say that millions of fish, or even hundreds of millions, have been planted into the Yellowstone River drainage outside the park.

This hodgepodge philosophy of planting fish came to an end in the late 1960s, when stocking of the main stem of the Yellowstone ceased and wild populations of trout were allowed to propagate. Interestingly, these trout soon began to increase in numbers a few years after stocking was curtailed and have since become self-sustaining. When this happened, the fish populations in the river began to shift. In areas with large concentrations of a particular species of trout, the fish began shifting to other areas for a number of reasons. Areas that held good populations of rainbows, for instance, now hold good populations of browns—the water isn't suitable habitat for the rainbows, but it is for browns. Most of the upper river experienced a shift in trout populations, which eventually stabilized to what we have today. As of this writing, the numbers of wild trout are increasing in the river, with historically high numbers of rainbows in certain sections. Cutthroat numbers have declined because of a number of factors, including dewatering of spawning tributaries, excessive harvest for food, the introduction of non-native species, and general neglect. They are making a comeback in most sections of the river, although there will never be as many as there were before man interfered with the environment. Brown trout are doing well in the river and through the years have been the species that the river's reputation as a fishery is based on. All things considered, it is because of the management of the Montana Department of Fish, Wildlife and Parks that we now enjoy good numbers of fish and superb fishing.

Regulations have changed from the early part of the century. The river has experienced seasons when anglers were allowed to keep pounds of fish, much of which seems excessive today. We now have liberal seasons, we can fish the river outside the park all year long, and we have restrictive creel limits. Cutthroats became protected in the upper river from the Pine Creek Bridge to the park in 1984 as catch-and-release went into effect for them. Later, in 1988, the catch-and-release of all cutthroats became mandatory riverwide. Then in 1994, the entire Yellowstone drainage in Park County became catch-and-release for cutthroats. The year 1984 also saw a section of the upper river from Pine Creek Bridge upstream to the Emigrant Bridge change to a slot limit for rainbow and brown trout: anything between thirteen and twenty-two inches must be returned to the river unharmed. This section also has an artificial-flies-and-lures-only restriction. As we learn more about what our fishery needs, we will probably see more and more restrictive regulations to protect the treasure we have now.

There have been some severe threats to the river in the past years, many of which have affected the fishing, and some still affect the fishing. There have been natural threats in the form of flooding, and drought years with extremely low water. Although these were serious, they have not affected the river as much as has the human factor. In the 1930s, arsenic leached out of the settling ponds of commercial mines in the Jardine area, killing fish and insects. The late 1940s and early 1950s brought spraying of insecticides that literally decimated all the green drakes and western march browns, among other insects, from the river. It has taken nearly forty years for these insects to come back to decent numbers. Timber cutting along some of the tributaries has altered their natural flow because of excessive clear-cutting. Sediment loads from agricultural land due to overgrazing and the removal of vegetation was a significant problem, as was erosion caused by poor land and water use. Human-caused channel alterations also threatened the river and the fish in it.

One of the major threats to the river was the proposal of the Allenspur Dam, which was to be located two and a half miles south of Livingston. This was first proposed in 1906, but it was not until the early 1970s that it became a real threat. The exploration of the vast coal reserves in eastern Montana and the development of an associated coal energy technology was the reason for the renewed threat. The reservoir that was to be formed behind the dam would have had a storage capacity of 4,012,000 acre-feet and would have been called Allenspur Reservoir or Paradise Lake. Thank the gods and the people who fought against this dam as it would have been environmentally criminal to change this magnificent free-flowing river into a holding facility.

Today, the river is healthy and probably in the best shape it has been in since people first started messing with it. Trout populations are increasing, and the fishing borders on fantastic. It is still threatened by overdevelopment, but the good news is that there are many of us who consider the river to be in our stewardship, and we'll be damned if we allow any more degradation to occur. And the agencies managing the river are doing their utmost to insure its continued protection.

The Yellowstone.

2

Yellowstone National Park Waters

The waters in Yellowstone National Park are perhaps some of the most famous in the world, in the sense that every fly fisher in the country, if not the world, has fished or would like to fish park waters. A veritable *Who's Who* of fly fishing has set foot in these waters at one time or another, and will continue to do so. Perhaps the lure of going back in time or having the opportunity for a wilderness experience attracts fly fishers to this pristine and scenic section of the country. There are few places left that can offer relatively untouched natural beauty, an opportunity to see unique topography and wildlife in great abundance, and the chance to catch cutthroat trout that have remained physically unaltered since they first evolved. It's not an everyday occurrence in the lives of most fishermen to fish among a herd of elk or buffalo or to encounter a grizzly bear off a remote trail yet still be within an easy drive of the amenities of hotels and restaurants.

Fishing the water in the park can be as simple as driving to the river, walking a few yards to the water, and beginning casting. Or it can be a wild and woolly experience by hiking into some of the more remote sections. It is truly a place to fulfill whatever fishing fantasy one might have, whether that be casting to rising fish in classic dry-fly water or throwing huge weighted nymphs in rough-and-tumble canyonlike water. One can be social in fishing sections that are popular; the ability to chat with other anglers, compare notes, admire gear and techniques, and talk "fly speak" is as important to some as is the actual fishing. Or one can be totally isolated for days on end, with the addition of an element of danger thrown in.

The trout that swim in these waters have remained relatively unchanged physically since they first became cutthroat trout, but that should not imply that they are inherently stupid fish. A very common error made by visiting anglers is to expect to catch tons of fish. After all, to most of us the park is a wilderness, and fishing a wilderness area should be relatively easy, or so we think. Although there are days on the river when every cutthroat seems bent on getting itself hooked, the fishing can be incredibly tough at other times. And midging fish in the estuary section below the lake can make one wonder if he'll ever catch another fish. A key to success is to understand where fish are at any given moment during the season. An angler visiting the park in September and fishing the Buffalo Ford area may be somewhat bewildered because he may not be catching as many fish as his buddy may have on opening day in July. What he may fail to realize is that in September many fish have already returned to the lake after the spawn, and there just are not as many fish to be had. And many of the insect populations have already hatched out over the course of the season and are not as available to the fish. The trout have seen literally thousands of fishermen in the more accessible stretches, and they know what drag and poor presentations are. These trout are like most other trout in the country: they are governed by instinct and they learn to adapt to pressure.

The waters in the park hold a special niche in the park's overall management philosophy: anglers are allowed to fish and in some areas to keep fish. This is considered by some to be a concession made by park officials—there is no other consumptive use of park resources allowed. Hunting has long been abolished, as has logging and other consumptive uses. There was a time when the fishery was abused and in danger, but protective management has brought it back to near the abundant levels it once reached. It is a privilege to fish the river in the park, one that we should cherish, protect, and preserve, so that the generations following us can enjoy the experience.

The Yellowstone River in the park can be divided into four different sections, not including the lake, and can really be considered three different rivers because of the radical changes in its character. The headwaters section as it enters the park has the characteristics of a wild freestone river and is perhaps the most inaccessible of all the sections. It then turns into a winding, oxbowed, wandering river as it enters the lake. This section is susceptible to the ravages of all weather that occurs upstream. The section of river below the lake is a tailwater fishery that takes on spring-creek characteristics and has the lake to filter out the roil and muck of runoff or weather. The third section occurs after the upper and lower falls, where the river runs through a couple of canyons and becomes much steeper and faster. We have broken this stretch into two sections because of the species of fish that inhabit them: from Yellowstone Falls to Knowles Falls there are cutthroat and rainbow trout, and from Knowles Falls to where the river exits the park in Gardiner there are cutthroat, rainbow, and brown trout. Each section of river is unique and offers the angler a challenging and rewarding experience. Because these sections of river are so radically different, we'll cover topography, water characteristics, accessibility, seasonal changes, and the fishing as we discuss each individual section.

Management Practices

As unique as the park is, its basic management philosophy is equally so. In most other water in this country, fisheries are managed for the protection of the fish, but with sport fishing as the motivating factor. Angling and angler satisfaction are very important elements in management philosophies so long as they result from biologically sound management practices. (Unfortunately, "biologically sound" is not always the case on some waters where anglers can exert political or social pressure on management groups.) Here in the park the fisheries are managed primarily for the preservation of predators: grizzly bears, river otters, eagles, ospreys, pelicans, and others. The angler is here not as a predator, although at times in the past he surely acted like one, but as a visitor allowed to experience the resources without making a negative impact.

Currently, certain animal-rights activist groups are taking a hard look at fishing in the park and questioning its validity. Until recently the act of fishing has escaped the scrutiny of these groups—fish

Fishing in the Big Bend area.

aren't as warm and cuddly as a baby harp seal. Apparently that is
changing, to the point where the National Park Service (NPS) and
the U.S. Fish and Wildlife Service (aquatic resources advisor to the
NPS in the park) have had some discussion concerning what to do
if the activist pressure becomes intense. There has been discussion
of totally banning fishing in the park, not because of biological
needs, but because of political pressures imposed by certain groups.
This will probably not happen in our lifetime, but it has been discussed. Also discussed was a novel approach to fly fishing—"hook-
less" fishing—actually cutting off the entire barb and point at the
bend of the hook, not just debarbing by bending the barb down. This
way an angler can present the fly to the trout, experience the strike,
play the fish for a while, but never land it. We can't envision the activist groups accepting this as a solution. There is a real concern, and
the Fish and Wildlife Service (USFWS) is examining ways of com-
bating what it sees as a potential future battle. It is in the process of
putting together a study to figure out what *exactly* is important to

fishermen in the act of fishing: is it the strike, the ability to hook a fish, land a fish, touch a fish? Is it enough to be out there in the environs dressed in the uniform of the day, flailing a fly rod socially? Or is the entire experience important? Entire tomes can probably be written about why anglers fish and still not get to the heart of it, but we guess that a semiscientific survey will partially answer this impossible question. Why one fishes is as individual as why one picks lifelong friends or spouses—it only makes sense to each of us on a totally individual level. Let's hope that some management solution can be found that will insure future generations the opportunity to experience what we have experienced and not be limited to having to read about what once was or be forced to fish using some quasi fly-fishing method.

Angling quality is defined in Yellowstone National Park as the opportunity to fish for wild trout in a relatively undisturbed environment. As a whole, the NPS and USFWS have done an excellent job, considering that about three million people visit the park each year, and in 1993 an estimated 398,000 angler days were spent fishing park waters.

According to the *Fishery and Aquatic Management Program in Yellowstone National Park, 1993 Annual Report,* published by the United States Department of the Interior, Fish and Wildlife Service, Fisheries and Federal Aid in June 1994, the goal of the aquatic management program in the park is to "Pursue an aquatic management policy that allows ecological processes to function as if uninfluenced by modern man, while providing for visitor use and education." This is quite an undertaking, and is as unique as the park. The management program objectives are to:

1. Describe the qualitative and quantitative characteristics of the fish populations, associated biota, and other aquatic resources of Yellowstone National Park;
2. Determine how visitor use and other factors affect the dynamics and trends of fish populations, associated biota, and other aquatic resources;
3. Recommend measures to minimize the effects of human

activities on the fish populations and other aquatic resources; and
4. Maintain or restore, in numbers sufficient to assure their long-term persistence, aquatic ecosystems and their fish-species assemblages representative of those present upon the arrival of European man in Yellowstone National Park.

This, however, was not always the case. The United States Congress established Yellowstone National Park as our nation's first national park in 1872 "for the benefit and enjoyment of the people and for the preservation, from injury and spoilation, of all timber, mineral deposits, natural curiosities and wonders . . . and their retention in their natural condition." The regulations started off to protect the "natural curiosities and wonders"; the question is, were fish considered a natural wonder and curiosity? In 1872 the general fishing regulations stated that there be "no wanton destruction of fish. No capture for merchandise or profit." Then, in 1878, the regulations changed to state that "All hunting, fishing, or trapping within YNP only for recreation, food for visitors or residents prohibited." And in 1908 the regulations went to a twenty-fish limit per person per day. Man was surely a consumptive user in those days. There were even rules on how to kill fish, as provided by the 1912 regulations: "Fish to be retained must be killed by sharp blow to back of head or knife into head."

In 1917 there was restricted fishing for meals by the Yellowstone National Park Hotel Company, but in 1919 regulations closed fishing to employees for meals and prohibited commercial fishing. It was also around this time that waters in the park began to close on a regular basis but catch limits on other waters remained relatively high. There were still ten- and twenty-fish bag limits. A curious regulation appeared in 1929 that stated, "Boiling or attempting to boil live fish in hot springs, pools or geysers prohibited." Apparently, that was a fairly common practice in some parts of the park, especially in the lake section. Then somewhere around 1937 regulations changed from numbers of fish to pounds of fish: "15 pounds of fish per person per day plus one fish not to exceed 10 fish." Then live minnows, salmon eggs, and other fish eggs were banned as bait, and the digging of worms within the park was prohibited.

As time progressed, the regulations became slightly more restrictive. More waters were periodically closed, but bag limits remained generous. As the 1960s approached, the bag limits became smaller, the seasons more restrictive, and the regulations more complicated. A regulation that went into effect in 1964 stated that, "No person shall wantonly waste or allow edible portions of fish to go to waste in the Park." The rangers were finding literally tens of thousands of dead fish in trash receptacles each year. Then in 1973, the park required a permit for anglers and the Yellowstone River had catch-and-release regulations established for it. In 1978 there was a general-regulation format change that broke the park into zones, each zone with its own set of regulations. In 1994, anglers were required to purchase a fishing permit for the park, and the use of lead was abolished. The 1994 regulations state that, "Because of the increasing number of anglers in the Park, more restrictive regulations have been adopted in Yellowstone. These restrictions include: season opening/closing dates, restrictive use of bait, catch-and-release only areas, and number/size limits according to species. A few places are closed to the public to protect threatened and endangered species, sensitive nesting birds, and to provide scenic viewing areas for visitors seeking undisturbed wildlife."

As of this date, anglers can still fish the waters in the park and can still keep fish from various areas. Although the park has seen some very strange regulations over the years and had its ups and downs with fish populations, abuse, natural disasters, and attacks from special-interest groups, the *privilege* to fish park waters has been retained and maintained throughout the years. Let us hope and pray that our offspring and their offspring's offspring will continue to enjoy that privilege forever.

Headwaters of the Yellowstone River

Many fly fishermen consider Yellowstone Lake to be the headwater of the river, but the actual headwaters are outside the park, in

Headwaters to Yellowstone Falls

the Washakie Wilderness Area of the Shoshone National Forest in northwestern Wyoming. The river starts as two branches at Younts Peak, a mere 12,156 feet above sea level, and flows in a generally northward direction to the park. This is a wilderness area in every meaning of the term. It probably has remained unchanged for centuries—a true backcountry. Many smaller streams flow into it, but it actually starts to become a river as Atlantic Creek and Thorofare Creek dump into it. The addition of Lynx, Cliff, Phlox, Mountain, Badger, Trappers, and Cabin creeks make up the Yellowstone as it flows into the lake inside the park. All this occurs at a relatively high elevation among some rather awesome scenery: the Continental Divide to the west, the Trident to the east in the Absaroka Mountain Range, the Thorofare Plateau, the lake itself, and not a road for miles and miles. As the river eventually reaches the lake it has the characteristics of wildly meandering, oxbowing, high meadow-like water. Where it actually flows into Yellowstone Lake it forms a delta caused by the depositing of runoff silt and debris.

Thousands of years ago, this section of the river held no cutthroat trout because it lies on the eastern side of the Continental Divide and flows toward the Atlantic Ocean (it eventually finds its way to the Gulf of Mexico). Cutthroat trout are a Pacific side or a "west of the Continental Divide" fish. How the species found its way into the Yellowstone is open to some debate, but the consensus is that it occurred during the last ice age, when glaciers retreated. Currently, Two Ocean Creek splits at the top of the Continental Divide and forms Pacific and Atlantic Creeks, which flow toward their namesakes' oceans. At this split, the trout had an opportunity to cross the Divide, and the cutthroats have taken advantage of that opportunity, making this section of river the entryway for cutthroats in the Yellowstone system. The series of waterfalls downstream of the lake would have prevented any fish from entering from the north, so now there are cutthroats here and a very interesting fishery.

Accessibility

To say that this area is accessible would be a gross exaggeration—it is anything but accessible. This is perhaps the most remote and inaccessible area within the entire park. Oh sure, there are trails that will lead one there, but they aren't for the casually curious. The headwaters section can be reached from all directions but with considerable effort, especially for the angler on foot. From the southern entrance of the park one could take the South Boundary Trail and head east for approximately twenty-five miles, a mere stroll in the woods. From the East Entrance Road about a mile or so from Yellowstone Lake one could follow the Thorofare Trail along the eastern side of the lake to the headwaters area. It's only a twenty- to thirty-mile jaunt, depending on what section is to be visited. There are many other trails into this area from many directions, so a good map should be consulted before embarking on a journey such as this.

For those of you who are into backpacking, this area is the ticket: a pristine wilderness, major solitude, and a step back in time. However, a word of caution: this is grizzly bear country, so take all necessary precautions when making this hike. Bells, loud talking, prudent handling of foodstuffs, and maybe some pepper spray should make the trip relatively safe and free of those face-to-face confrontations that make us wish we had an extra pair of drawers handy. If you have never seen a grizzly up close and personal, count yourself lucky and hope it never happens. These are dangerous wild creatures that can actually eat you and probably feel no remorse afterwards. Traveling safely in their territory is something every angler planning a trip to the park should take seriously.

There are some other, slightly easier ways into this area than hiking for miles on end. There are outfitters who will gladly pack you in on horseback for a nominal fee. This isn't a bad way to go, and it allows one to enjoy the scenery and let someone else worry about the route. Another alternative would be to hitch a ride or charter a boat at one of the marinas on the lake to the Southeast Arm of the lake, where it becomes a simple matter of joining up with the Thorofare Trail and walking a few miles to the river. The other alternative would be to charter a boat and tow your own canoe or nonmotorized craft and paddle or row to the delta area. However, do this very early in the day before the winds pick up—they can be extremely dangerous.

However you end up in the headwaters area, plan to spend a few days here; a minimum of three days would be about right. It's just too far a trek to fish for a day and head out. Take the time to fully appreciate this wilderness and the solitude it affords. If you happen to run into other anglers, you all probably have something other than the fishing in common.

Seasonal Changes: The Fishing

There is basically only one season on this section of river and that would be the month of August. Runoff, weather, and the natural instincts of the cutthroats inhabiting the river combine to make a very narrow window of fishing opportunity for the angler. For all intents and purposes, the fishable water lies between the lake and where Atlantic Creek flows into the river. This is around the 8,000-foot mark, and summer comes very late here. The runoff period occurs in May, June, and very often into late July and drains some very high peaks (12,000 feet plus). The snowmelt causes some torrential flooding as swift, powerful water races toward the lake, bringing muck, roil, and debris as it scours its way downstream. Insect life in the upper reaches is limited—very little can survive the annual scouring. Obviously, this period offers only mud, high water, and extremely cold water to the angler.

As the runoff conditions recede, the cutthroats from Yellowstone Lake begin their annual spawning run up the river. The extreme conditions that exist in this section insure that there are very few resident (year-round) fish here, especially as one travels farther upstream. The cutthroats come in vast numbers and at times fill areas beyond what one would consider carrying capacity, especially where the feeder streams flow into the river. These fish are all the fifteen-, sixteen-, and seventeen-inch fish that anglers are used to seeing on other stretches of the river. They are no larger or smaller on the whole. Many feeder streams are literally choked with cutthroats that are seemingly out of proportion in size to what one would normally expect in such small waters. These fish take care of business and begin to move back to the lake, lingering in the meadowlike stretches for a number of weeks. They don't all move at once—it usually takes most of the summer for these trout to make their way back to the lake.

Late July will still find plenty of cutthroats in the upper stretches and the feeder streams and available to the angler. Any small dark nymph or Woolly Bugger will take some fish, as will attractor dry flies like Royal Wulffs, Humpies, and such. The problem with this time of year is that the insects—particularly mosquitoes—can be especially bothersome. A good deal of standing water remains as the runoff recedes, and the lower stretch is somewhat marshy, making for excellent mosquito habitat. Bring a good head net with you if you plan an early trip. Late July can be an iffy month, depending on the water levels. In a high-water year the river may still be in the throes of runoff, so plan carefully: it's just a little too far to walk and find fishing conditions on the poor side. Also, any time one ventures into this section, he should be prepared for a thunderstorm to wipe out the river for a day or so. It does clear quickly, but know that there could be some unexpected down time. We suppose that careful attention to weather systems could help here, but unless you have a lot of time or are a local, you go when you can.

Hatch Chart for the Yellowstone River Above the Lake

Mayflies

Western green drake		
(*Drunella grandis*)	Size: #10–#12	July 20 to August 15
Gray drake		
(*Siphlonurus occidentalis*)	Size: #10–#12	July 25 to August 20
Pale morning dun		
(*Ephemerella inermis*)	Size: #16–#20	July 25 to August 15
Speckled wing dun		
(*Callibaetis nigritus*)	Size: #14–#16	August 1 to September 1
Trico		
(*Tricorythodes minutus*)	Size: #18–#20	August 15 to September 20
Blue-winged olive		
(*Baetis tricaudatus*)	Size: #16–#22	August 20 to October 15

Caddisflies

Little tan short horn sedge
  (*Glossosoma velona*)   Size: #14–#16   July 20 to August 25
American grannom
  (*Brachycentrus americanus*) Size: #12–#14   July 25 to September 1
Green sedge
  (*Rhyacophila bifila*)   Size: #12–#14   August 5 to September 5
Spotted sedge
  (*Hydropsyche occidentalis*) Size: #10–#12   August 10 to September 10

Stoneflies

Golden stone
  (*Calineuria californica*)   Size: #6–#10   July 25 to August 10
Yellow sally
  (*Isoperla* species)   Size: #14–#16   July 25 to September 1
Olive stone
  (*Isogenus* species)   Size: #12–#16   August 1 to September 1
Little olive stones
  (*Alloperla* species)   Size: #14–#16   August 10 to August 25

Other Food Forms of Importance

Midge (Chironomidae)   Size: #16–#22   August 20 to October 1
Leeches (Hirudinea)   Size: #6–#14   All season
Shrimp/scuds
  (*Gammarus lacustris*)   Size: #12–#16   All season
Ants (Formicidae)   Size: #14–#22   July 25 to September 5
Grasshoppers (Acrididae)   Size: #8–#14   August 1 to September 5

August is really the season to fish on this stretch of river. It does find some fish already moving back to the lake, but it offers an excellent opportunity to have some wonderful fishing. The hot, dry days of a normal summer have baked the mosquitoes into submission, and the weather is pleasant enough, almost idyllic. A good majority of the fish will be in the lower meadow section and willing to feed on almost anything that is properly offered. These fish usually do not see too many flies over the course of this area's short season, so they are a little on the naive side. Put a fly over them or swim a nymph by them and you will usually be rewarded with a take. Matching the hatch isn't particularly necessary—any good attractor patterns ought to do the trick. For dry flies we suggest the following patterns and sizes: Royal

Wulff in #12 to #18, Parachute Adams in #12 to #20, Green Drake Wulff in #10 to #14, Elkhair Caddis in #12 to #18, Golden Stone in #8 to #12, Griffith Gnat in #16 to #22, and Trico Spinner in #16 to #20. Due to the lead ban in the park we began using beadhead nymphs almost exclusively. Therefore, for nymphs we suggest the angler bring along a few Hare's Ears in #10 to #18, Pheasant Tails in #14 to #20, Princes in #8 to #16, and Girdle Bugs in #6 to #10. Also, remember to add a few Gray/Olive Scuds in #12 to #14, and Dark Olive Woolly Buggers in #6 to #14. The angler should also pack a few ants in #16 to #20, hoppers in #10 to #14, and crickets in #12 to #14 to round out the selection.

For those of you who are sticklers for matching the hatch, you are going to find several hatches crowded together in a very short time. Often, you will experience multi-complex compound hatches. Fortunately, the cutthroat are seldom finicky during this time period. Mayflies will be represented by *Callibaetis*, green drakes, gray drakes, pale morning duns, Tricos, and *Baetis*. In most years the salmon flies are generally long gone before the angler arrives on the upper river. However, you may encounter golden stones, along with a small host of little yellow and olive stoneflies. The fly fisher on the upper river will also encounter the little tan short horn sedge along with the American grannom, green sedge, and spotted sedge. There will also be prolific midge hatches during late August and early September.

As the month of August comes to a close, there will be fewer and fewer fish remaining in the river—most will be on their way back to the lake. September sees even fewer fish remaining and some potentially severe storms. At this altitude one should be prepared for serious snow at this time. We do not recommend trips into this remote area in September. If you do decide to go in, do so as early in the month as possible.

This section of river offers the angler a unique experience, especially for those who enjoy getting away from the crowds and don't mind working to do so. The fishing isn't really any better than on other parts of the river—the fish aren't any larger or more plentiful. But one cannot beat the feeling of stepping back in time and realizing that this is what it all must have been like. Besides, there is romance in the adventure of any headwater section of any river.

Attractors versus Imitations

For those of you who are just starting, you may find this talk of attractors and detailed hatch charts somewhat overwhelming. This confusion seems to center mainly around dry-fly fishing itself, though it really concerns all types of patterns and methods of fly fishing. However, for this discussion we will limit the talk to dry flies. For the person who is just starting to fish with dry flies and wants to know how to go about it, things can seem rather confusing at times. If some time is spent watching other anglers on any stream that has decent dry-fly fishing, one might see two very different methods of approach or schools of thought regarding dry flies. That would and does increase the confusion. Let's look at what the newcomer might witness that would cause this confusion.

There are those who will only cast to trout that are visibly rising and will only use patterns that they think imitate what the trout are feeding on. These individuals seem to spend a great deal of time looking at the bugs and discussing the size, shape, and color of the naturals. At times they even call these insects by funny sounding Latin names. Upon spotting the rising trout, they often resemble great blue herons in that they appear to be slowly and carefully stalking their prey. They often talk about feeding lies, line control, slack, and the problems of drag. And they are often successful in moving the trout to the fly. Then, there are those hard-bitten characters who never match the hatch or seem to care if the trout are visible or not. They employ patterns that seldom look like any mayfly found in creation, except perhaps in general shape, and seem to be casting here and there with little regard for feeding lies or careful approach. They refer to the insects as bugs and often ignore everything else, including the size. Still, they seem to land a fair number of trout.

Okay, now what! Who's right? Which method should be chosen? Or does it even matter? Sound familiar? Well it should. Many of us have been in this position at one time or another; it's called getting started, and it can be very overwhelming. But it doesn't need to be.

So now we're back to attempting to figure out what to do and which method is right. Both are! There are times when matching the hatch and carefully casting to visibly rising trout will be critical to your success. There will also be times when nothing is hatching or the hatch is very sparse and the trout don't seem to be keyed in on or interested in the hatch. During those periods you very often can use an attractor pattern and enjoy considerable success.

The major point is that no one method is always right. The upper Yellowstone River above the lake offers both types of experiences. For the fly fisher who enjoys matching the hatch, there are plenty of hatches and lots of rising trout. For beginning anglers, remember that these are trout who don't see many anglers and are seldom finicky.

Yellowstone Lake

Yellowstone Lake is perhaps the largest lake on the North American continent above 7,000 feet and the central dominant feature within the park. Although it only ranks about sixtieth in size among the world's natural lakes, it is indeed impressive. Its approximate 140 square miles and 87,500 acres is the remnant of an ancient volcanic caldera with a maximum depth of 320 feet and an average depth of 139 feet. Only about 15 percent of the Lake is less than thirty feet in depth, but this is the zone that most fly fishermen are concerned with. Over a hundred streams, including the headwaters section of the Yellowstone River, feed into the lake, adding to its volume.

This is the most popular fishery in the park and receives about 50 percent of total angler use in the park. The season generally opens on June 15, very often while ice is still on the water. In the past many different species have been stocked in the lake on an experimental basis, but it remains a pure cutthroat trout fishery. The lake has suffered many abuses over the past century and overharvesting fish was a major one. It has been estimated that prior to the 1960s, over 48 million cutthroats were taken from the lake by sport and commercial fishermen, leading to an almost total collapse of the cutthroat population in the 1960s. More restrictive regulations and

Yellowstone Lake.

prudent management have brought back to Yellowstone Lake good concentrations of fish but it still has a long way to go before it reaches the abundant fish populations of the 1880s. It's well on its way to recovery, though.

A major problem has been discovered recently under the shimmering surface of the lake that, theoretically, could spell disaster to the cutthroats and greatly upset the ecological apple cart of the park itself. A few fishermen have reported catching what appeared to be lake trout. However, until 1994, no biologist had been able to ascertain that these fish were indeed lake trout. Park biologists are now certain that these are lake trout, based on actual examination of captured fish. More startling is that the few that have been captured appear to be different age-classes. A major study is underway to determine whether these fish are actually reproducing or whether they are being dumped into the lake by dubious persons year by year. There is a reward of ten thousand dollars for any information leading to the arrest and conviction of those responsible for stocking the fish. Park officials consider this an "appalling act of environmental vandalism." New regulations implemented on the lake make it mandatory that anglers kill any lake trout caught, regardless of size.

Why the big deal? Once lake trout gain a stronghold they can and probably will eliminate the cutthroat trout from the Lake. They are prolific spawners with a relatively high fry survival rate, and they can grow to very large sizes: thirty-, forty-, and fifty-pound fish are not uncommon. They are also very aggressive and predaceous; they will feed heavily on cutthroats because there is very little else in the lake except some suckers, shiners, and chubs. By nature, they seem to prefer water below the forty-foot depth, so they will not be readily available to the casual angler unless one has the specialized gear to fish for them. Harvested lake trout will probably not put much of a dent in the potential population. Lake trout spawn at approximately forty feet, so the fry will not be available to the cutthroats as a food source, allowing for a very high survival rate. The future could see the decline of cutthroats in the lake, leading to possible elimination. That's one of the big deals.

Another big deal, maybe even more severe than the depletion of the cutthroat population—if there could possibly be anything worse— is the destruction and damage to overall wildlife populations. Eagles, pelicans, ospreys, otters, grizzly bears and others are dependent on the cutthroat trout as a major food source. Because cutthroat trout are basically a shallow-water fish, they become available as food to other predators in the lake. If cutthroats were eliminated from the food chain, other wildlife numbers would surely diminish. The annual spawning runs in the river and creeks are very important to the grizzly bears, because they eat the fish in an attempt to recuperate after a winter of hibernation. It is crucial to their survival. Lake trout cannot replace the cutthroats as a food source for other predators because they are not readily available to them. They spawn in the lake itself and prefer the cold depths when not spawning, making them inaccessible to predators. There is usually a very short time immediately after ice-out that finds lake trout in the shallows of a lake, making them somewhat more available, but not nearly enough so.

This is clearly as severe an abuse of the lake and park as there ever has been. It would spell disaster to the park, changing it forever. Let us hope that a solution can be speedily found to this problem.

Accessibility

This huge lake is easily reached, because all roads in the park eventually lead to it. There are approximately 110 miles of shoreline that an angler can fish from, though only about 30 miles can be reached by motor vehicle. That leaves about eighty or so miles that take some work to get to. One can reach the rest of the shoreline by traveling on foot, horseback, or by boat. There are two main trails along the lake; the first is along the eastern shoreline—the Thorofare Trail. The second is along the southern shore and accesses the South Arm and Southeast Arm. Take the Heart Lake Trail and hook up with the Trail Creek Trail at Heart Lake. Most visitors who fish the lake do so either by boat or where access is the easiest, leaving the rest of the shoreline to those seeking solitude or a wilderness experience. These trails make for pleasant day hikes with some fishing in between. There are also full-service marinas where charters or boat rentals can be had to access the other shorelines of the lake for a day's fishing or as a way to drop off and pick up anglers wishing to spend a few days camping and fishing. There are outfitters who will take anglers in by horseback for a day or more. Basically, the entire shoreline is accessible. It just takes a little more work getting to some areas than it does to others.

Seasonal Changes: The Fishing

The lake opens to fishing on June 15 immediately after ice-out. There are some years when remnants of ice remain, but it's usually gone by the season opening. Many local anglers eagerly anticipate the opener and plan their schedules around it because some spectacular fishing can be had. Before we go any further, it should be noted that this lake is potentially very dangerous and especially so at this time of year. The high altitude insures that summer comes late and water temperatures remain very cold—cold enough to cause severe hypothermia in the unwary angler. The fisherman who gets dumped out of his boat needs to get out and off the water as soon as possible. The water and daily winds will chill right to the bone, lowering core body temperature and causing hypothermia. Once it starts, the ability to make logical decisions is greatly impaired, and the threat to life becomes very real.

The wading and float-tubing angler also needs to pay attention to the cold water and should take occasional breaks, before getting too cold. A few anglers have found themselves in serious trouble while float-tubing; once the point of shivering is reached, it is time to get out and get warm. Although the air temperature may be in the seventies, the water temperature may still be in the high thirties or low forties. It does not take long to reach the point of being too cold to do anything about it. Neoprene waders and modern undergarments go a long way to extending the actual time that may be spent in the water, but even they cannot completely stave off the penetrating cold. Be aware, be prepared, and be cautious.

The other potential danger that needs to be discussed is the wind and its effects on big water such as the lake. One can usually count on the wind blowing around the lake at a hearty pace on a daily basis. Mornings are usually pleasantly calm, which can deceive the unaware angler and catch him off-guard, because the afternoon will generally bring winds out of the southwest. The fisherman in small craft such as canoes and little rowboats will soon discover that wind whipping across a large expanse of water generates some sizable waves, very often waves larger than safety warrants for the size of the craft. More than a few boats are swamped by such waves each year, and more than a few lives have been lost as a result. The wind, waves, and cold water temperatures make safety a major concern.

The float-tuber needs to pay particular attention to the changing winds and to stay within easy reach of the shoreline. The wind, at times, can push a float tube out into the big water faster than the tuber can kick against it. Once out in the big water, the real problems begin—the least of which is getting blown across the lake and figuring a way back. Stay close to shore and keep at least one eye on the wind. Float-tubers need to remember that a permit must be acquired before entering the water to fish. A permit may be obtained from any of the ranger stations within the park.

The cutthroats in the lake will average about fifteen inches, with an occasional fish going over twenty inches, pretty much the same sizes found in other portions of the river system within the park. The only real difference is that the lake does have some smaller fish, although an angler will be hard-pressed to find and catch great quantities of them. As of this writing, the bag limit on the lake is two fish under thirteen inches each. Fish of this size are generally out in the deeper water, at least deeper than a fly fisher really wants to fish in, and most are caught by boaters trolling lures. It may seem odd that an angler can keep two fish under thirteen inches, but there is a very logical and biologically sound premise behind the rule. The larger fish are the ones that do the most spawning, and therefore they should be protected to insure the survival of the species. A few small fish caught and kept does not make a negative impact on the entire population. Most of the fish caught by fishermen are the larger, sexually mature fish, and they must be returned unharmed.

The cutthroat trout are fairly evenly concentrated around the lake's shoreline, for two reasons. The first is because, as a species, they generally prefer the shallower water to the depths, and the second is because that is where the greatest concentrations of food are. Yellowstone Lake is not a particularly fertile lake. The cold temperatures, general depth, and low nutrient input of the insoluble volcanic rock in the area make it difficult for plant and insect life to flourish. There are areas in the lake where plants and insects do flourish on a limited basis. Those areas are mostly confined to the shoreline and shallow bays, where the warming effects of the sun raise the water temperatures a few degrees.

There are approximately eighteen species of plants in the lake. However, the two predominant species are Richardson's pondweed and duckweed. The major weed beds are found in three to thirty feet of water along the shoreline. This shallower, slightly warmer water contains most of the plants, which in turn hold a relatively limited number of food sources for the trout. A couple of crustaceans that are extremely important to young trout are *Diaptomus shoshone* and *Daphnia schodleri*. These very tiny creatures are fed on heavily by the young fish and, interestingly, have an effect on the coloration of their flesh. Ever wonder why some lake and pond fish have a decidedly pink or orange flesh color? These tiny crustaceans contain a reddish pigment that actually dyes a trout's flesh when consumed.

Besides these minute creatures, there are two species of scud, *Gammarus lacustris* and *Hyallela azteca,* which are main staples of the trout. There are also midges (Chironomidae), Leeches (Hirudinea), aquatic worms (Annelida), dragonflies (Odonata), and tiny fingernail clams. There are also a few species of mayfly and caddisfly that are important; however, these may be only locally abundant in certain areas. There are also some minnows (introduced in the past by fishermen using live minnows as bait) such as suckers, shiners (goldeye), and chubs, which serve as another food item on the trout's menu.

The cutthroat trout will move to the shallows in search of the food sources hiding and feeding in the plants. This simplifies life for the fly fisher—one needs only to be concerned with the shoreline to find fish. By breaking down the shoreline into fish-holding structure, the quest for trout should be even simpler. From opening day on June 15 until early July one can find large concentrations of fish cruising the shoreline searching for their spawning streams, so the areas near the mouth of any tributary would be an excellent place to start. The current that spills into and extends some distance into the lake from any of these tributaries will also hold goodly numbers of trout, but one needs to pay attention to the regulations, because there is a one-hundred-yard zone around these outlets that is closed. These areas are generally closed until July 15, except for the mouths of Clear and Cub Creeks, which are closed until August 15 because of bear activity. It is always a wise idea to carefully read the current park regulations, because they can change from year to year.

Other areas that hold fish during the course of the season are: sandbars, rocky points, springs, bays and small coves, and any shallow cruising area. Obviously, if one can connect a couple of these, it increases the chances of getting into concentrations of fish. The more remote shorelines will, as the season goes on and more anglers are putting pressure on the fish, offer better opportunities for success. The South and Southeast Arm have generally good reputations for fishing.

The only semi-difficult trick to fishing the lake is to find concentrations of fish and get a fly to them. Matching a specific insect isn't something that is critical in this fishery—finding fish and making a presentation to them *is*. Therefore, a real key to success on the lake is knowing what fly lines will allow you to present your imitation at the proper angle and depth.

Early in the season, right after ice-out, the water temperatures are very cold and there aren't many insect hatches to get the fish looking up. The crucial requirement at this time of year are to get the fly down to where the fish are and to fish fairly slow. It does not matter if you wade, float-tube, or fish from a boat—the fly has to get to the level of the fish. This is the time to pull out those sink tips or even the full-sinking lines of different densities. It is also a time when the fish seem to take anything that has a little motion. Any medium-sized dark nymph ought to do the trick, for instance a Woolly Worm, Zug Bug, Prince Nymph, dark Hare's Ear, or some special concoction. Allow the fly to sink, and retrieve it using a slow hand twist or stripping motion, just enough of a retrieve to move the fly without having it race back to you. The anglers who fish from a boat or float tube have a slight advantage over the wading fisherman here because they can cover the water farther from shore. They also can drift over a great deal of water and find the concentrations of fish, whereas the wading angler can fish only as far as he can wade and cast.

Even though the fish, at times, may be beyond a wading angler's reach, he should still attempt to cover water by walking and casting until he hits fish. There is a great deal of movement by the fish. They are not holding in stationary lies as they would in a river or stream, so eventually they will come by the angler. Look for the cruising fish and attempt to make casts to those fish—more often than not a strike will follow.

As the season progresses and more insects are available, the cutthroats begin to look up to the surface for food, and it is at this time that the angler can entice fish with attractor-style dry flies. Again, the fish that can be spotted feeding or cruising are the ones that can be readily taken because then the major problem is solved—finding fish. Very often an angler will make a ton of casts to water that doesn't hold any fish, only to give up fishless, while another angler arriving at this time will begin picking up fish. The first angler wasn't using the wrong fly or the wrong technique—it was just a matter of timing. The fish were cruising by the second angler. Covering the water in likely areas is certainly a valid way of fishing, but the more successful angler will be the one who actually sees fish. A cutthroat will rarely refuse a fly if it sees the fly. Adding an occasional twitch to a dry fly will call attention to it. A #14 Muddler Minnow fished dry and ever so slowly twitched across the surface can be deadly. Nymphs are also very effective if the angler can put them in front of visible fish.

Wind is something an angler has to cope with throughout the season. Most mornings on the lake are relatively calm, and the angler will usually have little trouble spotting fish. Very often, a short hike up a bluff will enable one to locate fish so that he may figure out how to make a good presentation to them. As the day wears on, the wind will generally pick up, putting a chop on the surface that makes sighting harder. Then it becomes a case of fishing the water.

The times when the wind really blows and causes the waves to crash into the shore offer some unique fishing opportunities. The windward side of a lake or pond is usually a good place to find fish feeding. The action of the waves in the shallow water will stir up the vegetation and dislodge many insects and other organisms, making them very available to fish. An area of discolored water will usually appear, caused by the wave action and forming an edge between the discolored water and clear water that is important to the fisherman. Interestingly, most anglers fish these areas incorrectly. In general, they will cast out into the lake and retrieve back toward shore, when they should be casting parallel to the shoreline in the seam between clear and roiled water. Some anglers will cast to this seam and begin a slow retrieve parallel to the shoreline. Others will cast and just let the fly settle and move along with the wave action or drift. Another, slightly different technique is to cast to the base of a small wave as it breaks into the shore and allow the fly to be pulled back out away from shore by the gentle undertow of the next wave forming. This is an extremely natural-appearing technique and is at times deadly.

Work these areas by moving along the shore until concentrations of fish are located. Of course, when the wind blows, most of us look for some sheltering structure to make fly fishing more enjoyable, but the windward areas should not be overlooked.

An interesting technique for the boat fisherman or float-tuber is simply to troll a streamer-type fly (a small Woolly Bugger works as well as anything) along the shoreline until some fish are located. Once fish are found, stop and work them with drys, nymphs, or small streamers, then move on until another pod of fish is found. It's not demanding fishing, but it *is* productive.

As the season moves into mid- and late summer there will be many insects on the surface. There are *Callibaetis* species as well as a smattering of other mayflies available, and they can offer the angler some very good dry-fly fishing. The inlets from tributaries will distribute many insects that hatch upstream into the lake, where the cutts will lie in wait for them. Anything that hatches upstream will usually drift down to the lake, offering the angler an excellent opportunity to take fish on a dry fly. At times, a spinner fall will end up in the lake, making for some interesting fishing to cruising fish that are sipping as they go. This presents an often amusing or frustrating problem—determining which direction a fish is going and attempting to place a

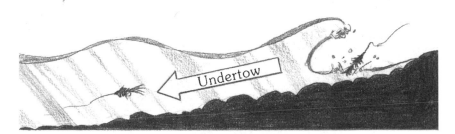

Casting to the base of a wave

1. Cast to base of wave near the shoreline.
2. Allow the undertow to carry the fly away from the bank.
3. Begin to retrieve.

fly in its path. These fish can be extremely erratic, so a guessing game takes place. A very dull but effective technique is to simply cast in the general direction of the sipping cruiser and wait and wait and wait and wait until it makes its way to the fly and sucks it in. The delta area where the headwaters dump into the lake is an excellent location for this kind of fishing.

Midges are prevalent in the lake and are an important food source to the trout. More important to the angler, they offer good opportunities to dry-fly enthusiasts. The problem with midges is that trout will very often key to a specific stage: pupa, emerging pupa, or adult, making some difficult choices for the angler. A good stuck-in-the-shuck pattern (usually a pattern with a trailing shuck such as a Griffith Gnat trimmed flat on the bottom and tied with some sort of shuck as a tail) retrieved very slowly across the surface can make things somewhat easier. The retrieve should be smooth, extremely slow, and even. Cutthroats are suckers for this, although the action seems to be contrary to most accepted methods of midge fishing.

Once the water begins to cool down in the very late summer and early fall, an angler may have to go back to sinking patterns to be really effective. But once these fish get conditioned to looking to the surface for food, it takes a while for them to forget. The Yellowstone Lake cutthroats can very often be coaxed into taking a dry fly when nothing seems to be on the surface, and especially so if a fish is spotted and worked.

This fishery is unique because of the environment in which it lies, its vast expanse of open water, and its position as the largest cutthroat fishery in the world. It offers anglers the opportunity to enter the ice cold waters of history and reap whatever reward is sought.

Hatch Chart for Yellowstone Lake
to Yellowstone Falls
(This chart covers the period from July 15 to October 31)

Stoneflies
Salmon fly
   (*Pteronarcys californica*)   Size: #2–#6   July 15 to July 25

Small western salmon fly
(*Pteronacella badia*)   Size: #8–#10   July 15 to July 30
Golden stone
(*Calineuria californica*)   Size: #4–#8   July 15 to August 10
Yellow sally
(*Isoperla mormona*)   Size: #14–#16   July 20 to August 25
Small golden stone
(*Hesperoperla pacifica*)   Size: #6–#10   July 20 to August 10
Olive stone (*Isogenus* species) Size: #12–#14   July 20 to August 25
Little olive stone
(*Alloperla signata*)   Size: #14–#16   August 10 to August 20
Giant western golden stone
(*Claassenia sabulosa*)   Size: #2–#6   August 5 to September 1

Caddisflies
Tan short horn sedge
(*Glossosoma velona*)   Size: #14–#16   July 15 to August 20
Little brown sedge
(*Lepidostoma veleda*)   Size: #14–#18   July 15 to August 10
American grannom
(*Brachycentrus americanus*)   Size: #12–#16   July 15 to August 10
Green sedge
(*Rhyacophila bifila*)   Size: #12–#14   July 25 to August 25
Spotted sedge
(*Hydropsyche occidentalis*)   Size: #10–#12   August 1 to September 15

Mayflies
Western green drake
(*Drunella grandis*)   Size: #10–#12   July 15 to August 1
Gray drake
(*Siphlonurus occidentalis*)   Size: #10–#12   July 15 to August 10
Small western red quill
(*Rhithrogena undulata*)   Size: #14   July 15 to August 15
Pale morning dun
(*Ephemerella inermis*)   Size: #16–#20   July 20 to August 20
Speckled wing dun
(*Callibaetis nigritus*)   Size: #14–#18   July 25 to August 25
Small western green drake
(*Drunella flavilinea*)   Size: #14–#16   August 10 to August 25
Mahogany dun
(*Paraleptophlebia bicornuta*)   Size: #14–#16   August 20 to September 20
Blue-winged olive
(*Baetis tricaudatus*)   Size: #18–#20   August 25 to October 25

Small western dark hendrickson
  (*E. tibialis*)   Size: #16–#18   August 20 to September 30
Trico (*Tricorythodes minutus*) Size: #18–#22   August 15 to October 10

Terrestrials

Grasshoppers (Acrididae)	Size: #8–#14	July 20 to September 20
Crickets (Gryllidae)	Size: #12–#14	August 1 to September 10
Black ants (Formicidae)	Size: #16–#22	July 15 to September 15
Cinnamon ants (Formicidae)	Size: #18–#20	August 1 to September 10
Black beetle (Coleoptera)	Size: #12–#18	July 15 to August 15

Other Important Hatches and Food Forms

Midge (Chironomidae)	Size: #16–#24	August 15 to October 31
Damselfly (Zygoptera)	Size: #10–#14	July 15 to August 15
Shrimp/scuds		
(*Gammarus lacustris*)	Size: #12–#16	July 15 to October 31
Sowbug (*Asellus communis*)	Size: #14–#16	July 15 to October 31
Aquatic worm (*Annelida*)	Size: #8–#14	July 15 to October 31
Water beetles (Heteroptera)	Size: #10–#16	July 15 to September 15

Yellowstone Lake to Yellowstone Falls

It doesn't get any better than this. This is the premier section of the entire river. Sure, other stretches have bigger fish, and some even hold more fish, but no other section has the quality of fishing found here. Quality is measured in terms of aesthetic beauty, numbers and size of fish, ease of access, methods of fishing possible, and the general over-all experience. The character of the water is that of a classic dry-fly fishery. Most anglers feel somewhat cheated if they have to resort to nymph fishing here to catch a few fish. The hatches are prolific and varied, the fish are willing and, at times, finicky. The water can be tough to fish or downright easy, and there is no hassle getting to the river. There is something for everyone—the super-technician and the rank novice can both find water, situations, and techniques that suit their needs, with a relatively high probability of catching fish. This is the true beer commercial of the river system—it doesn't get any better than this.

The Estuary, the Big Bend, Le Hardy Rapids, Buffalo Ford, and the Sulphur Caldron are names that attract a cultlike following

Yellowstone Falls and the Grand Canyon of the Yellowstone.

among visiting fly fishers. Annual pilgrimages to this section by individuals and fly-fishing clubs alike are common, many of whom plan to arrive during the same time period year in and year out. This creates a rather interesting phenomenon—the nonresident or nonlocal "expert"—the angler with intimate knowledge of a small section of water based on years and years of fishing it during the same season. These anglers know the water, the hatches, and the variable conditions that affect the fishing and allow them to be highly successful. There are few places in this country where this can happen, especially on the magnitude that it occurs here. In many of our trips around the country, we often meet anglers who are very familiar with this section of the Yellowstone and aren't averse to letting us in on how to fish it—it really is quite interesting because quite a few are right on target. Unfortunately, many of these anglers only know one short period of time and one short stretch of water—usually at the peak of the major hatches. As we'll discuss a little later, this is a multifaceted section, and although the season is relatively short, very complex with rapid changes. What appears in late July and early August is radically different in late August and early September, different enough that many anglers who normally fish the last two weeks in July would be very surprised by and hard-pressed for consistent action during September.

With the exception of Yellowstone Lake, this is the most popular stretch of water in the park and accounts for the most anglers and fishing hours. The stretch begins 1.6 kilometers below Fishing Bridge (this 1.6 kilometers is closed to fishing) and extends downstream to Chittenden Bridge in two reaches, with additional sections closed to fishing. The upstream reach extends from below Fishing Bridge ten kilometers down to Sulphur Caldron with a two-hundred-meter closure at Le Hardy Rapids and a side channel closed at Buffalo Ford. The lower reach begins at Alum Creek in the Hayden Valley and extends downstream to Chittenden Bridge. The river is closed below the bridge with good reason—although the water may seem gentle enough, it begins to pick up speed as it heads for the upper falls. A few fishermen have been foolish enough to attempt to fish this area and did not live to tell about it. Going over the upper falls is not our idea of a good time. Although these closures were not all primarily to protect the fish, the result has been the protection of the cutthroat trout from angler-caused mortality.

These fish that reside either in the river or migrate downstream from the lake to spawn, are perhaps the most intensely fished group of wild cutthroat trout in the country. It has been reported that each fish residing in the river has been caught and recaught an average of nine times a year. Even with this intense pressure on these fish, their size, weight, and age have continued to increase: the average fish is now about six years old. All this is due to the closures, restrictive regulations, and catch-and-release requirement; the overall quality of the fishery is second to none.

The opening of the angling season is July 15, which allows the cutthroats some protection while they are spawning, and remains open until the first Sunday in November. If any of you have fished this section in late October, you'll know that the only fish remaining in the river are the resident fish and that the numbers are far fewer than what could be encountered when the season opens. A good percentage of the fish migrate down from the lake to use the river to spawn. Once that is accomplished, they begin to make their way back to the lake. Anglers who aren't aware of this are often perplexed—leading to some misconceptions about the fishery itself. Many of these fish will begin returning to the lake once the season opens. If there is an exceptional low-water year, many fish will have already migrated back to the lake before the opening day. Usually mid- or late August finds the river with far fewer fish in it than on opening day. The angler who knows this and modifies his expectations and fishing techniques will have a good experience, while the unaware angler may go away mumbling derogatory things about the management of the river. This is still a very good fishery at any given time.

Opening day is an event that should be experienced at least once in every fly fisherman's lifetime, and it should be experienced at the Buffalo Ford access. It is truly amazing to watch the novice and expert, the individual angler, the small groups, the large fishing clubs, and even the occasional spin fisher all vie for position, casting every

which way in the pursuit of cutthroat trout. There are those who try
to escape by wading across the river to the far side, only to misjudge
the force of the current and end up taking a short swim. Every year
there is someone in the parking lot emptying water from his waders
and spreading clothes out to dry. It is the social event of the fishing
season in the park, and an experience that needs to be witnessed to
be believed. It is comical to watch the angler not familiar with this
stretch attempt to catch the fish that take up feeding positions downstream of his feet and very often actually bump into his feet. The cutthroat have grown accustomed to feet, which disturb the bottom and
release insects and foodstuffs into the drift, the old San Juan Shuf-
fle. It is amazing that fish that are prey for large carnivores like bears
have no fear of feet attached to large bearlike objects—people. The
crossing and wading of buffalo has probably conditioned these fish
to associate feet with the release of food into the drift, and the ones
that have fallen victim to predators aren't around to warn the others.
If you happen to be here on opening day, watch for the people gy-
rating strangely. They are the ones attempting to drop a fly at their
feet. When you do plan a trip during this time, keep your expectations in check and enjoy the social aspect—there are too many frustrated fly fishermen already. However, by electing to stay away from
the madding crowds an angler can have relatively large chunks of
water to himself even on opening day. One should avoid the major
parking areas and plan to walk some distance or use the trail along
the east side to avoid the "social" fishermen.

Accessibility

This is the most accessible stretch of river in the park, which is
why it is also the most popular section. The road runs along the west
side of the river, and there are many pull-outs and sites from which
to access the river. In many places the river runs right alongside the
road, while in others the river is but a short walk from the road.
Many of these spots have parking areas with picnic tables and rest-
room facilities. The angler who wants to leave some of the crowds
behind need only walk either upstream or downstream, away from
the parking areas. The casual fisherman or the other visitors usually

stay fairly close to the parking areas, leaving the distant spots to the more serious angler.

To really get away from most of the anglers, one could travel the Howard Eaton Trail, which follows the river along the east bank. This trail can be reached at the south end of Fishing Bridge or at Chittenden Bridge, or Tower Junction at the north end. Another way to access the trail is to wade across the river at Buffalo Ford or, depending on the water conditions, other spots. Buffalo Ford is traditionally the spot from which to wade across the river in all but the highest water conditions. By walking up- or downriver, an angler can have relative solitude and maybe even some fish to himself. As more and more fishermen use this area it is becoming increasingly more difficult to totally get away from other people, but the situation can be improved by walking short distances.

Water Characteristics

This entire section, with the possible exception of the Le Hardy Rapids area, has a spring creek or tailwater feel to it. It has been described as a huge spring creek, much like the Harriman Ranch section of the Henry's Fork. The lake acts like a large filtration system and eliminates the effects of runoff and keeps the flows clear and the temperatures fairly constant—much like a spring creek. Of course, the water levels fluctuate to a certain degree from year to year, but even they remain relatively constant. Also like a spring creek, the water is rich in insect life and usually clear and cold.

The upper reach, where the river exits the lake and one can legally begin fishing, is called the Estuary section. It is wide, slow, and deep, with weed beds, a silty or sandy bottom, and not much surface character other than the swirling currents that make getting a long dragfree presentation tough. Wading far out into the river is nearly impossible, but the good news is that fish generally cruise this area in search of food—so eventually some fish will make a pass nearby.

Toward the tail of the Estuary section above Le Hardy Rapids, the river narrows and picks up some speed. Wading becomes a little more practical and the surface has more character. One can see

The Estuary section.

current edges, drop-offs, holding and feeding lies, and can usually read the water. The fish tend to cruise less and use specific areas to hold and feed, probably because these areas are more defined and there is more of a current to contend with. Gravel bars are in evidence, and the character of the bottom begins to change to a large rock and cobble configuration.

The Le Hardy Rapids area is simply that—rapids. This section has the look and feel of a large western freestone river. It is relatively shallow and fast, with many boulders breaking the current. Although it is closed to fishing, it is interesting to walk along the boardwalk because one can often watch fish working their way back upstream to the lake: they very often look like salmon jumping their way up the rapids.

Just below the rapids, where one can legally fish again, the water has the feel of a large freestone river: it moves along at a good clip and there are many rocks breaking the current. Here there is some depth and good current speed with clearly defined current edges. The bottom is a mix of large rocks, cobble, and pea-sized gravel. Early in the season it acts as a holding or staging area for goodly numbers of fish migrating back to the lake.

As the river moves farther downstream, it again takes on the appearance of a large spring creek. There are very few areas of riffle, run, or pool-type water and although there are twists and turns, there is a large percentage of flat water. There are clear current edges and one can see depressions, drop-offs, shallows, weed beds, and gravel bars. Every so often there is some underwater structure that causes swirling currents, but most of this section down to the Sulphur Caldron has those even-looking currents that make it tough to read where fish should be. Around the Buffalo Ford area there are some small islands that the river braids around, giving the water all kinds of character. Current edges, current confluences, fast water, slow backwaters, shallows, bankside currents, midstream breaks, and more can all be found in this area. This adds to the area's popularity because there is a water type that suits everyone's personal taste.

The Sulphur Caldron area is unique because of the hot spots caused by the thermal activity in the area. Definite edges develop between the different temperatures, creating some unique fishing opportunities. There are some large back-eddies that make getting good presentations to feeding fish tough, and a few small islands that help add character to the water.

The Hayden Valley is closed to fishing, and the river here resembles a meadow stream on a large scale. It meanders here and there, oxbowing occasionally, even creating pondlike formations. This is a haven for fish from the fishing pressure upstream and is very important because of that.

The river upstream of the Chittenden Bridge area is somewhat deceiving—it looks slow and shallow, but care should be taken here. Wading very far out into the river is impractical because it is deep and the bottom is somewhat silty. This is an area for the angler who likes to fish to bankside feeders, sneaking his way up or downstream and searching for the riseform that will give a fish's position away. There is a fair amount of weed growth in this section and the fish have a tendency to cruise, often beyond an angler's reach, but careful observation will reveal fish holding along the banks and available to the wading fisherman.

Seasonal Changes: The Fishing

Due to the elevation, seasonal changes come quickly to the Upper Yellowstone. There is a narrow window of the peak hatch period that makes this section of the river very popular. From the mid-July opener till approximately the twentieth of August, there is a steady progression of hatches. As August draws to a close and September begins, we find that the number of different hatches that occur each day starts to diminish, as does the number of fish in the river. This cycle continues through October, until the season is finally over. This doesn't mean that the only worthwhile time to fish this section of the river is during the peak hatches. Let us start from opening day and fish our way through the season.

What opening day on the Upper Yellowstone generally means to us is insects everywhere, and we can either pick the type of water we want to fish or we can pick the hatch we wish to fish. However, for the sake of organization let's start the season off in the Estuary water. This section of water runs from the outlet of Yellowstone Lake to the Big Bend just above Le Hardy Rapids. It is often referred to by many anglers as some of the most challenging dry-fly water in the world, and justly so. This is deep, smooth, flat water that contains plenty of weed beds and other covers. The weed beds in turn hold lots of insects, and thus lots of trout. The trout in this smooth water are fussy. They have ample time to look over an offering and will seldom be fooled with a sloppy presentation. These conditions tend to make this an area the casual angler will not venture into. We have spent many an opening day fishing the Estuary water and have never felt crowded, and we've even fished sections where we haven't seen another angler all day.

The angler who opens the season on the Estuary water will generally encounter hatches of the gray drake, little brown sedge, tan short horn sedge, and even some early pale morning duns. The PMDs, if not there opening day, will generally show up by July 20.

However, all these insects lead to another problem for the angler to solve. Due to the type of water and abundance of available food, these trout are anything but easy. Often we have watched anglers wade into a section where the trout are actively feeding, fish for thirty or forty minutes and then move on, shaking their heads and talking to themselves. This frustration is often due to a lack of observation on the angler's part. This section of river, with its smooth-appearing currents, can be very deceptive, and the problem of drag is oftentimes the single greatest one the angler has to overcome. The billowing weed beds, which can grow to the top of the water or within inches of the top, create all kinds of mini currents that create drag for the angler who doesn't take the time to pick a fish, get into the proper position, and carefully cast, mend, and get a good drag-free presentation. One of the major keys to success here is letting your eyes do much of the fishing for you by picking a fishing spot and planning an approach with all the different currents in mind. Many follow the path of the dry fly, which is to fish up and across or up to a fish. This seldom works in the Estuary water due to the billowing weed beds and funny currents. The savvy angler will often fish down or down and across to a feeding trout. The angler fishing the Estuary water may also have to deal with trout that are selectively feeding on a certain stage of a certain insect. So be advised—know what is hatching and have well-stocked fly boxes.

Even though the Estuary is known as classic dry-fly water, the nymph fishing in this section can be equally as good and equally as challenging. The nymph fisher must be as careful of drag as is the dry-fly angler. A strike indicator, if used, must be carefully chosen so as not to spook the trout. The imitations of the nymphs and emergers are just as important if the angler is going to be successful. Choice of tackle can greatly affect the angler's success in this water. This is the place for the 2- to 4-weight rods and fine tippets. We often find ourselves fishing 6X and at times even 7X.

We will come back later in the season to the Estuary water. But before we move on, we need to again caution the angler about wading. This water is super clear and the depth can be very deceiving; therefore, wade slowly and with caution or you may be visiting the trout in their world. WET!

For the angler who would prefer to open the season where the fish are a little less selective, one might choose the half-mile section of water just above Le Hardy Rapids. Here the river changes and

starts to narrow up and gain a little more speed as it hurries on to
Le Hardy. The angler can open the season here with bigger stonefly nymphs and caddis imitations, along with larger dry flies. On
opening day the angler can expect to see salmon flies, small western salmon flies, golden stones, American grannom caddis, western
green drake, and small western red quills. After the Big Bend parking lot at the end of the Estuary water there is a hill the angler must
climb down to reach the river, and as the river starts to pick up
speed, the water can be very intimidating. However, this section offers some excellent angling with larger dry flies, and good nymphing
prospects. Le Hardy Rapids is closed to fishing. This water is just too
dangerous for the angler to be fooling about in.

In the half-mile of water just below Le Hardy Rapids, the angler
can expect to find just about the same conditions and hatches as
were found in the half-mile section just above the rapids. There is
one major difference for the angler—this section holds a lot of trout.
As the trout begin to move back to the lake, they hold below the
rapids as they feed and rest, building their strength for the trip up
through Le Hardy. Therefore, the savvy angler can always take a
few fish in this section. Once free of the influence of the rapids, the
river once again widens out and becomes a little more user-friendly.

From here down to Sulphur Caldron, the angler on opening day
can encounter western green drakes, pale morning duns, golden
stones, tan short horn sedge, little brown sedge, and American
grannom in huge numbers. This section of the river lends itself very
nicely to various nymph and dry techniques—there are water types
here for all skill levels. This section of river is also the most heavily
fished. However, if you arrive at the river around 7:30 A.M., you will
seldom see crowds much before 10:30 A.M., and the fishing can be
very good during these early hours. If you linger on after 7:00 P.M.
and fish till dark, you will notice a steady decrease in angler numbers.
This late-evening period ranks high as a favorite time to fish.

The Buffalo Ford area is a place that can enhance your observation skills not only in trying to figure out what is hatching and what
stages the trout are feeding on, but where these cutthroat trout lie,
hold, and feed. Early in the day when not much is happening in the

way of insects, the trout tend to hold in the deeper water. Depending on what section of Buffalo Ford one is in, the holding water might be something slightly deeper than the surrounding water. The fish that hold in the channels near the parking-lot bank will hold in significantly shallower water than the fish that hold in the water just down from the island. By carefully observing these areas one can actually see fish move to their feeding lies as the insect activity picks up. One of the all-time favorite feeding stations for a cutthroat in the upper river is anywhere there is a gravel bar with a depression, be it major or minor. Very often, these gravel bars will be adjacent to deeper holding water. Sometimes it is rewarding just to stand and watch the fish as they take their positions. Also, it's good to know that there are fish in the deeper sections, because one can begin fishing by nymphing these areas—it beats standing around while you're waiting for a hatch to start.

Due to the many and varied hatches, the upper Yellowstone provides some of the finest "spinner" fishing in the world. Seldom is the wind a problem for the evening spinner falls. However, if the angler is a grumpy sort, who doesn't care to fish around others, or feels that the trout below Le Hardy are just too easy, then he will want to open the season in the water below Hayden Valley. This runs from the mouth of Alum Creek down to Chittenden Bridge. On opening day this water means bank sippers and green drakes, gray drakes, maybe even pale morning duns, along with good hatches of the tan short horn sedge and little brown sedge. This is tough water to wade, so please be careful.

As one gets closer to Chittenden Bridge, one may even run into stoneflies. This section of the river also offers some very fine nymphing; however, we suggest that you stalk trout and only fish to the ones you can see. The nymphing angler may do very well with caddis pupa, along with imitations of both shrimp and sowbugs.

This pretty much takes you through the first ten days or so of the opening. Now, before we travel upstream to explore the second wave of hatches that will carry us into mid-August, let's discuss some of the skill the angler may need to work the selective trout found in some of these sections.

Tips on Fishing the Hatches

How to fish during the hatch, when the trout are selectively feeding on a certain stage of the hatching insect, can indeed be a perplexing problem. Careful observation is the key to understanding what imitation to use and how to fish it. Once again, the key to being successful is careful *observation!* Often we have used this phrase and then found that anglers either didn't know how to observe or what to observe. Therefore, we are going to explain each step we take when fishing a hatch, along with how and what we observe that influences what imitation we use and how it is used. We will use the Estuary water as an example, just above the Big Bend, and take you through a day in late July. What we are about to discuss is called "situational angling," and this topic could easily fill several volumes.

During a typical late-July day, an angler visiting this section can reasonably expect hatches of green drakes, gray drakes, pale morning duns, and speckled wing duns, along with tan short horn sedges, little brown sedges, and American grannom. Besides all that, the trout might also be feeding on midge worms, shrimp, scuds, leeches, and ants.

Now if we were concerned only with fishing the hatches, we could sleep in and not worry about arriving on the river until about 10:00 A.M. However, we prefer to arrive around 7:30 A.M., because we don't want to miss the gray drake or a possible spinner fall of green drakes or gray drakes.

Upon arriving on the bank of the section we are fishing, we would first take a few minutes and just watch to see what is on. The first thing that we might notice would be a few cutthroat cruising along the edges of a weed bed in a very established pattern, stopping now and then and turning toward the edge of the weed bed to take something, which might be a midge worm, scud, shrimp, or active PMD nymph. However, we also might see a few cutthroat cruising the currents of a back-eddy, gently sipping something from the surface film. Closer investigation reveals that the trout are feeding on leftover PMD spinners from the previous evening's spinner fall. Before we plunge right in and start casting about, we will carefully study the cruising patterns and the currents and plan an approach that will allow us to work the trout without spooking them.

As the day progresses we may find gray drakes or green drakes; however, we are going to skip past them and take you to the pale morning dun hatch. The first thing we might notice would be a few cutthroats "flashing" out along the edges of the weed beds. We would notice that a number of trout had moved into the channels between the weed beds, and others would be getting into position just off the major current lines. We would also notice that the trout were doing a lot less cruising and seeming to be holding in a more stationary area. This activity would suggest that the trout were indeed nymphing.

As the pale morning dun nymph prepares to hatch, it comes off the bottom or out of the weed beds and drifts with the current. This action can and does start as much as ninety minutes before the actual emergence. This action by the nymphs will start gradually and slowly build as the time for hatching grows near. In today's world of watching the clock and managing our time, we find that anglers often try to apply such measures to hatches. This is wrong. There is no whistle or bell that signals to the nymphs that it is time to start drifting. There is also no director yelling "Okay, it's time to hatch. On my mark!! *HATCH.*" No, this is a gradual process that *slowly* builds. Trout, being the opportunists they are, quickly notice this easily captured abundance of food and move to start feeding on it.

Once we had observed what the trout were doing, and because we already know the PMDs will soon begin hatching, we would select a nymph that imitates the nymph of the PMD and prepare to fish. For us, that might be a Sawyer-style PMD nymph. After selecting a trout and determining how to approach that fish, we then would proceed to work the feeding trout. Due to the gin-clear water, we would use a very delicate yarn type of strike indicator. Because the water in this section is deep, we would probably employ additional weight on the leader.

If we were on strange water and didn't know what to expect, we would get down below the feeding trout and sample the water to find out what they were feeding on. Upon hooking and landing the first trout, we would use a stomach pump to make sure of what the trout were feeding on.

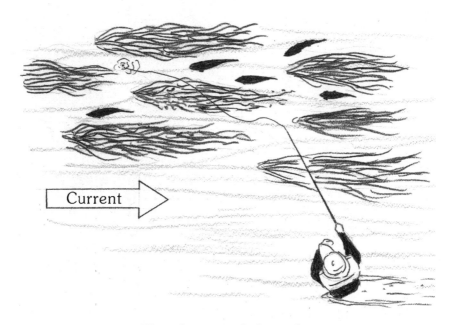

Nymphing weed channels

Drop a slightly weighted nymph and delicate strike indicator into the channel, up-stream of where the trout are holding.

For this angling situation, we would be using 2- to 4-weight rods. For leaders we would be using twelve-foot, 7X. In this situation we are working to visibly feeding trout. After a while, we would notice that the trout have moved up and are feeding in the middle water, and that the deep nymph action has slowed down. We would then remove the additional weight from the leader and continue to fish. The next thing we would observe is that the trout are taking nymphs that are just under or in the film. We would then remove the strike indicator and proceed to fish an imitation suited to the situation. For us that could be a Foam PMD Nymph or maybe a Curled Foam Emerger or a Harrop's PMD Transitional Nymph.

Finally, we would start to see the trout take the hatching nymphs in and on the film. For that situation we might use a Harrop CDC Transitional Adult or continue with the emergers. Through this whole process we would still be fishing to visible feeding trout, and for each trout we work we would be changing our position to get a good drag-free float. Oftentimes on warm days we will continue to fish the emergers throughout most of the actual hatch. We do this because observation has taught us that on warm bright days the insects hatch very quickly and the duns are only on the water a second or two. Therefore, the trout tend to ignore the duns and seem to concentrate on the emergers. However, on a cool damp day the duns will hatch out and ride the water for long periods of time, and trout will start to move on them. If this happens, it is time to switch over and use a thorax or parachute imitation. As the hatch starts we will often use a dun or spent dun. Why? Because there will still be what we call "feeders of opportunity," those fish that just haven't had enough and that will still move to adults.

Now this is a fairly simple, straightforward hatch, yet we still needed five to eight patterns to cover it effectively. Another thing to remember in this type of water: When you are stalking trout you can and will encounter trout that seem to be out of the mainstream of the hatch. These trout may be feeding on something different or on a different stage than most of the other trout. These are called situational angling problems, and the best way to solve them is with careful approach and observation.

Now let's continue with the seasonal changes on the Yellowstone. From July 15 to August 15 you are in the peak period of the hatches and there seem to be insects and trout everywhere, and as we stated earlier, you can pick your favorite water type or your favorite hatch.

Midseason

Starting in late August, many of the hatches fade and many of the trout have migrated back to the lake. The trout still in the river have become fussy and finicky. As all of this happens, the crowds of anglers start thinning out. Now this does not mean that the fishing has gone to hell. It *does* mean the angler needs to pay more attention and be a little more observant. By late August, hoppers, crickets, and ants can be very effective throughout the entire section. During the afternoon you still can find good hatches of caddis and the late afternoon brings the small western green drake (*Drunella flavilinea*) often referred to as just "flavs." There also may still be some caddis and small stoneflies. Up in the Estuary water, anglers will find the speckled wing dun, and the Tricos will start to appear. In the water below Alum Creek and up in the Estuary, wary anglers will also encounter the mahogany dun. In these sections the angler will notice more midge action.

By now the water levels have dropped and the wading is quite pleasant. As we get into September the Tricos, blue-winged olives, small western dark hendricksons, spotted sedges, and midges become the major hatches. All the while the trout numbers are decreasing. This is the time when the upper Yellowstone becomes a great training ground for anglers who are heading to New Zealand, because now those who enjoy the most consistent success do so by stalking the trout.

Late Season

Mid-September to closing brings us to the late season. Now the best fishing seems to be at the warmest time of the day, and the fishing on the upper Yellowstone becomes a gentleman's game, so to speak. You seldom need to arrive before 10:30 A.M., and the fishing is pretty much over by 5:00 P.M. The hatches continue to be Tricos, blue-winged olives, and midges. Most of the lake cutthroat are gone, and all that is left is the resident population. Most of the anglers have also moved on to easier trout that are more plentiful. This is one of our favorite times of the year to fish the park.

During the late season the savvy angler looks for areas where hot springs are entering the river. On the cooler current edges of these hot springs the trout will be very active, and during a hatch—wow— those are the places to be. Sulphur Caldron is one of those special places. The areas just above and below Le Hardy Rapids are excellent nymphing areas on which to bounce the bottom with stonefly and caddis nymph imitations. During the late season, shooting heads or full-sinking lines and Lite Spruce streamers can be deadly. By this time the water temperatures have cooled considerably, and the trouts' behavior will be affected by the cooler water. Tomorrow the season will close, and soon the lake will freeze over and a mantle of snow will blanket the earth, until warm south winds come back and another opening day draws near for one of the world's premier trout streams.

What flies should anglers carry with them? This depends so much on the section of water and the time of year. However, Royal Wulffs and Parachute Adamses, Elkhair Caddis, Griffith Gnats, and Black Crickets are patterns that we always have in various sizes. As for nymphs, we always have a few Princes, Red Fox Squirrels, and Bitch Creeks. We always have a few Muddler Minnows, dark olive Woolly Buggers, and Lite Spruce Streamers.

Locally Effective Patterns

PMD Para-Shuck

Hook:	Tiemco 101, sizes 16–14
Thread:	Light dun
Shuck:	Dun-dyed grizzly hackle tip
Body:	Pale yellow rabbit dubbing
Wing:	Light gray Z-lon, single post
Hackle:	Light dun, parachute-style

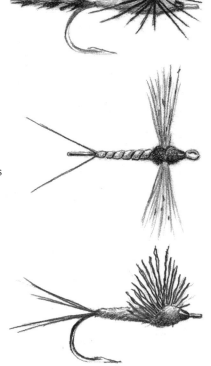

Biot Sparkle Spinner

Hook:	Tiemco 101, sizes 12–20
Thread:	Light olive
Tail:	Dun Micro Fibetts, split
Abdomen:	Light olive goose biot
Thorax:	Olive dubbing
Wings:	Medium-blue dun spinner-glass fibers

Organza Dun

Hook:	Tiemco 101, sizes 14–20
Thread:	Olive
Tail:	Blue-dun barbettes, split
Abdomen:	Light olive goose biot
Thorax:	Olive dubbing
Wing:	Medium-blue dun organza (spinner glass) tied Compara-dun style

Tom's Curled Callibaetis Emerger

Hook: Tiemco 2487, sizes 12–16
Thread: Gray
Tails: Mallard flank fibers
Shuck
 overlay: Grizzly-hackle fluff
Rib: Dark ultra translucent thread
Abdomen: Sheared natural gray muskrat
            fur, dubbed
Wing case: Gray mottled turkey-wing quill fibers
Post: Gray Scintilla fly foam
Hackle: Grizzly, undersized, parachute-style
Legs: Grizzly philo plume
Thorax: Pale bluish gray Scintilla dubbing #04
Head: Dubbed, same as abdomen

Callibaetis Parachute Sparkle Dun

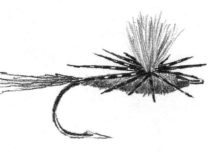

Hook: Tiemco 101, sizes 12–16
Thread: Gray
Shuck: Gray Antron body-wool fibers
Body: Scintilla dubbing, #10
            transparent gray
Wing post: White mottled turkey flat
            fibers
Hackle: Grizzly, parachute-style

Glass Bead Callibaetis Nymph

Hook: Tiemco 101, sizes 12–16
Thread: Gray
Bead: Pearl-Glass
Tails: Mallard flank fibers
Rib: Dark Ultra Translucent thread
Abdomen: Scintilla dubbing #10
            transparent gray
Thorax: Sheared natural gray muskrat,
            dubbed
Collar: Natural grizzly philo plume

Other Effective Patterns

Dark Olive Woolly Bugger   Royal Wulff
Hare's Ear Nymph   Yellow Humpy
Pheasant Tail Nymph   Parachute Adams
Prince Nymph   Green Drake Wulff

Black Girdle Bug
Gray/Olive Scud
Copper Nymph
Midge Pupa
Bitch Creek Nymph
Deep Caddis Sparkle Pupa
Peeking Caddis Nymph
Pale Morning Dun Emerger
Soft-Hackle Nymph
CDC Transitional Nymph
Pale Morning Dun Nymph
BWO Nymph
Red Fox Squirrel Nymph
Lite Spruce streamer

Golden Stones
Elkhair Caddis
Griffith Gnat
Trico Spinner
Dave's Hopper
Henry's Fork Cricket
Emergent Caddis Sparkle Pupa
Pale Morning Dun Thorax
Rusty Spinner
CDC PMD Emerger
Black ants
BWO Compara-dun
Muddler Minnow

Yellowstone Falls to Gardiner

Here the river and the fishing opportunities dramatically change character. Names like the Grand Canyon of the Yellowstone and the Black Canyon cause one to pause before considering a trip into these awe-inspiring places. "Rugged" would be an adjective that might border on the mild side yet still describe the countryside and the river itself. This section is for the adventure-seeker, the angler who wants to forgo the crowds and doesn't mind working for it. Most of all, it's for the physically fit. If you're one of those couch-potato anglers, consider getting into shape before even contemplating this stretch of river; it's one thing to get to the river, it's another getting back out. This can surely be the place for the "extreme" fly fisher.

The area between Chittenden Bridge and Inspiration Point is closed to fishing because of the Upper Falls (109 feet high) and Lower Falls (308 feet high). Both pour the water of the Yellowstone into the Grand Canyon of the Yellowstone, which is approximately fifteen miles long and ranks high in the rugged and spectacular scenery category. It is a wild river in the canyon, with steep drops and swift water. Sheer walls line a good portion of the canyon, preventing an angler from traveling up- or downstream. At the base of these walls is a river characterized by violent water; it's not a place

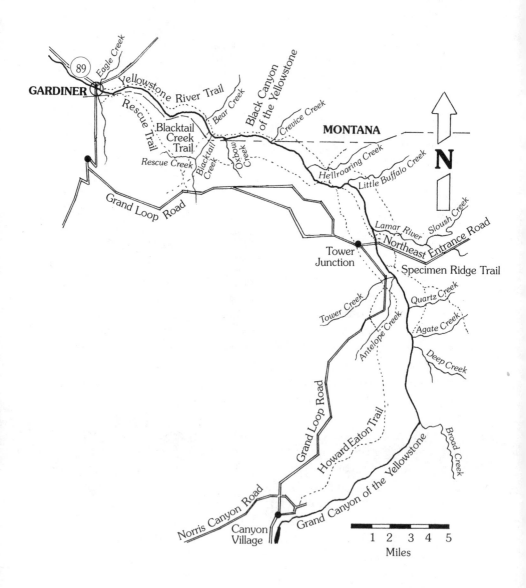

Yellowstone Falls to Gardiner

The river near Chittenden Bridge.

for a wading angler. However, when the water is low there are a few spots that may permit wading across, but use extreme caution.

This section sees water that is clearer earlier in the season than in the downstream portion because of the lack of tributaries that spill into it and dirty it in the spring and early summer. It opens to fishing on Memorial Day weekend and is at its best from that time to when the salmon fly hatch ends, usually around late July. The salmon-fly nymphs tend to migrate to shore so they can crawl out of the water and hatch as adults. This action puts vast numbers of nymphs near the shore, and the trout move out of the depths toward the shore in search of these huge morsels. Here the angler has a chance to fish to trout that are nearby and not sulking in the deep, swift water. Later in the year the large golden stones emerge, and similar fishing can be had. One constantly hears stories of the fishing being so good that the fishermen wear themselves out (maybe the hike in or the thought of the hike out has something to do with this).

Recent years have seen an increase in the number of anglers willing to make the fifteen-hundred-foot vertical descent into the canyon. Either we are in better shape than our predecessors or more information is available about the fishing here. We suspect there are more anglers in search of new uncrowded conditions than there were before, anglers that don't mind some physical hardships. It is getting tougher and tougher to find water that one can have to oneself.

The last section of the Yellowstone before it exits the park at Gardiner is known as the Black Canyon, and it is truly magnificent. It may even be one of the park's least-known and visited scenic wonders. The good news is that access to this twenty-mile stretch is easier and less strenuous than to the Grand Canyon: the bad news is that it still takes some good hikes to get to it, especially if you want to reach the middle portion, which is far from a road. More of the river can be fished here, because a trail runs along its entire length from Roosevelt to Gardiner, but not in one day. The Lamar River does dump into the Yellowstone in this section, which limits how early in the season one can fish it. The time of the year when this portion of river is fished the most is right after runoff, when the salmon flies are out and about. The Lamar does dump a considerable amount of roil into the river when runoff is full-blown, so much depends on when the Lamar clears. Usually the first few weeks in July, again depending on water flows, is the optimum period, with clear water and plenty of big bugs. As in the Canyon portion, the salmon-fly nymphs migrate to the shore, where they attract fish, and the fisherman has easy pickings.

Although July may be the optimum time to fish here, it is by no means the only time. Insects hatch throughout the season and bring fish to the surface in good numbers. Those who can nymph-fish deep pool-like water do very well most of the year. There is a giant golden stone that hatches throughout the summer, and the angler twitching an imitation can usually expect to bring a fish up from the depths. When the hoppers are in full strength, some excellent fishing can also be had. We have friends from out of state who would rather fish this section of river all summer long than anywhere else. They swear by the quality of fishing here—to each his own.

This entire stretch of river from the Lower Falls down has trout that are non-native. Inspiration Point down to Knowles Falls has cutthroats, rainbows, brook trout, whitefish, and a rainbow-cutthroat hybrid. The section from Knowles Falls to Gardiner has all the above plus brown trout. This section has experienced the effects of stocking outside the park because fish have run upstream. This entire stretch is among the least studied by the park fisheries people because it's just too difficult to do so. The rough water makes taking an accurate sample very difficult. As a matter of management practice the rainbow trout is protected here because novice fishermen might have a hard time telling one from a cutthroat. (As a side note, we find many novices commenting on how many brown trout they catch on the upper river near Buffalo Ford and on Slough Creek, although there aren't any in those areas.)

This entire stretch is well worth any effort in terms of fishing, beauty, and the solitude of a wilderness experience. It would probably be fair to say that there are parts of this stretch that don't see anglers every year and parts that have never even had a fly float on them. Many anglers who do venture into this section do so on a very limited basis. For some it may be a yearly trip, for others it may be once every few years, and for others still, it may be one trip in a lifetime. The anglers who make this section a regular part of their fishing are few and far between, and probably in better shape that most of us.

Water Characteristics

Mostly, the water is fast, violent, and unwadeable. The canyon sections with sheer walls narrow the river and force the water to move at a rapid pace—far too rapid to deal with except along the banks. This is a big, brawling river with deep, swift, and treacherous sections. Where the river emerges from the canyon at Tower Falls it is fast and powerful but fishable. The key is to fish close to the bank, where the contours of the bank create some calmer pockets that can be fished successfully.

Farther downstream in the Black Canyon section the river is still big and brawling, but there are more places where it widens out and becomes wadeable. It is almost like a pocket-water stream, but on gargantuan proportions. There are large boulders in the channels with deep swirling pockets behind them. There are spots with riffle corners that an angler could easily fish. A good way to characterize the river here is as challenging—challenging because of the fast-water character and challenging because the angler has to figure a way of fishing it successfully. The mix of water is runs, rapids, cascades, even a fall, and deep pools. Not your average let's-wade-out-a-bit-and-fish kind of water.

Stay near the banks even if a wadeable section is discovered—it is too far from any medical help if the need arises, and those who tire themselves wading and fishing are going to pay dearly on the way out. Keep some energy in reserve. We make the trip into these sections sound grueling—and it's really not—but it *does* take some effort.

Accessibility

There are quite a few spots from which to access this remote portion of the river, and all of them take some work. When planning a trip into this section, plan for the hike in and out as the first priority, and the fishing itself as the secondary one. Make sure you have a first-aid kit with you, a well broken-in pair of hiking shoes, a snack or lunch, and some spare clothing. Carry water, Halazone tablets, or a portable water purifier to prevent dehydration—some summer days take more out of you than you may think. If you plan to do some wading, a pair of lightweight waders and wading shoes fit nicely in a day pack. It's not possible to travel very far, fish, and get out again in one day, so carefully plan what you think is reasonable. Those of you looking for more of a trip can spend a few days along the trail camping. This is an area where grizzly bears are known to frequent, so take the necessary precautions. And there are rattlesnakes down there, too; be careful where you step.

Starting at Inspiration Point there is a trail called Seven Mile Hole Trail that will lead you down into the Grand Canyon and the river. Here the trail ends, and access to other portions is a tough go, cross-country. This is one of those areas with a lot of water that never sees a fly. Another way of reaching the river is along the

Howard Eaton Trail, but this trail only parallels eleven miles of river from a distance. By traveling across country off this trail, one could come to some pretty remote areas of the canyon. This would be the trail to take if one wanted to hike from Tower Falls campground.

At Tower Junction one can access the Specimen Ridge Trail and cover a three-mile section of river to the bridge that crosses from Roosevelt, the northeast entrance road. This trail runs along a section of river called The Narrows. Actually, from the bridge upstream there is some very fishable water, especially so in low-water years. Many anglers will also work their way downstream from the bridge, although there is no marked trail.

At Roosevelt Lodge and Cabins there is a trailhead for the Garnet Hill Trail that works its way five miles down to the river in the Black Canyon section. At this point is a suspension bridge that crosses the river—kind of neat in an adventurous way. There is a shorter way down to the river that meets the Garnet Hill Trail a short distance before the suspension bridge, but it isn't named on the park map. Look near the Floating Island Lake for this trail; it will cut a few miles off the hike. Check your maps before venturing off, or you could spend a long day walking and not fishing. By crossing the bridge, one hooks up with the Yellowstone River Trail, which follows the river for about twenty-four miles into Gardiner. For the angler looking to spend a few days or longer on a pack trip, this is the trail to do it on. By entering from the Gardiner side, a number of different trips can be planned: one could do the entire thirty miles to Roosevelt or a fifteen-mile hike coming out along the Blacktail Trail.

The Howard Eaton Trail parallels the river but from quite a distance, and it really isn't a feasible way to reach the river. The next access downstream is the Blacktail Trail—it is well marked with a trailhead marker. This trail leads down into the Black Canyon for about five miles, crosses the river at Blacktail Bridge, and hooks up with the Yellowstone River Trail. This trail gives the angler another option for an extended stay: take either the fifteen miles toward Gardiner or a twenty-four-mile trip back to Roosevelt.

Many fishermen use the Yellowstone River Trail out of Gardiner to spend part of their days devoted to fishing. It's about a six-mile hike up to Knowles Falls, with fishing in between, and this can make a pleasant two- or three-day campout. There are outfitters in and around Gardiner who will gladly take you to these areas on horseback if you so desire, for a price of course. This isn't a bad way to go, especially if you are out of shape (if you're not used to riding, you will have sore muscles) or only have a short time to see and fish this area.

This section of river offers the angler a chance to have a wilderness experience, get away from the crowd, fish some spectacular water, and view some unbelievable scenery. With some proper advance planning, a trip into the Grand Canyon or Black Canyon will be as rewarding an experience as you'll likely encounter in this lifetime.

Seasonal Changes: The Fishing

Due to the official park season, there is less time possible here than on the Yellowstone outside the park; therefore, we will break it up a little differently. The very first thing the angler planning a trip to this section needs to understand is that there is limited information on the hatches and no experts who have put in thousands of days working the water. The other day, Tom was saying that after going through twenty years of his fishing journals, that he had spent a total of fifty-six days on this section of river. Rod has spent about the same amount of time there. We have interviewed many anglers, both resident and nonresident, who have never fished this section and others who may have spent as little as two to ten days on it. Well-known fishing guide Bob Jacklin of West Yellowstone has been guiding around the area for twenty-five years. Bob told us that maybe he has spent fifty to sixty days on this section of river. Bob considers this section of the Yellowstone to be excellent dry-fly water and a good place to fish attractor-type dry flies as well as hoppers. Bob, who has run Jacklin's Fly Shop in West Yellowstone since 1974, made an audio tape with Gary LaFontaine on the Yellowstone River in the park (this tape is part of the River Rap Series, published by Greycliff Publishing). We mention this because the tape is a good way for the angler who wishes to fish the Yellowstone to pick up some very valuable fishing tips from one of the top fishing guides in the area. The information covered by Gary and Bob in this tape will give the visiting angler a much better feel for the river.

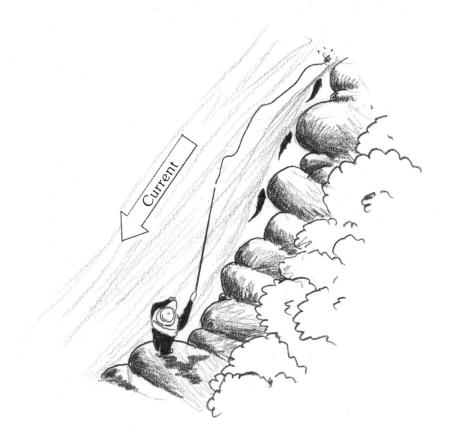

Current

Nymphing the shoreline

Walk and cast upstream to fish holding in the calmer, quieter water created by the rocky shoreline.

The Early Season: June and July

This section of river opens to fishing on the Saturday of Memorial Day weekend. The angler who wishes to try this section early will probably have to fish in the Tower Falls area, which is upstream from where the Lamar empties into the Yellowstone. Even in this section the angler may not find the water too clear! Upstream from the Lamar the angler can find the river milky during June. In a normal year, the higher water levels wash the sides of the canyon, thus the milky color. However, by late June the river will start to drop and the big salmon fly nymphs will begin migrating toward the shore in preparation for emerging. During this time the angler can find some excellent nymphing as the trout move toward the shore to feed. Generally, upstream nymphing methods are best, because the wading is very limited and the water is still high and fast. Generally, the salmon flies will start to hatch around July 4, and the angler can follow the progression up from the park line.

Once July arrives, the river has started to clear and drop, and the salmon fly hatch is just the beginning. It is followed by the golden stones, small golden stones, yellow sally stones, and olive stones, along with caddis. Once the hatches start, this section of river offers the angler some very good dry-fly fishing. Stonefly hatches go on throughout most of the summer. By mid-July the angler will also encounter good hatches of small western red quills. These are often lost among the stonefly hatches. Once the hatches get started, the trout become used to seeing a lot of larger naturals on the water. Also, this section holds a lot of the cutthroat trout that seem to enjoy rising to drys. Therefore, anglers can expect good dry-fly fishing with stonefly imitations as well as with attractor patterns like Royal Trudes, Royal Wulffs, Madam X's, and Stimulators.

Mid-Season: August to Mid-September

As August arrives, so does the hatch of the giant western golden stone, along with hatches of the spotted sedge and the green sedge. These hatches keep the trout looking up. Also during August we have hopper fishing. The hopper fishing in this section of river can at times be fast and furious; there can be days when you might think that the trout had never seen a hopper by the way they smash them. By August the river has dropped a considerable amount and the wading is a little easier; still, this is never a place to be careless. Though many anglers prefer the dry-fly fishing that this stretch of river seems to offer, there are also some excellent nymphing opportunities. In August, one of our favorite techniques is to fish a dry-nymph combination, like a hopper with a Beadhead Caddis Emerger three inches behind the hopper.

What to do about fishing the hatches? We advise that when you find them, fish them. However, you will seldom find the fishing tough when using attractor patterns, either dry or wet. During early September we have enjoyed some good fishing with small flying black ants. Because small ants are hard to see on some rough-water sections, we will often fish them in tandem with another dry that is more visible.

Late Season: Mid-September to Closing Day

Mid-September brings the start of the blue-winged olives. There are certain areas of the river that have excellent hatches of these insects. Two that come to mind are the section below Knowles Falls, that runs from the base of the falls downstream for three-quarters of a mile, and the area where Hellroaring Creek enters the river and downstream for a half-mile. There may be other sections, but these are the two that we have the most experience with during this period. During mid–September, and in some years clear to mid-October, the angler can still find hopper fishing here. With the exception of the blue-winged olives, most of the hatches disappear by early October. However, the nymphing is still very good.

Streamer fishing is another option that is very effective during the late season. Between the Lower Falls and Knowles Falls, one is fishing primarily for rainbows and cutthroats. In this section we find Lite Spruce streamers, Muddler Minnows, White Zonkers, mottled olive Woolhead Sculpins, and white sculpins to be very effective.

Below Knowles Falls the brown trout have entered the system, and by mid- to late September browns are moving and gathering for the fall spawning run. In this section we prefer Western Lite Spruce Feather streamers, along with dark olive Sculpin Buggers, dark olive Flash-A-Buggers, black Girdle Buggers, and standard Dark Spruce streamers. For whitefish we recommend—No, no, you probably don't want those recommendations!

If you want uncrowded water you can always find it in this section of the river, and that is especially true during the late season.

The river in Hayden Valley.

Locally Effective Patterns

Metallic Golden Stone

Hook:	Tiemco 5212, sizes 6–10
Thread:	Yellow
Underbody:	Closed-cell foam
Overwraps:	Strands of yellow Krystal Flash wound over foam body
Hackle:	Ginger, palmered and clipped
Underwing:	Light brown turkey quill
Overwing:	Light elk hair
Legs:	White rubber legs

Beadhead Golden Stone Nymph

Hook:	Tiemco 200R, sizes 4–10
Bead:	Gold, appropriately sized
Thread:	Brown
Tails:	Two amber goose biots
Ribbing:	Light transparent amber Swannundaze
Abdomen:	Fifty-fifty blend of hare's-ear and golden-stone dubbing
Wing case:	Brown mottled turkey quill section pulled over thorax
Thorax:	Same as abdomen
Hackle:	Grizzly and brown, mixed, and clipped on bottom

Yellow Sally Trude

Hook:	Tiemco 101, sizes 16–12
Thread:	Yellow
Tail:	Light elk hair
Body:	Rear third fluorescent red, the rest yellow dubbing
Wing:	White calf tail
Hackle:	Ginger

Tom's Extended-Body Gray Drake Spinner

Hook: Tiemco 101, sizes 10–12
Thread: Gray
Body
 extension: .017 Maxima monofilament
Tails: Three moose body hairs
Rib: Two or three strands
 of black Krystal Flash
Abdomen: Scintilla dubbing #61
 siphlonurus gray
Wings: Two grizzly hackle,
 oversized (one size),
 closely wrapped in the
 wing area
Thorax: Dubbed same as abdomen,
 using the dubbing in a
 crisscross manner to
 form the wings

Tom's Extended-Body Gray Drake

Hook: Tiemco 101, sizes 10–12
Thread: Gray
Body
 extension: .017 Maxima monofilament
Tails: Three moose body hairs
Rib: Two or three strands of
 black Krystal Flash
Abdomen: Scintilla dubbing #61
 siphlonurus gray
Wing post: Gray Antron body wool
Thorax: Dubbed same as the abdomen
Hackle: Grizzly, parachute-style

Tom's Gray Drake Flymph

Hook: Tiemco 947BL, sizes 8–12
Thread: Gray
Tails: Natural teal flank fibers
Rib: One or two strands of
 black Krystal Flash
Body: Tapered, dubbed, Upstream
caddis/emerger #08 gray
Wing pads: Black marabou tips
Collar: Black and grizzly hen hackle, mixed

Other Effective Patterns

Black Girdle Bug
Bitch Creek Nymph
Black Girdle Bugger
Dark Olive Woolly Bugger
Lite Spruce Streamer
Dark Spruce Streamer
White Zonker
Silver Zonker
Kaufmann's Black Stone Nymph
Kaufmann's Golden Stone Nymph
Burlap Nymph
Muskrat Nymph
Prince Nymph
Peeking Caddis
Hare's Ear Nymph

Royal Wulff
Yellow Humpy
Sofa Pillow
Yellow Sally
Kaufmann's Yellow Stimulator
Kaufmann's Orange Stimulator
Goddard Caddis
BWO Parachute
Dave's Hopper
Whit Hopper
Elkhair Hopper
Foam Skittering Caddis
SRI Irresistible Caddis
Parachute Caddis
Dry Muddler Minnow

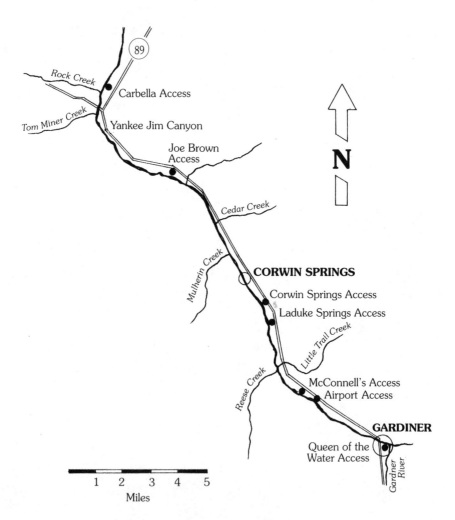

Gardiner to Yankee Jim Canyon

3

Gardiner to
Yankee Jim Canyon

The Yellowstone River exits Yellowstone National Park and the protection it offers to flow through numerous towns, ranches, and ter-
rains before meeting the mighty Missouri. The first of these towns is
Gardiner, a small western hamlet that blooms into a tourist town in
the summer months, caters to hunters in the fall, and is a staging
area for a limited number of snowmobilers during the winter. It is
also the north entrance to the park with all the amenities a park border town has to offer. There are a number of motels, lodges, restaurants, gift shops, places to camp, a few fly shops, more than a few
taverns, places to sign up for scenic raft trips, and many other things
to entertain oneself with. Because it is an entrance to the park it has
the feel, in the summer, of a family vacation area. Oddly, it hasn't
gained the reputation for being a fly-fishing town, as West Yellowstone or Livingston have, even though the river flows right through
town. This isn't to say that thousands of fly fishermen don't fish in
this area, because they do, but Gardiner just hasn't developed into a
perceived angling mecca.

Angling is an important element to this town because thousands
of fly fishers travel through it over the course of a year. Many who
stay in town look to other destinations than the waters nearby. Perhaps the mystique and glamour of the park have something to do
with this. This isn't to say that many visiting anglers do not fish this
stretch of river, for they do, but the numbers do not reflect the total
number of anglers in the area. This stretch of river has some quality
fishing available, especially during the salmon fly hatch, but for most

of the year it seems to be underutilized by the sheer number of anglers who pass through it. The traveling angler seems to want the experience of the more noted stretches of water, and the anglers who live in the surrounding areas seem to fish the sections of river nearest to them. It may be a little too far for the guides from Livingston and Bozeman to travel, day in and day out. Most of the fishery is left to the locals, a few guides operating and living in the area, and the occasional visiting angler.

As stated, there is some quality fishing to be had on this stretch on a daily basis. The greater numbers of cutthroats make even the dog days of midsummer productive—because of the cutthroats, this area is known as a place to take clients when the fishing is extremely slow on other stretches of the river. The salmon fly hatch is the premier event and draws anglers from all around the area—it even brings the guides over with their clients. This frenetic period is the time when this stretch is most crowded, and in some ways exciting. Catching trout on #4 dry flies is something that has to be experienced to be fully appreciated, and watching anglers in other boats whoop it up adds to the enjoyment. As the hatch wanes, so does the number of fishermen, and when the tourist season is over after Labor Day, a fisherman can pretty much have this section to himself.

Topography and Water Characteristics

This section, as it runs through the town of Gardiner downstream, has the feel of a small gorge, especially so in the heart of town. The banks are a rather steep drop to the river and are canyon-like. As one floats this section, the steep banks give way to more gentle slopes, but only on the west side of the river—the east side is still fairly steep. Both sides steepen as the river enters Yankee Jim Canyon, then gently ease as the canyon gives way to the broad expanses of Paradise Valley. Here the illusion is that the river seems to become larger or wider, even though the volume is the same. There is an almost confined feeling to this fifteen-or-so-mile section when one is on the water.

The Devil's Slide area.

A good deal of the upper stretch contains some significant white water under certain conditions; many white-water enthusiasts like to "do the rollies" right in town. Much of the river is boulder-strewn with some substantial rocks to maneuver around, so some interesting waves form. The floater who is not on his toes could get into some trouble in this first mile or so. However, not too many drift boats put in at the Queen of the Waters access because it involves carrying or dragging one's boat down a long steep bank. Most of the floaters who use this access do it in rafts or kayaks. This is the first access where one can legally enter the water with a boat of any sort.

There are all types of different water characteristics in this stretch, from the heavy fast rapids to long, smooth, flat glides and everything in between. Overall, one could characterize this stretch as large fast pocket water. The many twists and turns not only make for some interesting fishing but keep the oarsman on his toes. At certain times during the low water one has to carefully pick a path through the shallow riffles or end up dragging the boat over some nasty rocks. Also, during some of the high-water periods, a careful path must be chosen to avoid potentially dangerous confrontations with heavy water.

The first mile or so from where the Gardner River (spelled differently than the town name) flows into the Yellowstone has a series of rapids and rollers, especially right after runoff, and could prove to be a bit difficult for the novice oarsman. Since most fisherman do not use that access, it's not too big a deal. However, there are times when that section fishes real well and the temptation to launch there is great, but the water levels are usually down, so the danger is minimized somewhat. A dose of prudent judgment will go a long way for a safe and fun float. After this initial burst of adrenaline most of the rest of the floatable water is relatively easy.

Every type of water can be found in this stretch, and a floating angler will easily determine where fish should be found. There is an abundance of good banks with holding water abutting deeper lies; the twists and turns of the river create some great riffle corners and all kinds of current edges to cast a fly into. There is very little braiding, but the river does not need it because the water has enough character that an angler will know where he should fish based on his water preferences. Willows line some banks and hold many of the insects that the fish lie in wait for, especially during the salmon fly hatch. There is a very good ratio of riffle, runs, and pools, and long sections of typical "cutthroat water"—long, deep, slow glides. A few smaller creeks dump into the river in this stretch and provide some hot spots to cast to; there are even some thermal areas, the most notable being LaDuke Spring.

Yankee Jim Canyon is at the end of this stretch and is the only really dangerous place on the upper river. It is dangerous because there are three nasty rapids, classified as Class III whitewater, that could thoroughly ruin your day. Of course, water flows are an important factor in choosing to float this short section—some times and flows are safer than others. However, the angler in a drift boat would be well advised to stay out of this canyon—too many drift boats have been swamped by the waves that develop here. The odd part is that the water before and after these rapids is easy, but at least one of the rapids is positioned in a manner that prevents easy maneuvering to avoid its force and heavy water. Inflatable rafts, especially self-bailers, can handle this water most of the time, but count on getting wet, and make sure everything is securely lashed down. There are some pull-outs along the road that parallels the canyon and offer a chance to view the rapids before making any decisions about floating. If your raft-handling skills are toward the novice end of the scale, pass and take a shorter float—nothing ruins a good day fishing like dumping the raft and losing gear. If you are interested in some white-water fun, this little stretch will get the blood pumping.

The water between the rapids holds some of the largest fish in the river—so the temptation is great to fish the canyon. Water depths have been measured to over sixty feet deep here, and this, coupled with relatively fast water, make fishing the banks the only feasible way to present a fly to a trout. The banks are rocky in a riprap sort of way and provide great holding areas for fish. Floating and fishing the canyon verges on the "extreme" fly-fishing category. As one survives the third rapid the water begins to slow, get shallower, and broaden, and the banks begin to gradually slope away from the river. This section ends at the beginning of Paradise Valley.

Accessibility

One of the benefits of having the river run through a town is that there are usually many access points nearby, shuttle services available, and places to stock up on food and tackle. This section of river has a wide variety of access sites that are available to the public and make customizing a full-day trip or a few hours of fishing a snap. There are no long out-of-the-way shuttles to contend with, nor are the roads especially hard on one's vehicle. It's relatively easy to float the same section of water a couple of times in the same day—depending on how much time one has and how much time is spent out of the boat. Many anglers like to float shorter distances, getting out of the boat and working sections of water they particularly like, while other anglers prefer floating straight through and fishing from the boat. Unlike some other sections of river where the access points are few and far between, which makes stopping and covering *all* the good water impractical, this section allows the angler to tailor the trip to meet whatever suits him. As in any river section, especially one so near a town, there are many places to reach the river that are private and require permission to use. This local knowledge is sometimes shared if one asks around at the shops. Please remember that access to the water does not give one the right to trespass on private land—take care where you venture to.

The first of the access points is the Queen of the Waters site, at the junction of the Gardner and Yellowstone Rivers. This isn't an obvious site—it is tucked away behind the TWA (park concessionaire) building and appears to be on private land. It also isn't a very easy or practical place for the fisherman wishing to launch his drift boat, because there is a long steep bank leading to the river. Many of us cringe at the thought of dragging an expensive boat (usually our prized possession) over the rocks; besides, it's probably more work than we really want to do at the start of a fishing trip. However, the raft owner might be inclined, especially with help, to carry it down the slope, because this access starts a short white-water section that is fun to float, and the fishing is good. This is a good access point for the walking fisherman, because he can work upstream to the park or even fish the Gardner if he so chooses. Very often, when the fishing is exceptionally good, anglers will go to the trouble of dragging their boats down the steep slope in order to extend the distance of the float and have the opportunity to cover more water.

The next access point is one of those old locally known points that isn't on a map but is still in use because it adds a few miles and more water to extend a float trip. It's called the Airport access (actually it's a mile or so south of the airport), and it's best to ask for directions at one of the shops in Gardiner. The access is unimproved, with no facilities. At the river there is just a narrow opening in the willows where one can launch a boat.

McConnell Landing is the first improved site in this section where launching a drift boat is no problem. It's a day-use-only area that does not allow overnight camping. There is a handicapped-accessible rest room, a gravel ramp, and parking. It is clearly marked, so finding it is real easy. This is the access site most often used by those who float this section of river.

Next in line is the LaDuke Spring area, which has no ramp or space to launch a boat. It does have a large picnic area with barbecue grills and trash receptacles. There are rest rooms, but they are not handicapped-accessible. The walk fisherman could enter the water here and leave his vehicle parked in relative safety.

The Corwin Springs access site has no rest rooms or picnic area, but it does have a ramp area, mostly sand, to launch a boat. It is a little on the rough side but a good place to launch from if a short float is desired. It is clearly marked by a sign on the highway. Crossing the bridge at Corwin Springs and traveling about a quarter of a mile back upstream, one comes to another unofficial access that many people use. It is an area where there is a cut in the bank, and it is not marked in any fashion—but it's relatively hard to miss. Although many boaters use this area, it is on private land and permission should be sought before using it.

The Joe Brown access site is usually the end of the line for most floaters, because it is the last access before entering Yankee Jim Canyon. Some floaters have made the mistake of floating by it because the fishing was good or because they wanted to extend their time on the water (figuring it would be no problem to hitchhike back for their rig) and have paid dearly for it. There is some significant white water in the canyon, and there are times (most of the time) when a drift boat should definitely not be in there, nor should inexperienced rafters. This is a day-use-only area, with picnic tables, trash receptacles, and a handicapped-accessible rest room. There is a dirt ramp— actually it's sandy and relatively easy to get stuck in—on which to launch a boat or, in most cases, take a boat out of the water.

There are a number of pullouts along the highway that parallels the river through Yankee Jim Canyon where the walk fisherman can park a vehicle and reach the river. This will entail scrambling over riprap to fish. It is not advisable to enter the water and wade in much of the canyon unless you are very, very tall.

Another caution for the wading angler in the canyon is to beware of rattlesnakes. There are a number of these unpopular critters in the canyon, and an encounter of the wrong kind could definitely ruin a day. To say the least!

Those of you who do venture into the canyon with a raft will end up at the Carbella access. A good indicator that you're nearing it is the Tom Miner Bridge; the access is downstream of the bridge a short distance. Although some people use the bridge as an access site, it is on private land and it is posted. Carbella has a dirt ramp, no rest rooms, and no picnic tables, but it does allow camping with a fourteen-day limit.

This entire stretch of river is an interesting area to fish because of the variety of water and the accessibility of the water. There is something for everyone in this section, from the pulse-quickening white water to the calm, easily wadeable waters.

The Fish

This is a unique area because nowhere else in the entire river system do we find such an even mix of the trout species: approximately 33 1/3 percent brown, 33 1/3 percent rainbow, and 33 1/3 percent cutthroat. Each species is able to find suitable habitat, and there isn't an overabundance of any one species that would allow one to become more populous at the expense of the others. The cutthroats have good spawning grounds nearby that aren't dewatered by irrigators, and there is always the water within the nearby park to use.

There is an interesting theory floating around about the lack of large (sixteen-inch-plus) cutthroats in this stretch and the sections downstream into the valley. The theory goes something like this: The length of the cutthroats hasn't increased much beyond the fourteen-inch mark over the last five or so years because the "fast-growing" ones have been culled by past practices of overharvesting them. So what remains in the system are the slow-growers that may have an altered genetic pool. In effect, the ones with the "big" genes have been eliminated from the river, leaving only the "small-gened" cutthroats to reproduce. Thus, all we have are these smaller fish. It's an interesting theory, but as of now, only a theory.

The rainbows hold their own here because there is suitable water for them to thrive in, but no one seems to have pinned down where they spawn. According to people at the Montana Department of Fish, Wildlife and Parks there seems to be a mystery surrounding where these fish actually do spawn. The department is and has been studying the phenomenon but hasn't been able to locate the sites. There is speculation that rainbows use the main stem of the river, but that hasn't been proven, or that they migrate up into the Black Canyon area in the park. Interesting, but not a high priority in their understaffed and underfunded budgets.

The brown trout use the main stem of the river to spawn, in addition to some of the tributaries. The Gardner River has long held a reputation for holding huge numbers of browns in the fall. There have been magazine articles printed about the brown-trout fishing in this river each autumn, and many locals head there to attempt to get a big one. As mysterious as the whereabouts of the rainbow spawning grounds, the browns also have a mystery all their own. For reasons that are still unknown, a good percentage of the browns in this stretch are afflicted with blind-eye disease, which covers their eyes with a film, blinding them. Afflicted fish can't find food and eventually starve. Many of the brown trout in this stretch never grow beyond the eighteen-inch mark because of this. There is no known cause of this disease, but biologists believe it is probably water-quality or food-chain related. If you happen to catch a brown in this stretch, check out its eyes and see if you can tell if a film is developing over them.

There are quite a few whitefish in this stretch, probably in the ratio to trout of ten to one, although there aren't accurate counts. When the fishing is real slow, whitefish fill in the time between trout. Of course when the fishing is fast and furious, no one wants to deal with them.

Seasonal Changes: The Fishing

This is a most interesting section of river to fish during the winter months, because the influx of water from hot springs creates some unusual fishing opportunities that might not otherwise exist.

A rainbow taken during the salmon fly hatch.

During the spring we find that the caddis are not as strong as on the lower river. However, we find that the salmon fly hatch on this section of river is the strongest on the river outside the park. During late summer this section offers some excellent dry-fly opportunities due to the higher percentage of cutthroats. During the fall this section offers uncrowded fishing opportunities because it is underfished then.

Winter: Mid-November to February

The fishing during the winter months of November through February is limited by the weather, which is the single largest factor for the angler to consider. Fall can end and the winter can begin in the space of twenty-four hours as storm fronts come sweeping down out of the north, and soon the river might be frozen over and unfishable. However, this is Montana and not the North Pole, so even during the winter months there will be some warmer periods where the angler can get out and chase the trout. In November, that means spawning brown trout, and every year two or three really impressive browns are taken on this section by anglers using streamers and big nymphs. As we slide into December and January, the savvy angler who locates the current edges where hot springs dump into the river can even find some limited dry-fly action on midges. Even if there are no midges evident, the angler will be able to pick up several trout on nymphs like the Hare's Ear, Prince, Brownstone, and Montana Stones. As we get into late February the foam pools, back-eddies and quiet-water areas will begin to produce during the midge hatches. Due to the hot springs in this section of river there is always productive water to fish during the winter; the only limiting factors would be the air temperature and the wind.

Spring: March to Runoff

During a normal March, the midge hatch starts on this section of the river. By late March the angler may even encounter some early blue-winged olives, depending on the weather cycles. During March the rainbows start seriously to move and gather for spawning. Even though the water temperature may be hovering in the mid- to low forties, the thermal areas are still excellent places for an angler to work. As we approach April, the nymphing really picks up as the trout begin feeding on cased caddis and stonefly nymphs. With the exception of the midge and blue-winged olive hatches, the most productive way to fish during this period is with nymphs. Locally effective patterns, such as the Beadhead Prince Nymph, Brownstone, Black Girdle Bug, Montana Nymph, and Peeking Caddis Nymph can produce some excellent results.

By the end of April we start to see the western march brown mayfly hatch, which is soon followed by the caddis hatch. Throughout the end of April and during early May the dry-fly fishing can be excellent on this section of the river. Generally, the river will go out around the tenth of May. "Going out" means that, due to the warmer air temperatures, the runoff has made the river too high and discolored to effectively fish. In a normal year the river will not become fishable again until approximately late June.

Early Summer: June and July

For much of June the Yellowstone is high and unfishable. Somewhere around the twentieth of June the river will start to drop and clear. During this time the salmon flies first appear on the river, and the hatch will then travel upstream. The Gardiner to Yankee Jim Canyon is the premier section of the river for this hatch.

Each year many people travel to Montana to fish the fabled salmon fly hatch. Most of the time they miss the hatch. Still, they have some pretty fair fishing nonetheless. Catching the hatch just right is tricky business and requires as much luck as anything else. However, of all the famous Montana rivers that have the salmon fly, we believe the hatch on the Yellowstone is the most consistent and the easiest for the angler to plan for. But why do anglers return year after year in search of the "hatch"? Simply put, the salmon fly hatch can bring up some very large trout to the dry fly in addition to the excellent fishing opportunities offered by big nymphs and wet drowned adults. This hatch can produce, if timed right and properly planned, some of the most exciting fishing an angler will ever experience.

Hatching dates are greatly affected by weather cycles. During a warm mild winter and early hot spring, the hatch can come up to three weeks early. With a cold wet spring the hatch may be a week or two late. We have seen both extremes here on the Yellowstone. The best advice we can offer is to call one of the local fly shops. Generally by late April, local experts will have a feel for the weather cycles and upcoming runoff and can offer some reasonable advice on when to come for the best chance of hitting the hatch. The angler planning a trip to fish the salmon fly hatch should be somewhat flexible and plan for several days, not just one. Actually hitting the hatch when you have only allowed a day to do so is pretty risky.

Notes on the Salmon Fly, the Angler, and the Trout

The salmon fly (*Pteronarcys californica*) is a large stonefly; the mature nymphs are up to 2 1/4 inches long. The adults will range between 2 to 2 1/2 inches in length, and the females are larger than the males. As you can see, this makes a substantial meal for hungry trout. The salmon fly nymph lives in the river for a period of three years; therefore, this insect is always available to the trout, in various sizes. There are only three basic stages the angler/tyer must be concerned with: nymph, dry adult, and drowned wet adult. Once the time to hatch is on, the large *Pteronarcys* nymphs migrate to the edge of the river and crawl onto the rocks and willows to hatch. There they split their nymphal shucks and emerge as adult salmon flies.

The salmon fly hatch takes place just at the end of runoff, and the river is high and still somewhat discolored. During this time, the trout will also migrate to the edge, where they can find a better food supply and relief from the heavy currents of high water. Therefore, when the nymphs start to migrate to the shore, the trout are there, waiting and hungry. Early morning will generally find the adult insect hanging on the brush along the river's edge, where, due to wind, birds, ants, or other passing wildlife, they can be knocked in the water, where they may find themselves prey for some hungry trout. Around 10:30 A.M. to noon, the sun will have warmed things up enough that one can see some early flight activity. These insects are somewhat clumsy and a few often end up in the water. During the evening hours, from 5:00 P.M. to dark, the mating and egg-laying flights will occur. The females will lay their eggs by landing on the surface of the water. This is the prime time for drys.

As you can see, the salmon fly, whether in nymphal, adult, or drowned adult form, is very available to the trout, and this is not a feast the trout will pass up. The angler will find the action with nymphs to be best in the early-morning hours, and this action will taper off as the sun warms the air and the water. During the mid-morning and afternoon period, the angler may employ the use of adults, or wet adults, or maybe even some nymph-dry combinations.

Many anglers leave the water long before the best dry-fly fishing occurs. Some anglers arrive to fish the salmon fly hatch with no prior knowledge of the insects or the tackle it takes to fish the imitations properly. Tom has a story about his first experience with the hatch that is somewhat typical of the anglers we have interviewed.

Have You Heard the One About Big Nymphs?

I remember the first time I traveled to Yellowstone country to try my luck during the salmon fly hatch. It is indeed a painful memory. At 7:30 A.M. I strolled into the local tackle shop to ask what section of the river the "hatch" was on and what patterns they might suggest I use— you know, the normal questions asked by anglers when fishing waters outside their home area. Well, the place was packed! I never realized that fishing the "hatch" was so popular. As a matter of fact, I had never seen so many people in one place at one time that were all fly fishermen. Well, needless to say, by the time I got close to the counter and asked what patterns to use, I could see that the clerks were swamped. Not wanting to be a bother, I just grabbed about six of the #2 Bitch Creek Nymphs that had been recommended, paid for them, and beat feet out to the river. Being from the Midwest, I had never fished anything even closely approaching the size and weight of those monster flies. Much of the fishing at home had been done with 4X and smaller tippets and ten- to fifteen-foot leaders. So I proceeded to gear up with a nine-foot 4X, and started to fish.

Now in those days I couldn't afford a guide if I had wanted one, and let me tell you, I would have given almost anything for one that day. Sure, I had read about the salmon fly hatches and the methods

A real salmon fly checking out its imitation.

used to fish them. Now either I missed it or the writer forgot to mention it, but I didn't remember anything about leader lengths and tippet sizes. Let me tell you, I proceeded to beat the heck out of myself for the next hour. I had never tried casting anything like that in my life, and the 4-weight rod and 4X tippet just wasn't what was needed to do the job. The next hour is all it took me to lose the six huge nymphs I had purchased earlier. In the process of losing those marvels of fly tying, I had also hit myself in the head, shoulders, and back several times, and it was painfully clear that I needed help!

Does this story have a familiar ring to it?

Finally, a fellow approached me who had been fishing upstream. He said "Hi there, young fellow. I couldn't help but notice that you seem to be having a bit of trouble." (Now *there* was a definite understatement if I ever heard one!) "I would have been down sooner, but I was having a bit of a problem myself." I figured he was just being nice. I sure never saw him have any problems other than landing two nice trout. He probably figured it wasn't safe to come anywhere near me as long as I was slinging around those lethal weapons. Come to think of it, I don't blame him at all. After the introductions were over, I proceeded to explain the problems I was having. He quickly explained that the problems were easily solved. He then gave me a lesson on how to fish big, heavy nymphs. I have passed on his lesson many, many times throughout my eighteen years as a Montana fishing guide.

First, the nymphs are necessary when fishing the salmon fly hatches, because the mature natural nymphs can be two to three inches long. The salmon fly nymph doesn't hatch like a mayfly, by floating to the surface and emerging. It migrates to the bank, crawls out of the water up onto the streamside vegetation, and splits its nymphal skins and emerges. After reading this, you might ask "Why fish the big nymphs at all"? Because they become very available to the trout during this time when they are migrating toward shore. The current breaks them loose and drifts them along, and the trout will give up their deep pools and undercut banks and venture into the shallows to feed on this natural feast. What's that? Shallow, you say? Then why the heavy flies? Hold on and we will explain.

The period of time in which the salmon fly hatches coincides with the end of the annual spring runoff. The rivers are high, sometimes very high, and the water may yet be slightly discolored, so the trout feel perfectly safe moving into shallower water. Besides, the trout move to edges where the current will push the food to them. Why hold out there in that super-fast water and waste the energy? The trout will be in close because of the water conditions and because that's where the food is. Now remember, shallow water is a relative term. The water on the bank is slow and shallow compared to the water farther out, but it still may be two to three feet deep. Have you ever noticed how little fast water it takes to float a heavy fly up off the bottom? Using scuba gear, we have watched a heavy fly being presented in the wrong way with too fine a tippet and a leader with no extra weight, or a fly that is improperly weighted. The fly then whizzes by in the middle water, and that's not what you want. You want the fly bouncing along on the bottom if you are going to have any success at all.

The keys to success with fishing big heavy nymphs are few in number. While fishing #2s and #4s during the salmon fly hatch, use leaders no longer than nine feet. Use heavy tippets of OX or 1X. These leaders and heavy tippets will help the fly turn over properly. Next, you need a powerful rod suited to the purpose, we like an eight-and-a-half-to nine-foot rod for 7-weight lines. Some will use nine-foot rods for 8-weight lines, which tends to be a little slower and more forgiving. Be deliberate and powerful on your pickup (backcast) and on your delivery (forward cast). Pause long enough for the big buster to straighten out behind you. Remember, you're not fishing a dry—keep those false casts down to a minimum. Another technique for casting the big stuff is to use a single-water haul to load the rod on the forward cast; this way, no false casts are necessary. A single-water haul is on the pickup, or backcast: Allow the line and fly to land on the water behind you, then before the line and fly have a chance to start sinking, simply make your forward cast—the tension of the water on the line loads the rod for the forward cast. When possible, use floating lines and strike indicators—they give you a better chance to see the strike and react.

When fishing big nymphs, take your time. What's the rush? You'll better understand the need to take your time after you have an encounter of the *wrong kind* with a large, heavily weighted nymph.

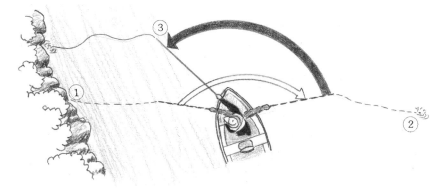

Single-water haul

1. Pick up from water.
2. Throw the line onto the water behind you.
3. As soon as the fly hits the water, make the forward cast, using the tension of the water to load the rod. This way, no false casts are necessary.

When wade-fishing, we prefer to fish upstream or right out in front using a dead-drift method, using the raising and lowering of the rod tip to help control some of the slack line. The trick is to keep that fly bouncing along the bottom and to take your time and be deliberate. Therefore, if you are coming to the Yellowstone to fish the salmon fly hatch, prepare yourself with the proper tackle and imitations, and you will have a much more enjoyable experience.

Where to Fish the Hatch

This question is often asked, *"Where should I fish? Ahead, through, or behind the hatch?"* This can depend on the kind of fishing you are looking for. We find that the best nymph fishing is most often ahead of the hatch. Please note that under normal conditions the hatch will move up the river three to six miles a day. We often find the best dry-fly fishing to be behind the hatch. During the time period of the salmon fly hatch, the river is high, and wade-fishing along some sections of the Yellowstone can be very difficult, if not impossible. However, the float fishing can be just the ticket. With a good oarsman to keep the boat properly positioned, the angler can work the banks with floating lines, strike indicators, and big nymphs. We also have had excellent results fishing drowned adults and nymph combinations, as well as dry/nymph combos. Another technique that lends itself nicely to float fishing is the *tip and strip* technique. (That's our name for it.) For this method we use a ten-foot Ultra Sink Tip and a five-foot 0X leader. Using a #2 Girdle Bug, Bitch Creek Nymph, Montana Stone, or whatever, we cast the fly straight into the bank and as close to the bank as we can without hanging up. Then we slowly strip the imitation off the bank. If it's bouncing its way off the bank, you're doing it right. If not, either you need to add additional weight to the leader or you're stripping too fast. Keep your rod tip pointed right at the fly as you strip. With this technique you will have no trouble detecting the strike. Just make sure that you have a good hold of the rod. For those of you who have chased the salmon fly hatch, you know the excitement and awe of seeing a truly large trout come up for the large dry, or possibly you have felt the jolting take on a large nymph. Many of you who

An adult salmon fly.

have chased know the frustration of being a week early or late. For those who have yet to sample your first salmon fly hatch, get ready for some of the most exciting fly fishing the West has to offer.

The angler who visits the Yellowstone River around the first of July can almost always find a section where the hatch is in progress. Often it will be here in the Gardiner section. After reading through this praise of the salmon fly hatch, the angler might think that this the only thing going on in the Gardiner section and that early July is the only time to fish it. Nothing could be further from the truth. During the same time the salmon flies are hatching, the angler may also find good hatches of golden stones along with yellow sally stones, which continue to hatch through the month of July. The angler will also en-counter the spotted sedge and the western green drake.

As July continues there is a whole host of caddis appearing on the river. As July gives way to August the river has dropped and cleared a great deal and the wade fishing becomes a lot easier. During late July we have often enjoyed an evening's fishing at one of the access sites along this section of river.

Late Summer: August to Mid-September

During August the angler will continue to enjoy the caddis fishing in this section. We also have the giant western golden stone, and of course hoppers. During late August and on into mid-September, when other areas of the river seem to slow down, this section can still offer some excellent dry-fly fishing. This is often credited to the numbers of cutthroat trout found here. Whatever the reason, the fishing here on an average is very good; however, this section is underfished during this time. We have often talked about this and find it amusing. If the fishing was so great during the salmon fly hatch, why wouldn't it be good now? Do anglers think that the trout move to another section after the hatch is over? We don't have the answer; however, we have enjoyed many a float in the late summer on this section and had the river practically to ourselves. It is, more than likely, that most other anglers simply fish water that is closer to their home bases.

Fall: Mid-September to Mid-November

By mid–September, the angler will see the return of the blue-winged olive hatches along with the midges. During the fall fishing with attractor dry flies such as the Royal Trude, Coachman Trude, and Royal Wulff can be delightful. During this time, nymphing with cased caddis and stonefly imitations can also be very effective. As we move into fall the brown trout start to gather and move as they prepare to spawn, and this section of the river holds some dandies Some local anglers prefer streamers now, while others choose nymph imitations. Whatever you decide, you have a chance of hooking a true trophy trout during this time of the year.

Hatch Chart for Gardiner to Yankee Jim Canyon

Stoneflies
Salmon fly
  (*Pteronarcys californica*)   Size: #2–#6   June 20 to July 10
Golden stone
  (*Calineuria californica*)   Size: #4–#8   July 25 to August 15
Yellow sally
  (*Isoperla mormona*)   Size: #14–#16   July 1 to August 10
Small golden stone
  (*Hesperoperla pacifica*)   Size: #6–#10   July 1 to August 10
Olive stone (*Isogenus* species)   Size: #12–#14   July 10 to August 15
Giant western golden stone
  (*Claassenia sabulosa*)   Size: #2–#6   August 1 to September 1

Caddisflies
American grannom
  (*Brachycentrus americanus*)   Size: #12–#16   July 15 to August 20
Spotted sedge
  (*Hydropsyche occidentalis*)   Size: #10–#12   June 15 to September 20
Green sedge
  (*Rhyacophila bifila*)   Size: #12–#14   July 15 to August 10
Tan short horn sedge
  (*Glossosoma velona*)   Size: #14–#16   July 10 August 10
Early grannom
  (*Brachycentrus occidentalis*)   Size: #12–#16   April 25 to May 20
Little sister sedge
  (*Cheumatopsyche campyla*)   Size: #14–#16   July 10 to September 1

Mayflies
Western green drake
  (*Drunella grandis*)   Size: #10–#12   June 20 to July 10
Gray drake
  (*Siphlonurus occidentalis*)   Size: #10–#12   July 10 to August 1
Western march brown
  (*Rhithrogena morrisoni*)   Size: #14–#16   April 20 to May 15
Pale morning dun
  (*Ephemerella inermis*)   Size: #16–#20   July 20 to August 20
Blue-winged olive
  (*Baetis tricaudatus*)   Size: #18–#20   March 15 to April 20,
                                                      September 15 to November 10

Terrestrials
Grasshoppers (Acrididae)   Size: #8–#14   July 15 to October 10

Crickets (Gryllidae)	Size: #12–#14	August 1 to September 10
Black ants (Formicidae)	Size: 16–22	July 15 to September 15
Cinnamon ants (Formicidae)	Size: #18–#20	August 1 to September 10
Black beetle (Coleoptera)	Size: #12–#18	July 10 to August 10

Other Important Hatches and Food Forms

Midge (Chironomidae)	Size: #16–#24	August 15 to October 31
Cranefly larva (Tipulidae)	Size: #4–#8	June 30 to August 15

Minnows

Mottled sculpin (*Cottus bairdi*)	Size: #2–#8	All year
Whitefish minnow (*Prosopium williamsoni*)	Size: #2–#10	All year
Long-nose dace minnow (*Rhinichthys cataractae*)	Size: #2–#10	All year
Long-nose sucker minnow (*Catostomus catostomus*)	Size: #2–#10	All year
Mountain sucker (*Catostomus platyrhynchus*)	Size: #2–#10	All year

Locally Effective Patterns

Himenator

Hook:	Tiemco 5212, size 6
Thread:	Red
Body:	Orange Rainy's Float Foam
Hackle:	Brown, palmered and clipped
1st underwing	Light dun Microweb
2nd underwing:	Mixed black and pearl Krystal Flash
3rd underwing:	Light elk hair
Wing:	Chocolate deer hair tied bullet-head-style
Legs:	Brown rubber legs

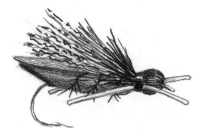

Rod's Stone Nymph

Hook:	Tiemco 5262, sizes 2–8
Thread:	Black
Tails:	Black rubber legs
Ribbing:	Copper wire
Abdomen:	Black leech yarn above orange chenile
Hackle:	Brown, palmered up the abdomen
Thorax:	Black leech yarn
Legs:	Black rubber legs, two pair
Hackle:	Black, palmered through thorax
Antennae:	Black rubber legs

Foam-Post Para-Caddis

Hook:	Tiemco 100 Sizes 16–14
Thread:	Olive or tan
Body:	Olive, tan, or color to match natural dubbing
Wing:	Light dun fly film
Post:	Yellow or orange closed-cell foam
Hackle:	Dun-dyed grizzly, parachute-style

Tom's Golden Stone Nymph

Hooks:	Tiemco 200, sizes 2–12
Butt:	Dubbed fox-squirrel belly fur
Tails:	Two brown goose biots, tied in a vee
Rib:	Two strands of root beer Krystal Flash
Abdomen:	Dubbed fox-squirrel belly fur
Wing case:	Dark turkey tail quill section

Thorax and Legs: Fur and guard hair
from the back of the
fox squirrel, spun in
a dubbing loop and wrapped
Head: Dubbed #60 brown Super Possum
Antennae: Two brown goose biots, tied in a vee
Note: Underbody shaped flat

Tom's Adult Salmon Fly*

Hook: Mustad 94840, sizes
2–6
Body extension: Orange poly yarn
2-ply, and 1-ply brown,
twisted & doubled
Wing: Fox-squirrel tail hair
Wing topping: Bleached elk
Hackle: Three to four brown
Eyes: Black mono
Head: Black sheared muskrat,
dubbed
Antennae: Two brown hackle
stems

Tom's Adult Golden Stone*

Hook: Mustad 94840, sizes
6–10
Thread: Tan
Body extension: Tan poly yarn, 2-ply,
and 1-ply brown,
twisted and doubled
Wing: Bleached elk hair
Hackle: Three to four ginger
Eyes: Black mono
Head: Dubbed hare's ear fur
Antennae: Two dark ginger hackle stems

*Note: These two adult patterns can be used as a fluttering stone, or the hackles can be trimmed off the bottom and can then be fished as a spent adult.

Other Effective Patterns

Hare's Ear Nymph
Brown Woolly Worm
Montana Nymph
Brook's Stone
George's Brownstone Nymph
Beadhead Prince Nymph
Black Girdle Bug
Peeking Caddis Nymph
Bitch Creek Nymph
Wet Adult Salmon Fly
Black Yuk Bug
Western Bitch Creek
Kaufmann's Black Stone Nymph
Deep Caddis Pupa
Soft-Hackles
Jacklin's March Brown Nymph
Hare's Ear Flashback
Muskrat Nymph

Blue-winged Olive Thorax
Blue-winged Olive Parachute
Griffith Gnat
Harrop's CDC Midge Adult
Elkhair Caddis
Goddard Caddis
Muddled Salmon Fly
Sofa Pillow
Improved Sofa Pillow
Irresistible Caddis
Orange Temptation Stone
Henry's Fork Salmon Fly
Henry's Fork Yellow Sally
Yellow Humpy
Royal Wulff
Royal Trude
Green Drake Extended Body
Gray Drake Extended Body

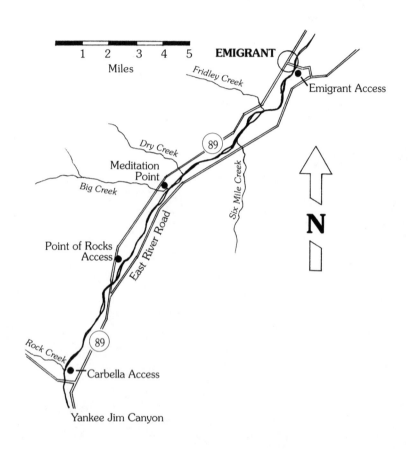

Yankee Jim Canyon to Emigrant

4

Yankee Jim Canyon
to Emigrant

The beginning of the Paradise Valley section has no equal in sheer scenic beauty, a quality that is easily overlooked when fishing. It is very common that floating anglers are so excited about fishing or so caught up in the act of fishing that when they finally do look up at the landscape, they express something akin to astonishment. The landscape is beautiful: the Absarokas towering to the east are a dramatic backdrop to some super fishing opportunities. The valley begins to widen at the upper reach of this stretch, and as one travels downstream the valley continues to broaden and is encircled by mountains on all sides. The river moves through some scenic property with evidence of old homesteads.

The area is rich in western lore. Many of the families that who settled the area still hold ranches in this part of the valley. This was still a very wild place in the late nineteenth century, and was considered Indian territory: the Crow tribe laid claim to the land. In the late 1860s, gold was discovered at Emigrant Gulch, which precipitated many conflicts as people sought their fortunes. The Boettler brothers were among the first to attempt to mine the goldfields and settle in the valley. After a few skirmishes with the Crows, they established one of the first ranches in the valley, at Emigrant. The Battle of the Little Big Horn opened this area for settlement when the Crow tribe was relocated. The 1870s saw many ranches springing up throughout the valley, many of which still belong to the founding families.

The ancestors of today's wild cutthroat bore witness to the many conflicts that occurred here and were probably washed with both

Native American and European blood. The cutthroat trout is part of the history of this section; it moved downstream from the park waters and established itself as a native fish prior to the time white men first appeared in the area. The Yellowstone cutthroat trout had many common names: cutthroat trout, native trout, redthroat trout, mountain trout, and the most common—black-spotted trout. If one reads some of the old journals or historical accounts of the area, these names are referred to, and there are many people who to this day refer to the Yellowstone cutthroat trout as the black-spotted trout.

This was the only trout species in this section of river until the introduction of brown trout and rainbow trout. At present the cutthroat trout numbers have been reduced, and special regulations are in effect in an attempt to bolster the population. Overharvesting is but one of the factors that have led to this decline. Cutthroats have always been a food source for the people who populated the valley, and until recently were the trout of choice for the people who take trout to eat. The catch-and-release regulation for all cutthroat trout is making a difference, but time is needed for the species to significantly reestablish itself. There probably will never be the number of cutthroats in this section as once existed here, but progress is being made by conservation groups. The good news to the angler is that cutthroats comprise a high number of the fish caught in this area, and they make fly fishing here a rewarding experience.

Water Characteristics

As the river exits Yankee Jim Canyon it appears to broaden (probably an effect of the valley broadening), slow somewhat, and then straighten to a degree. The water has less character than in the Gardner stretch because it doesn't twist and turn as much to form the riffle corners that are synonymous with good numbers of fish. The water here is certainly shallower than the depths of the canyon itself, and a lot more wadeable. Because of the distance between access points, most anglers float this section and do the majority of their fishing from a boat, occasionally getting out to cover some of

Typical water in the Yankee Jim Canyon area.

the more interesting water. There are some very good banks in this stretch that hold good numbers of fish, especially some of the high banks with adjacent deep water. Any bank that has some deep water and some structure and holding areas will produce fish, and some of the slower, deep banks seem to be the preferred habitat of cutthroats.

This section has a few areas with small islands breaking the water up and adding character by means of riffle corners, current edges, and current confluences. These areas are quite a distance apart, with the major grouping toward the end of the section. Plan on spending some time fishing these areas, because they hold quite a few fish and it's always a pleasure to get out of the boat to stretch, wade around, have the opportunity to systematically work the water and even hunt around the shore for petrified wood or agates. Rock hounds will find this area very interesting and may possibly add some unique pieces to their collections.

The bottom configuration consists of large rocks, bowling-ball-sized stones, cobble, and pea gravel. The banks in many places are lined with willows and provide good cover for fish lying in wait for a salmon fly or other insect. The salmon fly hatch is decent in this section, so it's always a good idea to hit these banks early in the season. If the water is high it is a good idea to look for fish on the off-bank—the nondominant side where the current is a bit slower. Otherwise, look for the dominant bank with current and some depth, and fish while floating. If pods of fish are spotted working the surface, the angler could get out of the boat and work back up to them.

There are a few creeks that dump into the river, and their mouths provide attractive areas to find fish: Big Creek, Dry Creek, Sixmile Creek, Fridley Creek, and Emigrant Creek all flow into the river, at least when irrigators haven't pulled all the water out. There is only one area where some care needs to be exercised, and that is about midway into the float—there is an area that has some underwater hazards, but they are clearly marked with a sign. Also, look for an irrigation ditch off the river on the left side: it resembles a channel, and some anglers have mistakenly floated down this ditch, only to be surprised by a small dam. It does put a damper on a day's floating. Otherwise, there is no water that can be considered difficult or dangerous in this section, and any type of craft, from canoes to drift boats, will have no trouble navigating it.

This is an area that still has visible scars of past abuses of the river. It was common in the past for folks who lived along the river to use it as a trash dump, and we still see the evidence along the entire river. There is an area called the Wanigan, with literally thousands of old rusty tin cans spilling down a high bank. This refuse is a reminder of what could have become of this river.

Accessibility

This approximately twelve-and-a-half-mile section has the fewest number of access points in the valley. There are only three options for floating: the entire twelve-and-a-half-mile float from Carbella to

Fishing from a drift boat.

Emigrant, a four-and-a-half-mile float from Carbella to Point of Rocks, or an eight-mile float from Point of Rocks to Emigrant. During low-water years, when the water flows at two to three miles an hour, some of these options could make for a long day on the water and possibly prevent one from getting out of the boat to work fish or cover water. When the flows are moderate (three to four miles an hour) or moderately high (four to six miles an hour), floating the longer distances becomes more practical.

The Carbella access point was covered in the previous chapter (see page 90). The Point of Rocks access is basically a spot off the highway that is clearly marked. It allows camping with a fourteen-day limit but has no rest-room facilities, nor does it have picnic tables. The ramp is a simple dirt slope cut into the bank. It's not a very pretty access point, but it serves its purpose of shortening a long float or providing for a short float. It is also an area that a walk fisherman can use to reach the river.

The next access downriver is Meditation Point. This is basically a rest stop off the highway for travelers. It has no ramp to launch or take out a boat, but one could probably put a light craft such as a canoe in here. It would entail carrying it down to the water and traversing some riprap. This access has a very large paved parking lot, a picnic pavilion, trash receptacles, handicapped-accessible rest rooms, and a phone. Camping is not allowed. The walk fisher can reach the river here and have some decent fishing along the riprap bank, or one can hike up- or downriver until suitable water is found.

The last access point in this stretch is Emigrant Bridge. If you float under the bridge, you have missed the access. This area has a dirt ramp cut into the bank, a picnic area, and rest rooms that are not handicapped-accessible. Camping is not allowed here. It is conveniently located near the town of Emigrant, and an angler could, after a day's fishing, stop at the Old Saloon and have a burger, a meal, or a few drinks. There is a gas station and convenience store nearby to replenish whatever stock is needed. Many of the folks who stay at the resort at Chico use this access to begin or end their day on the water. The walk fisherman can use this access to find areas to fish. Because the water is relatively shallow, he can safely wade to spots that look good.

The Fish

This is predominantly a brown trout fishery: at least fifty percent of the trout here are browns. There is a relatively even mix of rainbows and cutthroats at about twenty-five percent each. The percentages reflect the entire stretch, but the mix differs depending on what end of the stretch one fishes. The upper reaches hold more of an even blend of the three species because of the water type and the proximity of spawning areas. But for the most part, the slower, even current is not prime habitat for rainbows, as their numbers reflect, and there is little spawning habitat for them. The farther one travels downstream in this section the farther away one travels from any viable spawning area, so the number of rainbows decreases.

The cutthroats are native to this area and historically were the only trout species in this section, but as the years passed and the land became inhabited, their number started to fall off for a number of reasons: they were overharvested as food sources, other species were planted in the river and became competition for the same food, and finally, humans developed the land surrounding the rivers into ranches. These ranches needed water to irrigate crops, and it pulled from the tributary streams, further decreasing the cutthroat's chances for survival. Today, even though circumstances have changed, much remains the same. Although we can no longer take cutthroats to eat—it is catch and release only for cutthroats—there are still other species in the river as competition, and the ranchers are still taking water from the tributaries for irrigation. The depletion of the tributary streams is the main reason the cutthroats are not more populated in this stretch. When they spawn in early June there is still water in this stretch's tributaries, and the adult fish can enter them, but before the fry can get back to the main stem of the river these tributaries are dewatered, and the fry cannot reach the river. The only viable spawning streams are upstream above the Yankee Jim area. There is a correlation between how far away a spawning stream is and how many fish are in an area: The farther away the spawning stream, the less fish in a particular area. But even at only twenty-three percent of the total trout population, there are days on the river when it seems that every fish caught is a cutthroat trout. Their feeding habits make them easier to catch.

The brown trout, on the other hand, have flourished in this stretch of river. The habitat is more to their liking, and their feeding habits put them in less competition with the other species. The browns are mostly main-stem spawners, so they need not depend on the tributaries to sustain themselves. As one travels downstream, there is less and less evidence of blind-eye disease. Anglers wishing to catch decent browns would be advised to consider this stretch of river.

Oh yes, there are also good numbers of whitefish in this area.

Hatch Chart for Yankee Jim Canyon to Emigrant

Stoneflies
Salmon fly
 (*Pteronarcys californica*) Size: #2–#6   July 15 to July 25
Golden stone
 (*Calineuria californica*) Size: #4–#8   July 15 to August 10
Yellow sally
 (*Isoperla mormona*)   Size: #14–#16 July 20 to August 25
Small golden stone
 (*Hesperoperla pacifica*) Size: #6–#10   July 20 to August 10
Olive stone (*Isogenus* species) Size: #12–#14 July 20 to August 25
Giant western golden stone
 (*Claassenia sabulosa*) Size: #2–#6   August 5 to September 1

Caddisflies
Early grannom
 (*Brachycentrus occidentalis*) Size: #14–#16 April 25 to May 25
American grannom
 (*Brachycentrus americanus*) Size: #12–#16 July 10 to August 10
Green sedge
 (*Rhyacophila bifila*)   Size: #12–#14 July 5 to August 10
Spotted sedge
 (*Hydropsyche occidentalis*) Size: #10–#12 June 15 to September 15
Little sister sedge
 (*Cheumatopsyche campyla*) Size: #14–#16 July 5 to August 15

Mayflies
Western green drake
 (*Drunella grandis*)   Size: #10–#12 June 20 to July 15
Gray drake
 (*Siphlonurus occidentalis*) Size: #10–#12 July 1 to July 20
Pale morning dun
 (*Ephemerella inermis*) Size: #16–#20 July 15 to August 15
Western black quill
 (*Rhithrogena undulata*) Size: #14   July 10 to August 10
Western march brown
 (*Rhithrogena morrisoni*) Size: #14–#16 April 15 to May 15
Blue-winged olive
 (*Baetis tricaudatus*)   Size: #18–#20 September 15 to November 10
Trico (*Tricorythodes minutus*) Size: #18–#22 September 15 to October 15

Terrestrials

Grasshoppers (Acrididae)	Size: #8–#14	July 15 to October 10
Crickets (Gryllidae)	Size: #12–#14	August 1 to September 10
Black ants (Formicidae)	Size: #16–#22	July 15 to September 15
Cinnamon ants (Formicidae)	Size: #18–#20	August 20 to September 20
Black beetle (Coleoptera)	Size: #12–#18	July 10 to August 10

Other Important Hatches and Food Forms

Midge (Chironomidae)	Size: #16–#24	August 15 to October 31

Minnows

Mottled sculpin (*Cottus bairdi*)	Size: #2–#10	All year
Whitefish minnow (*Prosopium williamsoni*)	Size: #2–#10	All year
Long-nose dace minnow (*Rhinichthys cataractae*)	Size: #2–#10	All year
Long-nose sucker minnow (*Catostomus catostomus*)	Size: #2–#10	All year
Mountain sucker (*Catostomus platyrhynchus*)	Size: #2–#10	All year

Seasonal Changes: The Fishing

This section of river is perhaps one of the most difficult to fish on a year-long basis and be successful. Not only do you need to know the moods of the Yellowstone but you must also be able to read the water and to thoroughly understand the habits of each species of trout that resides in this section. If you accomplish all of this, then be assured that you will be successful as much of the time as anyone can expect!

Early Summer: June and July

This is without a doubt the easiest time to fish this section of the river, for a number of reasons. There are several insect species hatching during this time, and the river is just starting to drop and clear at the very tail end of June. When this happens the angler will have salmon flies, golden stones, yellow sally stones, green drakes, and a couple of caddis hatching. Due to the water height during a

Taking a mid-day break.

normal year and the wealth of food offered to the trout, the angler, whether wading or floating, can enjoy some fairly easy and relaxed fishing. During this time, dry-fly fishing is very popular on this section of river, and justifiably so. That does not mean that anglers should only fish "drys." There can be some very good nymphing, too. One of our favorite methods is to fish a deep caddis pupa and emergent caddis pupa in tandem. And the angler who wishes to work the bank with a sink tip line and a streamer-nymph combination can move some very big brown trout. However, during the early summer on this section, the dry fly is king! Attractor patterns like the Royal Wulff, Parachute Adams, Coachman Trude, and Yellow Stimulator are among the favorites, along with Elkhair Caddis, Goddard Caddis, and Madam X.

However, the angler who just fishes this section blindly with attractors may be passing up some very fine hatch fishing. With the exception of the major caddis and stonefly hatches, many of the mayfly hatches do not occur riverwide. Oftentimes one will float into

Get out of the boat and work the hatches.

a hatch of green drakes or PMDs that goes on for a half-mile or so, then suddenly ends. We have learned to stop and work these hatches, and by doing so have found some trout that are every bit as picky and selective as the toughest fish found on the spring creeks. The Yellowstone River seems to have developed this reputation as an attractor river. Some of you may be surprised to learn that there are times and places where matching the hatch can be very effective. The key to such fishing is observation and a willingness to put the boat over if you are floating and work to the rising fish. As we move into late July and on into August this section of the river can become less productive for many, and the fishing pressure falls way, way off.

Late Summer: August to Mid-September

There is no doubt that as the river water levels drop, so do the angler numbers in this section. That is not because the trout have moved on, and it's not because the hatches have come to a standstill. It is simply that the water levels have changed where the trout will hold and anglers are now catching a lot of those fabulous Gray Ghosts of the Montana Flats, commonly referred to as whitefish. Therefore, soon most anglers move on to what is perceived as more productive water. However, for the angler who will take the four- or eight-mile float, or for the angler who is wading, the fishing can be super. How's that, you ask? By the angler being observant and covering water that will hold trout and not whitefish. We often see floating anglers casting into a bank that may have only ten inches of water and we have asked, "why? " We are told that "Hey, we caught them here last week." Well that may be, but with the water levels dropping, the trout are moving away from those shallow banks and out to deeper water.

We often have our boat out in the middle of river, casting to drop-off edges. We are also not afraid to stop and work the hatches. Another tip: Fish the deep, slow, almost dead-looking water. Cutthroat trout prefer this kind of water, and a well-placed imitation will often bring one of those slow, lazy, deliberate takes the cutthroat are so famous for. Finally, know the habits of the species you are fishing for. It is not often that you will take a large brown trout on a dry fly during a hot, bright day. For Mr. Brown you might try fishing very early in the day or very late in the day, and you might try putting the imitation down where the fish live with the use of a sink tip or full-sinking line. We know an older fellow who used to fish this section all the time during August and September, and he took a number of large browns using streamers and wet flies. During August and September anglers will enjoy good terrestrial fishing in this section along with hatches of stoneflies, caddis, and mayflies.

Fall: Mid-September to Mid-November

Early on in this period, anglers can still enjoy good terrestrial fishing. During the fall you will encounter hatches of Tricos, fall baetis, and midges. Look in the back-eddies and mouths of creeks for areas that will hold the best action during the hatches.

Fall also means that the brown trout are beginning to move and collect for the fall spawning run. Here in the West, browns and streamers just seem to go together. This section is an excellent area for the angler who wishes to learn about streamer fishing. There are excellent pools and runs that can be fished with sinking tips and full-sinking lines, where the river doesn't seem overwhelming. Streamer flies often seem to be tied to catch anglers as well as trout. Some anglers seem to have that dreaded disease called *collectoritis*, which sometimes leads us to acquire impractical patterns. But impractical or not, it sure is fun, and we don't believe any angler *ever* has enough flies.

But there are some important factors the angler should consider before rushing off to the local fly shop or sitting down at the tying bench to lay in a stock of streamers. First, consider why trout take streamers. What type of waters will be fished? Shallow, gentle flows, or deeper, heavier water? Are there are any special patterns for certain times of the year? What minnow forms are available to the trout in the waters that will be fished and what are popular local patterns? It would be silly to tie or buy a bunch of smelt imitations if there are no smelt in the waters to be fished. Then, what tackle will be required to present the imitations at the proper depth and angle to be effective? Once these questions are answered, the angler can make the proper choice of streamers.

We believe trout take streamers for three main reasons: hunger, anger, and curiosity. Hunger is something everyone can readily understand. Oftentimes when streamers are mentioned, the angler thinks of brown trout, but rainbows and cutthroats will also feed on minnow forms. Anger manifests itself in three ways: trout will hit a streamer because it has invaded their territory, in defense of the redd (nest) during the annual spawning cycle, or because it is "in their face." Curiosity can be recognized as those lazy swirls after the streamer. They rolled on it or bumped it simply because it looked like something to eat, but they really were not hungry. Or, in the case of some of our creations, maybe they were thinking "What was *that*!"

Now that we understand a little bit about why trout take streamers, we need to investigate what minnow forms are available to the

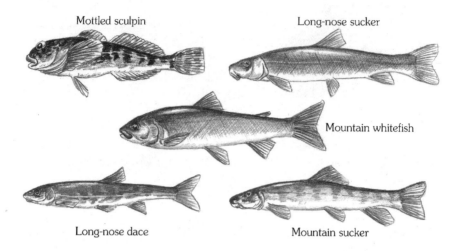

Mottled sculpin

Long-nose sucker

Mountain whitefish

Long-nose dace

Mountain sucker

The five minnows.

trout in this section of the Yellowstone. We also need to know what they look like and how they swim. Here on the Yellowstone, there are several species of minnow available to the trout, perhaps the most famous being the sculpin. Besides the sculpin there are also long-nose suckers, long-nose dace, mountain suckers, and whitefish as well as brown, rainbow, and cutthroat minnows. All these minnow forms are eaten by trout at various times, and the angler must decide how to properly imitate them in both general appearance and action. To do this we must know a little more about the minnows.

Mottled sculpin (*Cottus bairdi*). At first glance, this sculpin looks like a baby bullhead or catfish. The sculpin prefers to live in the riffle areas or sections of the river with a rocky bottom and fast-flowing currents. Sculpins live up to five years and vary in size from 1.7 inches to over 5.5 inches. The back is mottled, and the intensity of the coloring will vary depending on the natural colors of the habitat. Unlike most fish, sculpins have no swim bladder. Therefore, they dart in six-to eight-inch "jumps" from rock to rock as they feed. If one is swept away by the current it will dead-drift until it reaches the bottom and then will dart under a rock. Sculpins spawn during the spring and during this time are very active; many will fall prey to foraging trout. Because of the sculpin's inability to swim for long distances, brown trout will often chase them into shallow water, where they are easily exhausted and caught.

Long-nose sucker (*Catostomus catostomus*). This sucker spawns from April to June in smooth gravel in riffled water. Trout, especially rainbows, will follow this sucker to its spawning area and feed heavily on the eggs. The long-nose sucker growth rates are: first year up to three inches, second year up to five and half inches, and the third year up to nine inches. Long-nose suckers live eight years or more. The minnow is a dark olive-slate on the back with lighter sides and a white belly. Because these are bottom-feeding fish, the unwary minnow is often taken by trout.

Mountain whitefish (*Prosopium williamsoni*). The Yellowstone River has an excellent population of these native fish. The whitefish has a grayish back with silvery sides and a dull white belly. The minnows have a dozen or so blackish parr marks on each side. Whitefish are fall spawners, spawning during the months of September and October. Often, anglers will find trout mixed in with spawning whitefish to prey on the eggs. Growth rates are up to three and half inches in the first year and up to eight inches by the end of the second year. The minnows tend to school up after hatching out and remain in schools during the first couple of years. Trout will surround a school of small whitefish and drive them into shallow water, where they can be captured.

Long-nose dace (*Rhinichthys cataractae*). This minnow is a favorite of the trout and heavily preyed on. The body color will vary from black to light olive on the back and upper sides, with silver to yellow on the belly, and a very dark lateral stripe. The experts think these dace spawn in the late spring and early summer, but little of the life history has actually been studied. They will vary in size from .03 inches to 6 inches and live up to five years. They feed on small forms of aquatic insects and are constantly moving about in search of food, which brings them to the notice of the trout.

Mountain sucker (*Catostomus platyrhynchus*). This minnow has a darkish olive-green back and sides with fine black speckles and a grayish white belly. Spawning is in June and July. The growth rate for the mountain sucker is very slow, and trout continue to prey on them for several years. First year growth is up to 1.2 inches, second year is up to 2.2 inches, third year is up to 4 inches, and fifth year is up to 6 inches. Studies have shown that this species is an important forage fish for the trout.

Trout, being opportunistic feeders, will feed on any trout minnow, given the chance. Many times we have seen adult cutthroat trout slash through a school of cutthroat minnows on the Yellowstone. Now that we have learned a little bit about the minnows available to the trout we should make sure that we have the tackle to properly present the imitation.

For the Yellowstone River, we recommend an 8-weight system for any hard-core streamer fishing. In a later chapter we will discuss the use of 9010 systems and shooting heads for big heavy runs and deep pools. Sure, you can fish streamers on a 5- or 6-weight and be effective some of the time but often you find that you are not getting the imitation down to the proper depth and angle in order to take trout consistently. We would rather cast sinking lines and larger flies with a system that will do the job without making more work of it than necessary. The well-prepared streamer angler should have sink tips and full-sinking lines in various sink rates along with 8- and 9-weight Hi-Speed Hi-D shooting tapers. We are often asked what lines we prefer; for this type of fishing 3M/Scientific Anglers makes the best lines.

Because the angler fishing streamers should carry several different types of lines, we will explain some of the uses for the different line types we are recommending.

Ultra 3 Wet Tip V 13' (WF 8 S). This has a sink rate of six inches per second. To be used when fishing heavy riffles, heavy narrow runs, plunging drop-off riffles, and where the presentation may be upstream and additional line control is needed. Also used when fishing from a drift boat, for stripping streamers off the bank.

Uniform Sink V (WF 8 S). This has a sink rate of 4.75 inches per second. Used in deep slow pools where you need to get the imitation down and keep it there.

Uniform Sink I (WF 8 S). This has a sink rate of 1.65 inches per second. Used in medium to shallow riffles and flats where a floating line doesn't allow the angler to present the imitation at the proper angle. We use this line a lot.

Wet Cel IV Shooting Tapers (ST 8 S) and (ST 9 S). These are Hi-Speed Hi-D shooting tapers attached to some kind of shooting line—we prefer Amnesia. They have a sink rate of 4.75 inches per second. These lines are used for covering large pools where the water is a little deeper and faster. By using a double- or single-haul cast we are able to cover the larger pools very effectively with this line.

Ultra 3 Floating (WF 8 F). This is used when presenting a streamer imitation on or near the surface, as when skipping a frightened minnow across the surface. You may find it interesting to know that the late Joe Brooks fished a lot of streamers on the Yellowstone with a great deal of success. All of his streamer fishing was done with floating lines.

The leaders you need will vary according to what you are trying to accomplish with your presentation. But for the most part the leaders we use for sinking lines are all four to five feet in length. The leaders used on the floating line may vary due to pattern and technique being employed.

Now that we have outlined information about why trout take streamers, the minnow food forms available, and tackle, let's delve into popular local fly patterns. The following is a list of ten of the most popular local patterns.

Whitlock's Olive Matuka Sculpin. Sizes: #4–#8. This is a sculpin imitation that may be used throughout the year.

Muddler Minnow. Sizes: #4–#10. This is used as a sculpin and general minnow imitation throughout the year. Just because this pattern has been around for a while, anglers should not ignore it. It is still very effective.

Dark Olive Flash–A–Bugger. Sizes: #2–#12. This is a general attractor that is used throughout the season.

Lite Spruce Streamer. Sizes: #1–#6. This is thought to be an imitation of a whitefish minnow. It is used primarily in the fall for spawning browns and in the spring for spawning rainbows. One of the most popular and effective local patterns.

Sculpin Buggers. Sizes: #2–#6. This pattern is simply a combination of the Woolly Bugger and the Woolhead Sculpin, and it is very effective on the Yellowstone. There are several color variations. This pattern is a good imitation for sculpins and is often used as a general attractor or searching fly.

Marion Western Feather Streamers. Sizes: #1/0–#2. This is an excellent general minnow attractor and was developed right here on the Yellowstone by fishing guide Chester Marion of Livingston, Montana. There are various color variations. This pattern has proven to be one of the most effective of the streamer patterns due to its lifelike movement in the water.

Dark Olive Bunny Bug. Sizes #2–#8. This general minnow attractor tied almost entirely out of rabbit strips sinks very quickly once it gets soaked, and has a very tantalizing action.

PRS Lead-eye Feather Streamer. Sizes #2–#8. This combination of brown and yellow seems to be real effective for brown trout, and the lead eyes add extra action, almost a jigging motion, when the fry is stripped in on the retrieve.

Olive and White Clouser Minnow. Sizes #2–#8. This is an effective dace imitation that sinks quickly.

Big-eyed Bugger. Sizes #2–#8. Another general attractor that also has a jigging action and sinks rapidly.

Now that we have covered the local patterns, let's talk about what items the angler or tyer should consider before buying or tying a streamer selection. The important elements for a successful streamer pattern are shape, color, movement, balance, durability, and what we call castability. Let us examine each of these elements individually.

Shape. Shape, or silhouette, can be influenced by several factors: the material being used to construct the pattern, the type of water the imitation is to be fished in, and of course whether or not the pattern is an imitation of a particular minnow or just a general attractor. The shape can also affect the castability of the pattern just as the materials used in construction can affect the sink rate, which in turn will affect how the pattern is presented. For shape we recommend you follow the lead taken by known effective patterns of the same type, or imitate the shape of the natural as closely as possible. The type of water to be fished may influence the overall shape. In heavy water you may, for example, want a fuller and heavier wing so the fish will be able to see the fly. In smoother water you may want the imitation to be dressed a little more sparsely.

Color. Some claim that color is of no importance. But if that is the case, why not tie everything in black, white, or maybe hot pink! Studies have shown that trout do indeed see color. Now, the color they see in six feet of water may indeed vary from what we see while holding the imitation in our hand. When tying flies that imitate a certain minnow, we try to match the color of the natural as closely as possible. When tying attractors, we try to use colors or combinations of colors that have been proven to be effective on trout in the Yellowstone. Often, the tyer must mix and match several materials to give the overall appearance of a color that is desired. When working on new patterns we always put the finished fly in a tank to see if wetness will change the overall color. Some materials turn very dark when they get wet and may then alter the overall shade to something that wasn't desired.

Movement. Use materials or combinations of materials that will move and flow in the water. This movement is what creates the illusion of life and attracts the trout. More often than not, flies that are stiff and lifeless are ignored by the trout. What movement you create will, in part, depend on what you want the fly to do and the type of water you will be using it in.

Balance. This is how you want your fly to sink in the water and what you want it to do when you are retrieving. For example, If you put the weight forward on a Flash-a-Bugger or use a bead, it will sink nose-first and dive nose-first on the retrieve. If you place the bulk of the weight back toward the tail, then it will dive tail-first. Think about what you want your pattern to do before putting the weight on the hook so that you can balance the pattern to act properly in the water.

Castability. We once watched an angler try to cast a size 1/0 Whitlock Matuka Sculpin that was weighted with twenty-five wraps of .035 lead fuse wire with a 6-weight rod. Well, you could say that he had an encounter of the wrong kind with his fly. When weighting a fly, take into account the type of line and rod you will be casting with and balance the fly accordingly. Also take into account the absorbency of the material you are using and adjust accordingly. For example, weighting a Woolhead Sculpin with twenty-five wraps of .030 lead wire may make the imitation heavier than you wish to handle, because the wool head, wool body, and rabbit-strip wing all will soak up water.

Durability. Make sure you have flies that are constructed with materials and tying techniques that will stand up under the abuses of fishing. Make sure that heads are glued and well finished. Nothing will upset you more than to make a dozen casts and have the fly fall apart.

Biteable. The patterns that seem to work the best are always flies that move well in the water and are soft and chewable. Stiff flies look pretty in the fly box, and that is the best place for them.

Typical water in the area between Yankee Jim Canyon and Emigrant.

If an angler takes knowledge of the trout and its food forms, tackle, and imitations and mixes them together, the end result will be increased success while fishing streamers on the Yellowstone. In a later chapter we will cover the presentation methods used in streamer fishing. The Yankee Jim Canyon to Emigrant section of the river holds some excellent brown trout and is underfished in the fall.

Winter: Mid-November to February

What can we say about this section during the winter? Weather permitting, there is good nymphing, and most of it is done at the three access sites. Due to their distances from the surrounding towns and the fact that the local anglers don't tend to venture far afield during the winter, much of this section never sees an angler. However, for those who wish to explore or to have a section of the river to themselves, this would be a good section to fish.

Locally Effective Patterns

Stillborn Caddis

Hook:	Tiemco 100, sizes 16–14
Thread:	Olive or tan
Shuck:	Dun-dyed grizzly hackle tip
Body:	Olive, tan, or color to match natural dubbing
Hackle:	Dun-dyed grizzly, clipped on bottom
Wing:	Light elk hair

Foam Humpy

Hook:	Tiemco 100, sizes 10–18
Thread:	Light yellow
Tail:	Light elk hair
Body:	Pale yellow olive dubbing
Hump:	Dark closed-cell foam
Wings:	White calf tail, divided
Hackle:	Ginger

Hairwing Spot Dun

Hook:	Tiemco 100, sizes 12–18
Thread:	Gray
Tails:	Light blue dun barbets, split
Body:	Pale yellow olive dubbing
Hackle:	Blue dun, cut a vee out of the bottom
Wing:	Medium brown elk hair
Spot:	Fluorescent orange egg yarn

Western Lite Spruce Feather Streamer

Hook:	Tiemco 700, sizes 1/0–4
Thread:	Hot red
Tails:	Four matched silver badger hackles, two per side, with two strands of pearl Krystal Flash per side
Rib:	Fine dark Ultra Thread, reverse-wrap
Body:	Four to six silver badger hackles, tied in by the tips and wrapped forward tightly
Head:	Hot red thread

Olive Sculpin Bugger

Hook:	Tiemco 5262, sizes 2–8
Thread:	Olive
Tails:	Olive marabou with two strands of olive Krystal Flash per side
Rib:	Copper wire
Body:	Olive chenille
Hackle:	Grizzly, dyed olive
Collar:	Black deer hair
Head:	Olive wool, spun and clipped to shape

Tom's Dark Olive
Bead-A-Bugger

Hooks:	Tiemco, 947 BL, sizes 4–12
Thread:	Olive
Bead:	Gold
Tails:	Olive marabou with two strands of olive Krystal Flash on each side of the tail
Rib:	Fine dark Ultra Thread
Body:	Dark olive chenille
Legs:	Dark green Flex-i-Floss, two sets of two per side
Hackle:	Grizzly, dyed olive, and palmered

Other Effective Patterns

Royal Wulff
Parachute Adams
Coachman Trude
Yellow Stimulator
Elkhair Caddis
Goddard Caddis
Madam X
Muddled Salmon Fly
Muddled Golden Stone
Pale Morning Dun Parachute
BWO Parachute Sparkle Dun
Gray Drake
Dave's Hopper
Yellow Foam Hopper
Griffith Gnat

Whitlock Matuka Sculpin
Muddler Minnow
Dark Olive Flash-A-Bugger
Lite Spruce Streamer
Olive Sculpin Bugger
Black and Orange Sparkle Stone
Black Simulator
Murray's Black Strymph
Tom's Golden Stone Nymph
Pheasant Tail Nymph
Feather Duster Nymph
Deep Caddis Sparkle Pupa
Beadhead Olive Hare's Ear
Beadhead Caddis Emerger
Beadhead Copper Nymph

5

Emigrant to Mallard's Rest

There's gold in them thar hills, or something to that effect got this little community started back around the late 1800s as people came to mine Emigrant Gulch. Emigrant was the site of some of the first ranches and settlements in the Paradise Valley. Currently, it's a small hamlet that is a convenient place to stop for gas or lunch on the way to or from the park. To the angler, it's a convenient place to begin or end a day of fishing. To the recreational floater, it's a super spot to get on the river and absorb the breathtaking beauty of the valley—some exquisite photographs can be taken here. As a matter of fact, many of the photos in sporting and travel magazines of the Yellowstone River are taken on this section.

This section of river is one of the most popular sections to float. Many of the locals and many guides rarely fish other stretches. It's popular for a number of reasons: it's convenient, has a fly shop, a grocery store, a gas station, a few restaurants, a tavern, and good access sites. There are many bed and breakfast places in this end of the valley, and there's Chico, a resort area noted for its hot springs. Emigrant is a good place to meet for a day's fishing, as do many visitors who stay in the valley. Anglers who like to fish from a drift boat or who don't want to get all geared up in waders prefer this section because a float can last all day and one rarely needs to get out of the boat. Many local guides have clients who prefer this kind of fishing, so they use this section with regularity. It has become a great staging area, as evidenced by the number of drift boats parked in some of the lots and by the additional number one can see coming down the highway from both directions.

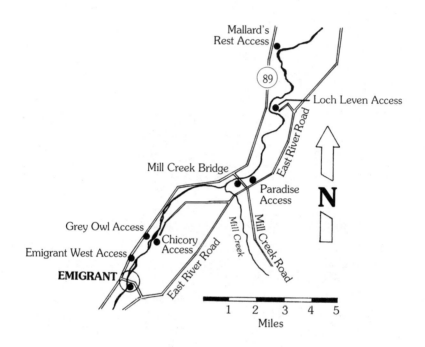

Emigrant to Mallard's Rest

There was once a production hatchery at Emigrant that for a while shaped the fishing in the area. It was easier to dump fish into the river in nearby sections than it was to haul them to other stretches of the river. For many years this was the area that had the greatest populations of trout. It's not that way at present, and ever since stocking ceased on the river the trout population centers have changed. However, there is still a good number of trout in this stretch, and, better still, there are relatively large fish in this part of the river. The slot limit that went into effect in 1984 resulted in a higher concentration of large fish here (eighteen inches and better) than in areas without the slot. In many rivers throughout the country a slot limit has the effect of increasing total fish populations if the habitat can support it, but that isn't the case in this section. What happened here is that the population shifted to larger browns. The angler looking for larger-than-average brown trout can expect to find them in this area.

Although there is a fair number of anglers who use this stretch on a regular basis, even more use it sporadically, depending on what is happening on the water. As some insects hatch out and move upriver, many of the local anglers follow their movements. Early in the season, when the Mother's Day caddis hatch is on and the river cooperates, a fly fisherman can get his last licks in on this stretch. This area becomes popular as the hatch moves upstream, and it is often the last place on the river to fish this hatch before the river blows out. The same thing happens with the salmon fly hatch, except then one doesn't have to worry about the river blowing out.

When the salmon flies are thick up here, so are the fishermen. Later in the summer when the grasshopper season is in full bloom and the water levels are normal, some spectacular fishing can be had. Sometimes, when the ranchers are mowing their hay fields, the hoppers are so thick and the trout so active that fishing is ridiculously easy. It almost becomes a time when one can cast anywhere and have a fish strike. When a day like this is reported, the news doesn't take long to spread around this small fishing community, and one can expect significantly more river traffic for the next few days.

Water Characteristics

Although this area is very popular, the water probably has the least amount of character here than on any other stretch of the river. Most of this section is relatively shallow with very few riffle corners and braiding. The width hardly changes—basically it's a straight shot from point A to point B. What this section does have is great banks,

Typical water in this stretch.

the kind that trout seek out to hold along and feed. This is what makes this section so popular: an oarsman in a drift boat can almost put it on autopilot, making minor adjustments as he floats. Constant, major maneuvering isn't something one has to contend with here, except for the occasional crossing of the river to a better-looking bank. In most cases it is fairly obvious which bank is the dominant one.

The first mile or so does have some braided channels that are worth spending some time fishing. They have all the character one needs in the form of riffle corners, clearly defined current edges, backwater, converging currents, drop-offs, and such. Where the channels flow back into the main stem are other areas that should be worked very carefully. Past these islands, before one reaches the Grey Owl access on one side of the river and the Chicory access almost directly across the river from it, the river makes a sharp, slow bend, and there almost always seem to be cutthroats working here. From Grey Owl down to Mallard's Rest there is very little in the way of water character. Where Mill Creek dumps into the river there is an excellent riffle corner, but that's about it until the very end of the float.

What this section *does* have is subtle water character along its banks, the kind that one has to look for and recognize. Sure, some of it is obvious, like the current edges along the larger backwater, but some isn't, like minor changes in the bank's structure or barely noticeable pockets. As the summer progresses and the water levels start dropping, it becomes harder and harder to read the banks. It is easy to spot newcomers to the area when the water is low because they are the ones fishing tight to the banks. This area is relatively shallow to begin with, and as the water drops one has to fish farther out from the bank. Usually a noticeable drop-off or trough can be seen (don't forget your polarized sunglasses) at various distances from the bank. These are the areas that will hold trout and therefore are the areas that should be fished. If you are catching more whitefish than you think you should be, move out a little farther from the bank and try it there. Okay, so some of you think one whitefish is too many. But be realistic and remember that there are something like five whitefish to every trout in the river.

These banks are mostly lined with willows and other forms of vegetation that become holding places for a number of insects after they hatch. The trout seem to know this and hold along these banks. Very often, when the river is high, one can see fish rising in the willows. This is frustrating, because you are surely going to lose your share of flies trying to catch these fish. But in order to catch fish, one has to fish where they are. Salmon fly time is a case in point. Very often these large insects will fall or get blown off the willows and land in the water at their bases. Of course the fish key on this, so it is mandatory that the angler place his imitation where the fish are looking to find food. If the water is high and you are in this area, bring plenty of flies—you'll need them.

Accessibility

Downstream from the Emigrant Bridge are six public accesses from which to reach the river. They are varied and spread out so that one can customize a trip. Some are merely walk-in access points and others are facilities with all the trimmings. It does seem that the closer one is to a town the more access sites there are. These are all relatively easy accesses to get to, and there are shuttle services available to make everything easier. The river has access points along both banks because there are two roads paralleling the river, Highway 89 on the west bank and East River Road on the east bank.

The first access downstream of the Emigrant Bridge is Emigrant West, on the west side of the river off Highway 89. This is nothing more than a very small space to park in and then walk to the river. There is a gate to go through the fence and little else—no rest rooms, no tables, no camping, and no ramp. This access is simply a way to get to the river across private land.

A few miles downriver are two access points almost directly across the river from each other. Chicory is on the east side, off East River Road, and it looks like a turnaround. Camping is not allowed, there are no rest rooms or picnic tables, and there really isn't a ramp. There is a space cut into the bank that could possibly serve as a launching area—it'd be tough but possible. The Grey Owl access is on the west side of the river, off Highway 89. It has more of what a float fisherman needs. It is a popular access because it cuts down on the distance one has to float to get out at Mallard's Rest and makes a day on the water a little more reasonable, especially when the flows are low. The downside is that it eliminates most of the upstream water with character from the trip. Grey Owl has handicapped-accessible rest rooms, a small area to camp in, and a dirt ramp to launch from. It is a little cramped for space, but one can park in an area near the highway if space is at a premium.

Farther on down on the east side of the river is the Paradise access area, a popular spot to stop and have lunch because it's about midway through the section. It is located atop a high bank along the river and has picnic tables, rest-room facilities that are not handicapped-accessible, and camping up to fourteen days is allowed. There is no ramp to launch from. A number of the local guides stop here for lunch because of the picnic tables and the scenery. However, if you are new to the area this access can be difficult to find from the river.

The absence of a ramp and any signs makes it a little hard to spot. When you float under the Mill Creek Bridge stay to river right and look for a table.

The next access point downstream is also located off East River Road on the east side of the river—Loch Leven. This is a full-blown access with a number of spaces to camp in. There is a fourteen-day limit. There are picnic tables, barbecue grills, rest rooms, and a concrete ramp to launch from. Many visitors to the area set up their base camp here, and it is a popular spot for RV enthusiasts. This is a large area, so it is not unusual to see anglers walk-fishing in this area.

The last access in this stretch of river is located off Highway 89 on the west side of the river—Mallard's Rest. This is another large access area and it's a very popular place to set up camp. The scenery is magnificent, and it's conveniently located close to the town of Livingston. It's centrally situated, so a wide variety of trips can be planned from here. There is a good ramp facility, picnic tables, and rest rooms. It is a popular spot with both visitors and locals. It can add a few miles of floating to the next section of river. Besides some of the water both up and downstream, it has some great character and good fishing of its own.

This entire stretch is one of those sections where an angler can plan any kind of trip that suits him. There is excellent walk-in access and enough sites with ramps for very short or very long floats. The campsites are good, and the valley is hard to beat for scenic vistas.

The Fish

The blend of trout species in this section comes out to about sixty percent brown trout, twenty-five percent rainbows, and fifteen percent cutthroats. And yes, there are a number of whitefish to be had. Prior to the late 1960s and early 1970s when stocking was in full swing, this section of river had a large number of fish, and the blend was significantly different. In researching old creel surveys from the early 1960s, we found that this section of river exhibited the highest trout catch rate and that the Livingston and Carter's Bridge section had the lowest catch rate for the survey. Today, the highest concentrations of trout outside the park can be found in the river in and near Livingston. This is the difference between managing for wild trout and stocking programs. When the river was planted with trout, this section was heavily stocked, probably because the hatchery was right there at Emigrant. When stocking took place, the entire blend of trout species was different, for many of the stocked fish were rainbows.

Today, the rainbow population makes up only a quarter of the total trout population because the habitat isn't particularly suitable for rainbows. That percentage will probably never change because of the lack of a habitat niche; the rainbows here are at or approaching maximum saturation. An interesting fact about the rainbows that reside in this section is that the vast majority of them tend to be larger fish, most above fifteen inches. There is very little spawning habitat in this section, so most rainbows use the spring creeks located a ways downstream for spawning. These spring creeks have become the prime spawning grounds for the river rainbows. Because only the larger trout pioneer upstream after spawning (the smaller ones usually move downstream), the resident rainbow will be on the large side. It is relatively rare to catch small, ten-inch or so, rainbows up here.

The cutthroat numbers are low in this section because the species is reproductively limited here. There is very little in the way of spawning tributaries for them to use, and they don't seem to use the spring creeks as rainbow trout do. Cutthroats look for the cold water of mountain streams to do their spawning in and haven't made an adaptation to spring creeks. With little in the way of spawning tributaries (Mill Creek does see some spawning activity if water can be kept in it) in this stretch and the one immediately above it, there is little reason for these fish to take up permanent residence.

Brown trout, on the other hand, are flourishing in this section. The habitat is good, they make good use of the gravelly bottom in the main stem to do their spawning, and they are protected by a slot limit until they are large enough to be tough to catch. The slot limit

A nice brown that is typical of this section of river.

in this section protects fish that fall between thirteen and twenty-two inches; they must be released unharmed. Recent research about slot limits on larger rivers that aren't overfished is interesting. This section of the Yellowstone has not been overharvested—quite the contrary—the stocking programs made sure of that. Rainbow and cutthroat populations are down because they are limited reproductively and not taken in creels. On various other rivers where fishermen seem to outnumber trout, slot limits have a tendency to increase, in some cases greatly, the numbers of fish, but this isn't the case on the Yellowstone. What the slot limit has done here is to decrease the numbers of trout (remember, this was a heavily stocked section) and shift the population to larger brown trout, greater than eighteen inches. It has done this at the expense of smaller browns and rainbows. These larger fish have been protected from the harvest and their inherently low mortality rate has allowed them to take up residence and move the smaller fish from the prime water. This seems to be a typical result of a slot limit on rivers like the Yellowstone. The upside of all this is that there are good numbers of large brown trout to fish for, and the downside is that as the browns get larger, anglers have less success fishing for them. Guess we can't have our cake and eat it too.

Hatch Chart for Emigrant to Mallard's Rest

Stoneflies
Salmon fly
(*Pteronarcys californica*)   Size: #2–#6   June 25 to July 10
Golden stone
(*Calineuria californica*)   Size: #4–#8   June 25 to July 15
Yellow sally
(*Isoperla mormona*)   Size: #14–#16   July 1 to July 30
Small golden stone
(*Hesperoperla pacifica*)   Size: #6–#10   July 1 to July 20
Olive stone (*Isogenus* species)   Size: #12–#14   July 15 to August 15
Little olive stone
(*Alloperla signata*)   Size: #14–#16   August 10 to August 20

Giant western golden stone
(*Claassenia sabulosa*)   Size: #2–#6   August 1 to September 10

Caddisflies

Early grannom
(*Brachycentrus occidentalis*)   Size: #12–#16   April 25 to May 20
Spotted sedge
(*Hydropsyche cockerelli*)   Size: #12–#16   August 15 to October 20
Little brown sedge
(*Lepidostoma veleda*)   Size: #14–#18   July 10 to August 10
American grannom
(*Brachycentrus americanus*)   Size: #12–#16   July 10 to August 30
Long horn sedge
(*Oecetis avara*)   Size: #12–#16   June 25 to August 1
Spotted sedge
(*Hydropsyche occidentalis*)   Size: #10–#12   June 15 to July 20
Plain brown sedge
(*Lepidostoma pluviale*)   Size: #14–#18   July 1 to July 31

Mayflies

Western green drake
(*Drunella grandis*)   Size: #10–#12   June 25 to July 15
Western march brown
(*Rhithrogena morrisoni*)   Size: #14–#16   April 15 to May 15
Pale morning dun
(*Ephemerella inermis*)   Size: #16–#20   July 5 to August 15
Western black quill
(*Rhithrogena undulata*)   Size: #12–#14   July 1 to August 15
Western yellow drake
(*Heptagenia elegantula*)   Size: #14–#16   July 20 to August 20
Blue-winged olive
(*Baetis tricaudatus*)   Size: #18–#20   March 10 to April 20,
                                                  September 15 to November 10

Trico
(*Tricorythodes minutus*)   Size: #18–#22   August 15 to October 10

Terrestrials

Grasshoppers (Acrididae)   Size: #8–#14   July 20 to October 15
Crickets (Gryllidae)   Size: #12–#14   August 1 to September 30
Black ants (Formicidae)   Size: #16–#22   July 15 to September 30
Cinnamon ants (Formicidae)   Size: #18–#20   August 20 to September 20
Black beetle (Coleoptera)   Size: #12–#18   July 15 to August 15

Other Important Hatches and Food Forms

Midge (Chironomidae)	Size: #16–#24	February 15 to April 20, September 20 to November 10

Minnows

Mottled sculpin		
(*Cottus bairdi*)	Size: #2–#8	All year
Whitefish minnow		
(*Prosopium williamsoni*)	Size: #2–#10	All year
Long-nose dace minnow		
(*Rhinichthys cataractae*)	Size: #2–#10	All year
Long-nose sucker minnow		
(*Catostomus catostomus*)	Size: #2–#10	All year
Mountain sucker		
(*Catostomus platyrhynchus*)	Size: #2–#10	All year

Seasonal Changes: The Fishing

This section of river is paradoxical in nature. First, it is one of the most popular floating sections. Second, by late summer anglers are complaining about the lack of trout and the increased numbers of whitefish they are catching. This section of the river perhaps above all others proves that the angler working the Yellowstone must be aware of the changing water levels and how that fact is going to change where the trout are holding. Due to the depth and speed of the river in this section, the floating angler can stop and wade a great many areas. Unfortunately, many anglers do nothing more than float through this section, fishing only from the boat; thus, they never get to really know and understand this part of the river.

Spring: March to Runoff

During March this section will see some action around the access sites and by anglers who have homes nearby. But for the most part it sees few floating anglers. In March the angler can expect to see good midge hatches and the start of the spring Baetis or blue-winged olive. Anglers should not overlook nymphing possibilities during this time. We often like to work a double nymph rig using a #6 or #8 stonefly imitation as the lead fly and cased caddis imitation as a dropper. We

High water means no fishing.

also find this a good section in which to fish streamers. Our favorite pattern is a Western Lite Spruce Feather streamer or Olive Mottled Sculpin Bugger on a type 2 or 3 uniform-sink fly line. And when the rainbows start their annual spring spawning run in March, egg imitations can be very effective.

As we move into April we still have the midge and spring Baetis hatch, and by mid-April the western march browns start to appear. The angler will find the best hatches of the western march brown in the riffle sections. As the end of April nears, we start to see the early grannom caddis appear. This is the first major mega-hatch of the year, and it seems to bring up every trout in the river. The fishing during this hatch is something you have to experience to believe. This hatch carries on into May. However, we generally lose the river to the annual runoff by the tenth of May. The river will remain high and discolored until late June.

Early Summer: June and July

In a normal year the river will start to become fishable around June 20 to July 1. Salmon flies will also start to appear about that time, along with golden stones and the long horn sedge. From the end of June until about the third week in July this section of river offers some of the finest float fishing found anywhere. That is not to say that floating is the only way to take fish here; however, the float fishing can be so good that many anglers have no desire to stop and wade. In July the angler will also see yellow sally stones, small golden stones, little brown sedges, American grannom, and spotted sedges. Now if this isn't enough, the angler will also see hatches of western green drakes, pale morning duns, western black quill, and western yellow drakes. Now you must understand that not all these hatches are section-wide. Often, the hatch may cover as little as a quarter-mile or as much as a mile or so of the river. However, for the angler who stops and works the hatch, the fishing can be very rewarding. Some of these hatches will carry over into August. By the third week of July we start doing a lot of wade fishing in this section of river.

Rick Smith, a fishing guide as well as manager of Montana's Master Angler Fly Shop in Livingston, can launch his boat at Emigrant and spend the whole day fishing the three miles of river between Emigrant and Grey Owl with some rather impressive results! Rick works the various hatches and uses the boat mainly for transportation. This three-mile section is easy wading and has lots of small islands and back channels, riffle corners and flats. We have often floated from Grey Owl to Mallard's Rest, using the boat only to move from place to place, and enjoyed good fishing.

Late Summer: August to Mid-September

Many of the hatches already mentioned will continue into August. In addition, anglers will also encounter the little olive stones, giant western golden stones, and ants and hoppers. This can be an excellent hopper section if you know where to fish them. As the river drops and clears, the trout move off many of the banks in this section due to their gentle, sloping nature. The banks won't continue to hold the trout because of a lack of cover. Therefore, if the angler is going to continue to be successful, a clear understanding of trout habits and behavior is needed.

Because dry-fly fishing is so popular, we will deal with this problem from the standpoint of the dry-fly angler.

Tips and Tactics for the Dry-Fly Angler

Of all the ways there are to fish for trout with a fly, none are as popular as fishing with the dry fly. Dry flies will work in all types of water— rapids, riffles, smooth-flowing flats, and even along the edges of deep pools. The key to successful dry-fly fishing is using the flies in the right places. The matter of fishing the dry fly could fill several volumes, and many other authors have written in-depth on dry-fly fishing. For those who wish to further their knowledge, we suggest reading: *Selective Trout,* by Doug Swisher and Carl Richards; *Trout Strategies,* by Ernest Schwiebert; *Dry Fly Fishing,* by Art Lee; and *Dry Fly—New Angles,* by Gary LaFontaine. All these are excellent books that will each in its own way enrich the angler in the ways of fishing the dry fly.

The major groups of insects the angler has to deal with while fishing dry flies are: stoneflies, caddisflies, mayflies, midges, and terrestrials. We are not going to discuss entomology other than to say that you must know the basic types of insects. The important question to consider when choosing an imitation to fish with is: Does the pattern match the general size, shape, and color of the natural?

Stoneflies tend to be large and hold the wings flat over the body. When the stoneflies are on the water, the rises can be violent. Good patterns for the dry stones are the Travis Fluttering Salmon Fly or Golden Stone, Stimulators, Coachman Trudes, Muddled Stones, and Low-Floating Stones.

Caddisflies appear to be small, mothlike insects. They carry their wings over the body like a tent. The rises to caddis tend to be very splashy and quick. These insects are very swift, and sometimes trout will leap clear of the water in their efforts to capture the adults. Good all-around caddis patterns are Royal Trudes, Elkhair Caddis, Goddard Caddis, Parachute Caddis, Foam Skittering Caddis, and Foam Spent Caddis.

Caddisflies on the water.

Mayflies resemble little sailboats on the water, and rises to the newly hatched insect can be very deliberate, with the trout leaving a telltale bubble and ring on the surface. Once the mayfly duns have become spinners, rises to them are much harder to detect because the flies float flush in the film and are unmoving. The trout have all the time in the world and almost kiss them off the surface. Good rough-water patterns for mayflies would be the Royal Wulff, H & L Variants, or Goofus Bugs (Humpies). Just about any good, busy pattern will work, in the proper size. For smooth water, try patterns like Compara-duns, Parachute Duns, or Extended-Body Duns. Also try spinner imitations in the proper sizes and colors.

Midges are tiny insects that sometimes hatch in astounding numbers, and the trout feed on them very readily. The midge looks like a mosquito, but it doesn't bite. The best all-around midge imitations we have found are the Griffith Gnat, New Dubb Adult Midge, and the New Dubb Para Midge.

Terrestrials. If you see a lot of rising activity during the middle of the day in the summer months yet don't see any insects, look closer. Chances are the trout are taking small ants or beetles. Because these are land insects and are out of their element in the water, rises to them are steady and deliberate; however, the rises to grasshoppers can be very harsh and violent. Good all-around terrestrial patterns are Foam Floating Ants, Fur Ants, Foam Beetles, Whit's Bright Spot Beetle, Dave's Hopper, Whit Hopper, Yellow Madam X, and Henry's Fork Hopper.

Remember, if there is a major hatch in progress and lots of flies are on the water, the trout may become very selective to one particular insect. Using these major insect groups, the dry fly angler can find decent dry-fly fishing from March to October on the Yellowstone.

The Needs of the Trout

The trout has certain requirements that must be understood if an angler is going to be successful fishing the dry fly in this section of the river. These are protection from predators and heavy currents, along with a good source of food. The trout's survival is based on energy taken versus energy expended. The places where the trout lives in the river are called *lies*. There are *sheltering lies, feeding lies,* and *prime lies.* These are the areas in which the angler will find trout. Now we will discuss what these lies are and how to recognize them.

Sheltering lies offer protection from heavy currents and predators. They also offer *some* feeding opportunities. Sheltering lies are found around boulders, under logs, in the deepest parts of the riffles, and off the deep sides of weed beds. A hooked trout will often head straight for its sheltering lie.

Feeding lies are often found in shallower water and offer little cover. Trout in feeding lies can be spooky, so be careful in your approach. In riffle water, feeding lies will be along current edges, off the shallow side of gravel bars, or anywhere there is a concentration of currents. In smoother water, the trout often can be found in the shallow water on top of weed beds or in shallow water very close to shore.

Prime lies offer both shelter and a good feeding station for the trout. Good places to look for these are in water that isn't deeper than waist-deep, in the riffles, behind big boulders, in current tongues along sunken logs, the drop-off edges of riffles, around undercut banks and brush piles in the river. Look carefully for these places, for they can hold large trout.

Fishing the Dry Fly in the Fast Water

Fishing the dry fly in fast water can be both fun and challenging for the angler. The fly will float through the water quickly, the angler casts more often, and the strike can be startling and fast. Once hooked, the trout will use the currents to its advantage in trying to rid itself of the fly. The fishing in riffles and rapids can be very rewarding, because there are many places for the fish to hold. On this section of the Yellowstone there are many riffle corners and edge currents along the pools for an angler to work.

Riffles are waters that run over a stony, rocky bottom with lots of choppy water but very little white water. There are several factors that make fishing riffles so attractive and effective for the dry-fly angler. Our favorite method of fishing riffles is the upstream technique. In riffle water the surface is choppy, and this distorts the trout's view. Also, the trout is facing upstream, looking for food. The camouflaging sound of the rushing water will allow the angler to approach the feeding fish from behind and get quite close, sometimes as close as within fifteen or twenty feet.

The method we prefer for fishing the riffle upstream is to cast up and slightly across the stream. If you cast straight up, the trout, when rising to the fly, may bump the leader and push the fly away. If you are fishing to a rising trout, remember that the riseform moves quickly downstream in the current, so cast six to eight feet above the rise because the trout may not be just where you thought. If you see no rising trout, fish the water carefully, looking for those sheltering and prime lies discussed earlier. Take your time and cover the water—don't just make a couple of casts and move on, thinking there are no trout here. At the same time, don't let your feet get glued to the stream bottom.

Pocket water generally has lots of big boulders and heavy currents, with lots of whitewater. An area with plenty of boulders is at the Pray Bridge and a short section just below the bridge. Remember, as a rule, that if the water is more than waist-deep, the trout won't come up to the surface for a dry fly. Behind those big boulders or other obstructions there are pockets, and it's these pockets on which the angler will want to concentrate. The wading in pocket-water areas can be difficult, but the rewards are worth it. These sections of the Yellowstone receive very little attention from the angler yet many times hold some of the largest fish in the river. Here again, the best method is the upstream technique. Remember, due to the fast flows and obstructions, the currents are many and varied, so keep the cast short and pick your spots—such as the tails of the pockets, in front of the boulders, near overhanging brush alongshore, or at a point where many currents come together. A long cast for pocket-water fishing is twenty-five to thirty feet.

Line Control and Fighting the Fish

If you are going to fish the Yellowstone, or anywhere in Montana, you are going to have to deal with wind. Wind is a fact of life in the West. When fishing during windy days, the angler should try to keep casts as short as possible and should cast as tight a loop as possible. If the wind is very brisk, don't fight it—go with the flow. If it's blowing downstream, then fish downstream. This may not be the best hooking angle, but it's better than hooking yourself by fighting the wind.

When fishing in the faster water we grease the entire leader so it won't sink and then pull the fly under or cause drag. Under any dry-fly fishing conditions, the most important factor the angler has to deal with is drag. Learning how to use a "reach mend" and learning to mend your line on the water will go a long way toward solving many of your drag problems.

The reach mend is accomplished by reaching the rod to the left or right after the cast is completed but before the line has reached the water. Mending your line on the water is most often done by flipping the *belly* of the line upstream to put some slack in the line and leader. For better line control while casting, try shooting the line through your line hand but not releasing it, then placing the line

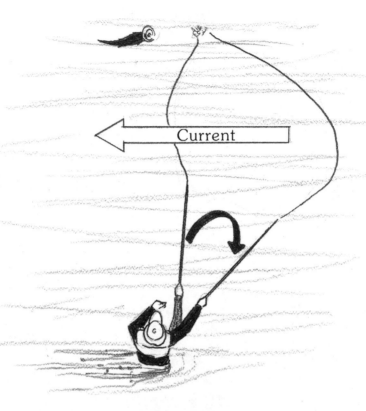

Reach mend

1. Cast to rising fish.
2. Roll the rod in an upstream direction so a belly forms upstream.

under a finger of the rod hand, lowering the rod to a horizontal position, and stripping in the slack line with the line hand as the currents feed it back to you. With a little practice you will find that you never have to look down at your hands and can pay closer attention to the drift of the imitation.

Sometimes when fishing upstream, the angler has problems picking up the line for the next cast. Try using a roll-cast pickup to start the cast. All one needs are a couple of false casts before putting the fly back on the water; that's where the trout reside. Watching some anglers, a nonfishing person might get the idea they are fishing for birds with as much time as they spend false casting. Most of the new floatants will float the battleship *Missouri*, so just take a couple of false casts and put the fly back where it will be the most effective.

Once the fish rises to the fly, set the hook—smoothly and firmly. That doesn't mean trying to rip the jaw off!! Once you see the take or feel the fish, give a little and let the trout have line if it wants it. If the fish runs at you, strip in the slack, but put that slack on the reel as soon as you can. Do so by hooking the line under the little finger of your rod hand and putting the slack on the reel under tension. Putting the line on loose will cause *real* problems if the fish makes a second run. Follow the fish downstream if you have to. If you let the trout get too far below you, the weight of the current on the line will pull the fly out or break the tippet. If the fish jumps, bow the rod tip to the fish and once the fish is in the water, pick up the rod smoothly. Work the trout into a quiet water pocket or into shore and net the fish. (Use only nets with soft cotton bags.) Quickly remove the fly, then properly revive and release the trout in quiet water to increase its chances for survival.

Dry-Fly Fishing in Smooth Water

Many of the techniques used in fishing fast water are also used while fishing in smooth, quiet water. On smooth water, the angler must use care and approach the trout with caution. Trout in smooth water tend to be a little more spooky than those found in fast water. The presentation angle of the fly is also much more demanding when one is working trout feeding in smooth water. Trout will often take the most abundant food form available in this type of water, so the angler should watch closely to see what the trout are taking. When approaching a rising fish, try to break up your body silhouette with some brush in front or behind you. Bending over also helps to present a smaller object for the fish to see. However, this only applies when your approach brings you into the trout's line of vision.

If the trout is lying very close to the surface, his window is very small and he can't see very far. Under these conditions the angler can sometimes approach within fifteen feet. However, this also means that the trout's feeding lane is very small, and an angler is going to have to put the imitation in that feeding lane if the trout is going to be taken. We often hear that you don't find selective trout on the Yellowstone. That is *bunk,* and don't you believe it! If the trout is lying a foot or more under the surface, then the closest the angler better approach is about thirty feet. When wading in smooth water, do so slowly and carefully, because the trout will spook if you go charging about like a wounded buffalo. Remember to look for the lies in flat water, such as weed beds close to shore, under overhanging brush, and around the edges of logs or other obstructions.

Sometimes the upstream approach isn't getting the job done, and other techniques are needed. Try the downstream method using a parachute cast. Remember to wait until the fly is past the trout, then lean the rod off to the side and pick up the line gently. Don't cast directly over the trout—the shadow on the water coming off the line during casting can put the trout down, as can the water drops coming off the line. When you are fishing smooth water and find yourself fishing with fine tippets and small flies, remember to set the hook gently. Just tighten until you feel the fish and then give back the rod and fight the fish with the combination of the rod and reel.

If the take is downstream, hold up a second and let the trout turn down or away before you set the hook or you'll pull the fly right out of the trout's mouth. If the trout runs below you when fishing with fine tippets, and following downstream is not an option, then use gentle, steady pressure and work the rod from side to side. By doing this you will be able to walk the trout right up the stream.

When fishing down and across to a rising fish, use a parachute cast with a reach mend. This will allow you to put the fly to the fish before the line or leader will be seen. In some cases you can cast down and across, lift the rod and skate the fly directly into the trout's feeding lane, and then lower the rod tip to obtain the proper slack.

Float Fishing

On the Yellowstone the angler can do a lot of fishing from a boat. This adds a new dimension to dry-fly fishing. Float fishing is a fun way to fish the water and allows anglers the opportunity to casually cover a great deal of water during a day. The single most important item for the dry-fly angler to remember while fishing out of a boat is that *everything is moving*—the water, the fly, and the boat. The placement of the cast depends upon the speed of the current in relation to the speed that the boat is moving downstream. More often than not, an angler will have to immediately make a quick mend upstream after casting so that a belly doesn't form in the fly line and cause the fly to drag out from the bank. This is essential when there is an upstream wind blowing, because during the cast the light leader and fly will usually blow back upriver and the heavier fly line won't. This causes a belly, and the fly will immediately begin to drag. When the current between the boat and the bank is significantly faster than the current along the bank, an upstream mend should be made.

Under normal conditions, anglers are casting slightly ahead of their positions in the boat. An angler fishing from a boat should also be mindful of the lies and cast the fly accordingly. Many times, an angler must rely on the oarsman to point out the best areas to cast to.

There is no doubt that fishing the dry fly is both fun and productive, whether you're floating down the river or wading along its edges. Many anglers are leery of big western rivers like the Yellowstone. Just remember to look at these rivers, think about what the trout needs and about the various types of lies, and you'll be able to read the water.

Fall: Mid-September to Mid-November

Many anglers think that by mid-September the dry-fly fishing is over. This simply is not true! Mid-September brings the Tricos. It also sees an increase in midge activity, and during those cloudy days the return of the blue-winged olives. And the fishing with hoppers and ants can continue clear into late October. During this same time period the brown trout begin to gather for the annual fall spawning run. This section of river holds a large number of browns, and the streamer fishing can be excellent.

The fishing continues to hold up until mid-November, or until the first major storm of the season drops the water temperature from

Some stonefly nymphs taken from this stretch of the river.

the mid- to high forties down into the thirties. This same storm may also drop the air temperature into the uncomfortable zone for anglers, thus sending them indoors and back to the fly-tying vises to dream of warmer days and the trout of tomorrow!

Locally Effective Patterns

Heavy Metal Beadhead

Hook:	Tiemco 2457, sizes 12–16
Bead:	Gold, appropiately sized
Thread:	Brown
Tail:	Hungarian partridge soft-hackle fibers
Abdomen:	Kreinik metallic braid, small, various colors
Thorax	Dark olive brown dubbing
Hackle:	Hungarian partridge soft-hackle

Fluorescent Trude

Hook:	Tiemco 101, sizes 10–18
Thread:	Brown
Tail:	Light elk hair
Body:	Peacock herl
Wing:	Fluorescent orange calf tail
Hackle:	Brown

Gray Para-Shuck

Hook:	Tiemco 100, sizes 10–18
Thread:	Gray
Shuck:	Grizzly hackle tip
Body:	Gray poly dubbing
Wing:	White Z-lon
Hackle:	Grizzly, parachute-style

Tom's PMD Nymph

Hooks:	Tiemco 101, sizes 14–20
Thread:	Rusty dun
Tails:	Wood-duck flank fibers
Rib:	Copper wire
Abdomen:	Olive pheasant-tail fibers
Wing case:	Olive pheasant-tail fibers
Thorax:	PMD sheared muskrat dubbing

Tom's PMD Floating Nymph

Hook:	Tiemco 101, sizes 14–20
Thread:	Rusty dun
Tails:	Natural wood-duck flank fibers
Rib:	Copper wire
Abdomen:	Dubbed, sheared muskrat PMD
Wing case:	Gray Scintilla fly foam
Thorax:	Dubbed same as abdomen
Legs:	Four to six natural wood-duck flank fibers, per side
Head:	Dubbed same as abdomen

Tom's PMD Stillborn Dun/Spinner

Hook:	Tiemco 101, sizes 16–20
Thread:	Rusty dun
Tails:	Brown or olive Z-lon fibers
Abdomen:	Sheared muskrat PMD, dubbed
Wings:	Light dun turkey flat fibers, tied spent
Thorax:	Dubbed same as abdomen

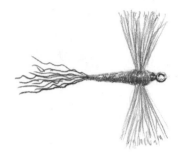

Other Effective Patterns

Borger Dark Brown Hair-leg Woolly Worm
SRI Olive Squirrel Nymph
Brown Simulator
Early Brownstone Nymph
Bett's Black Stone Nymph
Troth's Stonefly Nymph
Kaufmann's Tan Stone
Black Sparkle Stone
Pheasant-Tail Flashback Nymph
Olive Hare's Ear Nymph
Jacklin's March Brown Nymph
Mottled Pheasant-Tail Nymph
Olive Sassy Brassy
Feather Duster Nymph
Beadhead Copper Nymph
Beadhead Burlap Nymph
Baetis Nymph
Copper Nymph
Red Lace Midge Worm

Emerging Black Para-Midge
Foam-head Midge Emerger
New Dubb Midge Adult Gray
CDC Rabbit Foot PMD Emerger
Harrop's Olive Captive Dun
Baetis Para-Nymph Emerger
Lempke Extended-Body PMD
Tom's Green Drake
Tom's Gray Drake
Schroeder's Para-Hare's Ear
LaFontaine's Olive Airhead
Parachute Irresistible
Harrop's CDC Rusty Spinner
Hi-Vis Black Foam Beetle
Schroeder's Para-Hopper
Ugly Rudimas
Turck's Tan Tarantula
Olive Crippled Caddis
Foam Spent Caddis

6

Mallard's Rest
to Ninth Street

It would be fair to say that this section is the most popular stretch of
river outside the Park. Besides being located near Livingston and really convenient to get to, this stretch has some of the most interesting water in the river. Early in the year, when the Mother's Day
caddis hatch is on, an angler can be hard-pressed to find parking for
his rig at access points. Many an angler has finished his float only to
wonder where his rig is—the shuttle service had to park some distance from the access point. Of course, this has happened to us, and
we know what to expect. Almost any Sunday when the weather is
nice, this section is crowded not only with fishermen but recreational
floaters, as well.

Because this section sees a fair amount of activity each year and
because many who use these accesses are occasional floaters or
novices, it might be appropriate to mention a little about ramp courtesy. Nothing is more frustrating, especially when you're anxious to
get on the water and do some fishing, than to have to wait while
someone pulls down the ramp, unloads his boat, gears up, and then
spends half an hour talking with everyone. At the end of a long day
on the water it is just as frustrating and annoying to have to wait for
someone to reverse the procedure. In all fairness, most guides and
veteran anglers are quick, efficient, and courteous at access sites.
They should be, because they spend so much time doing this that
the procedure is second nature.

A little common sense and proper planning will make things
smoother for all. We are strict adherents of the "Seven P's of Life":

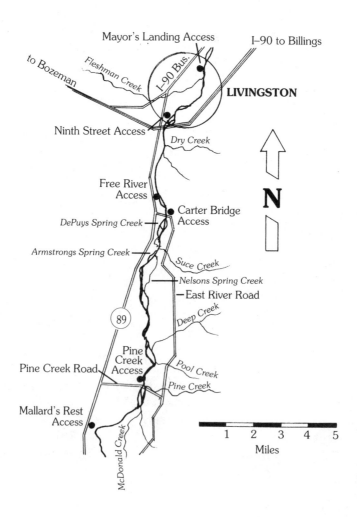

Mallard's Rest to Ninth Street

Proper prior planning prevents piss poor performance. When one first arrives at an access site with his outfit, it is a simple matter to pull over out of the launch loop and out of the way. Here an angling group can take all the time they need to unstrap the boat, put all the necessary equipment into it, organize their stuff, suit up, and assemble rods. When all this is done, then get in line or go down the ramp. Then all that needs to be done is to launch the boat and pull it over to the side, leaving room for others to launch, and then to pull the rig up to the parking area. After the boat is pulled out of the way, groups can take all the time they need to rig up the rods and make other adjustments. We see far too many groups that are completely disorganized, unfortunately, at the expense of all.

At the other end of the trip, when it's time to take the boat out (and many of us are slightly burned out), it is equally important to be as courteous as possible. Before pulling into a ramp area, look to see if there are other boats anchored there. If there are, pull in far enough downstream of the other boats—downstream so you don't inadvertently allow the current to force you into someone else's boat (guys are very touchy about their boats). If you haven't arranged to have your vehicle and trailer shuttled to the access and you have to make a vehicle move, pull your boat out of the way so other anglers have room. If your rig is waiting, do not start unloading and stacking gear on the shore—wait until your boat is out of the water, on the trailer, and pulled up into the parking area out of the way of other anglers. Then take all the time you need to store everything away, take apart your tackle, take the waders off and get the boat and trailer ready to leave. Nothing is more annoying than having to wait while guys make a thousand trips to their vehicles, putting stuff away, before they take their boats out of the water. If there is something that may be broken as the boat is pulled onto the trailer, have one of your party remove it while you are getting in line to pull out. Consider that all the other floaters are just as tired and want to get to where they need or want to be as much as you do. We realize that all this is sermonizing, but if you are ever on this stretch on a beautiful Sunday or holiday weekend, you will join the ranks of the highly agitated.

On most other sections of the river it is easy to tell if the fishing has been good by the amount of traffic on the water and rigs in the parking areas. In this small fishing community it doesn't take long for word to spread from shop to shop and guide to guide if some-one had a great day on a particular stretch of river. Usually the next few days will see that stretch fairly crowded with boats trying to cash in on the fishing. This stretch is difficult to read because it gets so much use. If you arrive and see the parking lot spilling over out onto the highway with rigs, it would be a good bet that someone had some great fishing in the past day or so. Otherwise, a full parking lot only means there are floaters on the river. Very often in the late sum-mer, when other stretches are fishing far better than this section, the parking areas will be full even if the fishing is really slow. This is par-tially because it is near to town and simply convenient, and partly be-cause many anglers like the variety of water types here, and partially because many anglers and guides do not know the other sections as well.

This is a beautiful stretch to float, with the Absarokas looming in the background, so the crowding is understandable. We may con-sider this section to be a crowded stretch as a rule, but compared to other rivers, especially the Big Horn, it really isn't too bad. No mat-ter how many boats are on the water there is still plenty of room to fish—you may not be able to stop at the riffle corner of your choice, but there are plenty of others. Over the course of a season the river here does at times reflect the fishing pressure. When the water be-gins to drop, and during low-water years, anglers out early and hav-ing first crack at the fishy-looking spots will be the most successful. A steady stream of boats fishing along a bank tends to make for some slow fishing for those at the end of the line.

This is one of those stretches where an angler can get out of the boat and work interesting water because there is plenty of it. Some anglers will float fast and hard to get to particular pieces of water, some will even float until they reach the mouth of Nelson's Spring Creek. Here they can walk a short distance up the creek and have a spring-creek experience with light rods, fine tippets, and small flies. This is a section where there is something for everyone to enjoy.

The beautiful Paradise Valley.

Water Characteristics

This stretch has more character from a fisherman's point of view than any other portion of the river. The only other section that comes close is the water near Gardiner. Any and everything a fly fisherman needs in the way of water types can be found here. There is interesting water right from the start as one floats down from Mallard's Rest and continues right through the town of Livingston. Interestingly, this is a section that changes, sometimes radically, from year to year because of the effects of the high water of runoff. There are a number of channels here that shift from year to year as the force of the heavy water shifts gravel and bottom structures around. The first float of the year, right after runoff, is always interesting in order to see how, not if, the river has changed. Some years there is very little change and some years bring significant change. When one does decide to take a side channel, it is necessary to be careful the first time through. There is nothing like finding a fallen tree blocking the channel when you're coming around a bend at a good clip to get everyone in the boat moving in different directions. It does tend to wake you up.

There is a great deal of braiding in this section, particularly in the upper and lower reaches. The Pine Creek islands force the river to braid around them for a mile or so, giving the floating angler a number of choices. Those fishing immediately after runoff would be wise to select the main channel until they know the other ones are safe. They usually are, but why chance it? Each channel takes on all the characteristics of a small river as it twists and turns to converge with the main stem. There are good banks, riffle corners, pockets, and even riprap to fish as one floats or wades down. The Pine Creek channel has a reputation of fishing well, and especially so in the fall.

Farther down toward the end of this stretch are a number of channels that veer off to the right before entering town. These channels have all a fly fisherman needs or wants. However, when the flows are low toward the end of the season or in a low-water year, it could be a little difficult floating through some of them because the water gets really shallow. Very often you have to float over water that should be fished. This is a very popular area with wading fishermen, because they can reach this section from town by walking to it. It is a super area to fish in the winter months when the midges and Baetis put an appearance.

The sections between also have some braiding because many smaller islands form, creating small side channels. Do not overlook the major channel that flows past DePuy's Spring Creek—there can be some awesome fishing in it. Very often, when the water of the main river is high and fast, this channel is very fishable. Many a hatch has come off here while most anglers blow by it, fishing the main river. As a matter of fact, most of these channels are more fishable than the main river when the water is high and fast.

The Yellowstone twists and turns through this section as it courses to town. The twists and turns create numerous inside bends that fly fishermen so love, with the accompanying riffle corners and current edges. As one works his way down this stretch, all kinds of

Fishing a channel by a gravel bar.

water character will be available to fish. There is a good deal of riprap in this section, because landowners have attempted to curb the effects of erosion. Many of these riprap banks are in the form of rock walls and create extremely good holding water for trout. The little pockets behind the many rocks generally have a fish or two waiting for a goody to float by. The erodible quality of these banks tends to slow the speed of the water alongside, which in turn makes it ideal habitat for trout. Whenever there is a hatch taking place, the first place an angler notices it is usually along one of these banks. The odd thing is that they are situated on the dominant side of the river, where the force of the current is the strongest, but the rocks break it up and considerably slow it down, at least right next to the rocks. Here fish have a chance to feed in leisure on the hatched insects that get forced to the banks. Although in some spots these banks seem unfishable because the water is moving so fast, they are really very fishable, especially so in the pockets.

Fishing these banks is fun because it all happens so quick. The floating fisherman is out in the fast current casting toward the riprap and the very slow current. Here a good oarsman is a blessing as he continually back-rows to slow the speed of the boat. Everything happens quickly—boom, boom, boom. Cast into a pocket and try to extend the drift by making a mend upstream, or reach cast or curve cast to keep the fly from dragging. Usually there is but a second or two of drag-free drift before one has to pick up and cast to a different pocket. It is amazing how fast trout seem to pick the fly up, very often hitting as soon as the fly lands on the water. It becomes a matter of cast, pick up, cast again, pick up, cast again, and so on all the way down the bank, almost as fast as you can say it. Usually toward the downstream end of these banks the current slows, so the pace is less frenetic.

The fisherman who can drift by these banks and find a spot to pull over (this can be difficult in many of these places) can walk back up along the banks and have some excellent fishing. The way the access points are located in this stretch, the wading fisherman has an opportunity to reach some of these great banks. As a matter of fact, the walking fisherman has the opportunity to cover a great deal of good water in this section, probably more so here than anywhere else, at least without a major hassle.

For anglers who relish throwing heads in the fall, this section has some super streamer water, with deep long runs and pools. The nymph fisherman will find a number of inside bends with current edges to dead-drift a nymph through. The dry-fly enthusiast has access to the slower water, where the bugs tend to gather as the currents concentrate them. The float fisherman has super banks to throw to along the entire stretch. There are even some hot springs that dump into the river below Carter's Bridge at which to stop. There has been many a trip when we stopped to sit in the springs and warm up. There is definitely something for every angler in this section.

Accessibility

Coming down the river from Mallard's Rest, one comes to the Pine Creek access site about three miles downriver, immediately after floating under the Pine Creek Bridge. It would be fair to say that this is the most-used access site along the entire river. It has a good ramp, plenty of parking, and rest rooms that are not handicapped-accessible. It does not have tables or barbecues. Many anglers take this short float after work, and others use it as an access to the channels just upstream for wading trips.

From Pine Creek down to the next access point, Carter's Bridge, is about seven miles. This is one of the most popular floats on the entire river. Here there is a good concrete ramp, parking, and handicapped-accessible rest-room facilities. There are no tables, and camping is not permitted. Finding it is no problem because it is immediately after the bridge. All the access points along this section are well marked with signs and are easy to get to. Many fishermen who want to walk use this access because there is good water nearby.

The next access downriver is the FreeRiver FAS site located off Highway 89 a mile or so from Carter's Bridge. This is nothing more than a place to park and walk to the river. Although there is a sign here, it is hard to see and looks as if it's in somebody's yard. At this time, there is a small bridge at the site, but it is in need of major repair, so this is not an effective access

As one floats down toward town from Carter's Bridge, two options become available. If one stays to the main channel, keeping river left, the next access point down is the Ninth Street Bridge access in the town of Livingston. This is a small-town park with a ramp, a few picnic tables, and benches. Stay to the left and don't miss it; it is before the Ninth Street Bridge. This bridge is extremely dangerous and has claimed the lives of a few unfortunate floaters.

If you float and stay to the right you can take the channels past this dangerous bridge—you'll be in a different channel and never even see the bridge. You will eventually be returned to the main stem in the middle of town and have to use the Mayor's Landing access point to get off the water. This is a full-service access and makes for a good place to take out after a short float from Carter's Bridge.

All these access sites allow an angler to plan his day, whether that be short, an all-day affair, or a quick hour or so of wade-fishing.

The canyon section immediately upstream of Livingston.

Situated in and near Livingston, these accesses make for easy shuttles and close proximity to the amenities the town offers. There are a number of shuttle services available—ask at one of the local fly shops for a recommendation.

The Fish

As we move down this stretch of river, the fish populations begin to change slightly. This section of river borders the town section, which has the highest numbers of trout per mile than any other part of the river, and the lower end down from the spring creeks falls into it. The upper reach of this section, around Mallard's Rest, has a greater percentage of brown trout in the population mix than do the lower reaches. Closer to the spring creeks the population of rainbows increases. The percentage of cutthroats is unfortunately low in this section.

As we work down this stretch the population breakdown comes out to eighty percent rainbow trout, fifteen to twenty percent brown trout, and three to five percent cutthroat trout. There are more browns in the upper reach for a couple of reasons. The first is that the habitat is ideal for them, and the second is that there is ample spawning ground for them. The Pine Creek channels are a case in point. It is amazing and interesting to see all the spawning redds in these channels every fall.

Since the rainbows tend to use the spring creeks to spawn (the spring creeks are the most important areas for spawning rainbows), their numbers are high around them. According to the fish and wildlife studies, we are experiencing an all-time high in numbers of rainbow trout in this section of river. Since the improvements made on the spring creeks, particularly DePuy's, rainbows have increasingly used them for spawning, which has increased their population. There is very little in the way of spawning tributaries downstream of this stretch, so rainbows will move a fair distance upstream to get to the spring creeks. Another factor affecting the high number of rainbows here is the habitat, which is ideally suited to their needs. The fast aerated water is much to their liking.

Cutthroats, on the other hand, are not doing too well in this section. Mostly this is because they are reproductively limited. There is hardly any water for these trout to spawn in, so there are relatively few here. They haven't yet adapted to using the spring creeks to spawn in, and the tributaries that do flow to the river are usually dewatered as irrigators pull water for their crops. We hope something can be worked out to keep a minimum flow in these critical tributaries for the sake of the Yellowstone cutthroat.

Problems in Paradise

This section of the river offers the angler great fishing and great hatches. We will be discussing the misnamed Mother's Day caddis hatch, the spring Baetis, the green drakes, and a couple of other special caddis hatches that only occur in this section. Due to the distance from town and the way the access sites are placed, this is the one section of river where anglers may encounter social problems. However, we have both traveled and fished extensively around the country, and we are here to tell you that the Yellowstone is *not* crowded, nor is it overfished. Nor, for that matter, is any other stream in Montana, based on what we have observed on other waters around the country. While we were doing research for this book, one of the old-timers we interviewed related that when one went fishing along the Yellowstone in years past, if he saw another angler he would immediately leave the area, moving three or four miles upstream. He went on to relate that the Yellowstone in recent years had become too crowded; therefore, he had given up fly fishing. We do not agree with this viewpoint and find it sad that someone would give up fly fishing.

In recent years much has been written about overcrowding, yet the problem can be easily solved if people do their part by observing *fly fishing etiquette*. However, there is an up side to this influx of anglers. We are finding groups like Trout Unlimited, the Federation of Fly Fishers, and others are gaining more members and more influence and that more anglers are becoming aware of the need for clean water and better management practices. With the increase in numbers and increased awareness of fly fishers, we are making better and faster progress in protecting our fisheries. We are not saying that everything is okay, and that nothing needs to be done. There are a great many battles yet to be fought. In an audiotape entitled *Fly Fishing with Ernie Schwiebert* (an interview conducted by Jim Bashline), we think maybe Ernie said it best when he stated "we get lost rock-rolling and arguing about trivia." That we do; we argue about barbless versus barbed hooks, catch-and-release versus keeping fish, whether this river or that river is overcrowded. We do this instead of concentrating our major efforts on protecting the fisheries we have and reclaiming those we have lost. As for the social aspects of fly fishing, we offer these simple words.

Fly Fishing Etiquette

We have schools that teach basic introductory-level fly fishing. We have several magazines that deal solely with fly fishing. There are many books published each year on the various aspects of fly fishing, yet we see very little in print on fly-fishing etiquette. As the sport continues to grow, everyone must take the responsibility to educate newcomers, and even some of the old hands, on proper fly-fishing etiquette. If we don't, the problem will only get worse! Now we will climb down off our soapbox and tell you how to avoid problems and what we think fly-fishing etiquette is all about. *Basic fly fishing etiquette is nothing more than simple courtesy and good common sense.*

First, let's discuss off-stream etiquette. We anglers as a group seem to spend a lot of time and energy on silly issues like what fly fishing is or isn't. We argue that indicator fishing is unfair or that streamer fishing is nothing more than spin fishing with a fly rod, or that if you're not dry-fly fishing you are not fly fishing, and so on and so forth. These conversations can be tiresome and pointless. Furthermore, *who the hell really cares?* If it's not your way, fine don't use that method, but to say it is wrong and argue about it is a waste of time. As this happens to be the land of the free, you probably won't change the other person's mind anyway. So be kind to and tolerant of those who don't happen to fish the way you do. We have found that if we worry less about how someone else is fly fishing, we tend to enjoy our own fishing a little more. If you wish to contribute some good to the sport of fly fishing, channel your energy toward protecting and enhancing the fisheries.

In *Webster's New World Dictionary,* the word *etiquette* is defined as follows: "The forms, manners and ceremonies established by convention as acceptable or required in society, or in a profession." After reading this definition you would think that fly fishers would have no problems with one another, that acceptable manners come very naturally to most fly fishers, and therefore seldom would there be a clash between them. A very old and dear angling friend of ours once said that fly-fishing etiquette is nothing more than common sense, and the best way to define etiquette was "Do unto others as you would have them do unto you."

Now after reading these two definitions, you might think that with good manners and common sense how are fly fishers going to cause problems either on or off the water? But, alas, that is not always the case. Unfortunately, there are those few who, either by deeds, words, or both, show that they have no manners or common sense, thus creating problems for themselves and the anglers around them. There are also those individuals who feel that etiquette is only something practiced on the water, that their right to *freedom of speech* covers them when they wish to cast aspersions on fellow anglers. These individuals often forget that though they have certain *rights,* those rights only extend as far as the next individual who holds the same rights Therefore, each individual needs to practice *etiquette* while exercising his rights, both on and off the water.

For the wading fly fisher, most problems can be avoided if common sense is used and an honest attempt at being courteous is made. Here are a few simple rules that work for us:

1. When you are fishing along a stream and chance upon another angler, get out and move around the angler, giving him plenty of room so you don't spook the fish he is working.
2. Never crowd anyone. Other anglers have the right to their own space without someone edging in on them.
3. If you are fishing an area like Buffalo Ford on the Upper Yellowstone where there may be lots of anglers, ask before you step in between two anglers—they could be friends fishing together.
4. Don't be unreasonable about how much space you need, and be willing to share the water. We once listened to an angler complain about how he was being crowded—but there wasn't an angler within five hundred yards of him in any direction.
5. If you encounter an angler who appears to be sitting on the bank resting an area, be kind enough not to jump in and start fishing. You might also ask about the situation, so you can move around the angler without spooking the trout being rested.
6. Don't trespass or litter, and make sure that you treat all property and streams with care. If a gate is closed make sure you keep it that way. Don't build unauthorized fires.

The angler who floats faces some other problems that must be considered. We covered ramp courtesy earlier in the chapter.

1. Never float over the water someone else is working. If the river is narrow, stop the boat and ask where you can go around.
2. Never yell at or harass other anglers because they are fishing with a method different from yours.
3. Remember that being in a boat doesn't give you any special rights, and simple courtesy extended to other anglers who are floating or wading will make for a more enjoyable day for everyone.
4. Don't race your boat to beat someone else to a spot. If that is the only spot to fish on the river, we say try another river.
5. Always be aware of the other anglers in your area regardless of whether they are wading or floating. This will keep you from crowding others and help you avoid accidents.

These are the rules to operate by regardless of whether we are fishing or guiding. Speaking of guiding—we are both guides, and we would like to point out that most guides are very courteous; however, for the very few who aren't, that guide's license doesn't confer any special rights to abuse others. Guides who act like dolts reflect on the good guides, who do not appreciate it *at all.* So to those guides, and you know who you are, chill out and clean up your act!!

The next time you run into someone who is not showing proper manners or good common sense, instead of yelling and screaming, try quietly offering to explain the definition of etiquette. Maybe that person missed those lessons earlier in life.

Seasonal Changes: The Fishing

This is indeed an interesting and complex section of the river to fish. We find hatches in this section that don't appear in other sections, and there are hatches that don't gain the intensity in this section that they do in others. There are also the effects of the spring creeks entering the river in this section. These factors alone, to say nothing of the ever-changing water levels, make this a very intriguing and complex section of the river to fish.

Hatch Chart for Mallard's Rest to Ninth Street

Stoneflies
Salmon fly
(*Pteronarcys californica*)   Size: #2–#6   June 20 to July 5
Golden stone
(*Calineuria californica*)   Size: #4–#8   June 20 to July 10
Yellow sally
(*Isoperla mormona*)   Size: #14–#16   July 1 to July 30
Giant western golden stone
(*Claassenia sabulosa*)   Size: #2–#6   July 20 to September 10

Caddisflies
Early grannom
(*Brachycentrus occidentalis*) Size: #12–#16   April 25 to May 20
Spotted sedge
(*Hydropsyche cockerelli*)   Size: #12–#16   August 15 to October 20
American grannom
(*Brachycentrus americanus*) Size: #12–#16   July 10 to August 30
Long horn sedge
(*Oecetis avara*)   Size: #12–#16   June 25 to August 1
Spotted sedge
(*Hydropsyche occidentalis*)   Size: #10–#12   June 20 to July 20
Plain brown sedge
(*Lepidostoma pluviale*)   Size: #14–#18   July 1 to July 31
Little western weedy-water sedge
(*Amiocentrus aspilus*)   Size: #14–#16   July 15 to September 20
Speckled peter caddis
(*Helicopsyche borealis*)   Size: #14–#16   July 1 to July 20

Mayflies
Western green drake
(*Drunella grandis*)   Size: #10–#12   July 1 to July 15
Western march brown
(*Rhithrogena morrisoni*)   Size: #14–#16   April 15 to May 15

Pale morning dun		
(*Ephemerella inermis*)	Size: #16–#20	July 10 to August 10
Gray drake		
(*Siphlonurus occidentalis*)	Size: #10–#12	July 1 to July 15
Blue-winged olive		
(*Baetis tricaudatus*)	Size: #18–#20	March10 to April 20,
		September 15 to November 10
Trico (*Tricorythodes minutus*)	Size: #18–#22	August 15 to October 10

Terrestrials

Grasshoppers (Acrididae)	Size: #8–#14	July 20 to October 15
Crickets (Gryllidae)	Size: #12–#14	August 1 to September 30
Black ants (Formicidae)	Size: #16–#22	July 15 to September 30
Cinnamon ants (Formicidae)	Size: #18–#20	August 20 to September 20
Black beetle (Coleoptera)	Size: #12–#18	July 15 to August 15

Other Important Hatches and Food Forms

Midge (Chironomidae)	Size: #16–#24	February 15 to April 20,
		September 20 to November 10

Minnows

Mottled sculpin		
(*Cottus bairdi*)	Size: #2–#8	All year
Whitefish minnow		
(*Prosopium williamsoni*)	Size: #2–#10	All year
Long-nose dace minnow		
(*Rhinichthys cataractae*)	Size: #2–#10	All year
Long-nose sucker minnow		
(*Catostomus catostomus*)	Size: #2–#10	All year
Mountain sucker		
(*Catostomus platyrhynchus*)	Size: #2–#10	All year

Early Summer: June and July

On the average, the Yellowstone will become fishable around June 25 to July 1. We often see the start of the salmon flies around the twentieth of June. Sadly, the hatch is no longer very heavy in this section as a general rule. Why? Nobody knows whether this is natural in an ever-changing system like the Yellowstone or if the cause is man-induced. The golden stones also appear about this same time. This hatch is a little stronger, but not overly so. Also, the angler will encounter the spotted sedge. Now this hatch is much stronger, and the trout will definitely feed on it. Toward the end of June the long horn sedge will appear, and the sheer numbers of these insects will soon have the trout looking up. Due to the popularity of the salmon fly and golden stone hatches, you will find few anglers on this section in late June or the first few days in July, unless it is a low-water year. The bulk of the anglers head upriver, chasing the hatch to other sections. We have seen years when the river didn't become fish-able until mid-July; however, this is the exception rather than the rule. Many anglers claim that the river is too high and the banks are too fast during this time of year for the angler to be successful. This is simply not true; the insects are there and the trout sure haven't moved to another section. Look for the off-speed banks and slower water, and the fishing can be just as good as anywhere else on the river. Very often these off-speed banks will have fish rising right in the willows, a strange sight and one that makes a proper presentation a little tricky. During this time we often have two or even three rods apiece with us. One rod will be set up for dry flies, one for nymph-ing, and one with a sink tip for throwing streamers and larger nymphs. Often, we have the river to ourselves.

As we move into July it seems that everything starts hatching. We see yellow sally stones, American grannom caddis, plain brown sedges, and two other species of caddis that we will discuss a little later. During July the angler will also see hatches of western green drakes and pale morning duns. Also during the month of July bee-tles can be important, and late in the month the hoppers start to show.

Except for some of the caddis species, most hatches are not riverwide—you have to look for them. Take the green drakes, for ex-ample. One section where we have found consistent green drake ac-tion is about a mile below the Pine Creek Bridge in an area called the Weeping Wall. As you're going downriver from Pine Creek you will come to an area where there is a high clifflike bank on the right and a forested section of land on the left. The Wall contains small springs entering the river, and the lower portion appears to be wet (thus the "Weeping" Wall). Over the years we have found the drakes there many times and enjoyed some super fishing.

During mid-July the angler can enjoy some excellent PMD fishing in the areas below where the spring creeks enter the river. Also in these same areas the angler will encounter the speckled peter caddis, which hatches throughout the month of July. By mid-July the little western weedy-water sedges will appear. This hatch will continue until late September. Anglers working the areas below where the spring creeks enter the river need to be aware of these hatches and plan accordingly.

As July progresses and the water levels begin to come down and the salmon fly hatch tapers off, you will seldom have this section to yourself. Be prepared to share.

Late Summer: August to Mid-September

Many of the caddis hatches continue on into August, as does the PMD hatch. The angler will begin to see the giant western golden stone during early August, and hoppers will also become more important. By now the banks are in fine shape for the floating angler, and there is lots of wade fishing as the riffle corners and edge currents become more defined.

As we move into September, ants become very important in this section of the river. Sometime from mid-August on you can encounter Tricos in various sections of this stretch of river. This hatch seems to be gaining in strength each year.

Fall: Mid-September to Mid-November

During the fall, anglers will still encounter an occasional Trico hatch, and on those cool, cloudy days the blue-winged olives will return. Also during the fall the midge hatches will return.

Fall is a beautiful time of year to fish this section: the water levels are down and the river is well defined. During the fall the brown trout start to move and gather for the fall spawning run. It is during this time that the names of pools are mentioned and anglers talk of big trout, big flies, and shooting heads. In this stretch of river there is Car Body Pool, the Pine Creek Bridge Pool, Joe Brooks #1, and the Nelson Rock Wall Pool, to name just a few. Of course, the angler can also find some excellent nymphing, as well as some dry-fly fishing. It's just that, well, streamer fishing is a favorite of ours.

A nice autumn brown.

Winter water.

Winter: Mid-November to February

During this period the weather is the biggest factor in determining how much fishing is done. However, even in a normal winter there will be plenty of days when the angler can be on the water. Much of the winter fishing is using streamers or nymphs as the water temperatures drop. The presentations must slow down, and the angler should take more time to thoroughly cover the water in the area being fished. During late November and again during February the angler can see midge hatches and find trout feeding on them in foam pools or back-eddies. Most of the fishing done during the winter is wade fishing. Anglers are out floating only if there has been a long warm spell or the whole winter has been very mild.

Spring: March to Runoff

March means an end to winter, and more opportunities to fish the river. Now, we are not saying that the storms have ended, or anything like that; anyone who goes afield in March should go prepared, because the weather can vary greatly.

We generally start the month nymphing. By midmonth we will begin to see the blue-winged olives. The Baetis will hatch during the warmest part of the day, which means the afternoon. This means you don't have to rush out to the river at the crack of dawn. During the month of March the water temperature starts to rise, and as this happens, the trout become more and more active.

During March and on into April the rainbows gather and move to the mouths of the spring creeks. They use the creeks as spawning grounds; therefore, the fishing below these areas can be very good on nymph and egg imitations. April brings warmer days and increased activity from the insects, the trout, and the anglers. Anglers will continue to see blue-winged olives and midges, and around the middle of the month the western march brown will appear. The best western march brown hatches will occur below riffle sections of the river. The angler may encounter western march browns, Baetis, and midges hatching all at the same time. This will make for some very interesting and challenging fishing for those who like to work over selective trout.

Toward the end of April we see the start of the first *mega-hatch* of the year, the misnamed "Mother's Day" caddis hatch. We often talk to anglers who wish to come and fish the hatch and are making plans for arriving on May 10. This hatch starts in late April, and the river generally becomes unfishable by May 10. If you want to fish the hatch, try the last few days of April and first five days of May. Sure, we have had early years when we were unable to fish the hatch due to runoff; however, most years we are able to get in a few good days before the river becomes too high and discolored. As we stated earlier, this is the first *mega-hatch* of the season and every trout in the river takes advantage of the bounty.

To become more efficient anglers during the caddis hatch, we must have a clear understanding of the caddisfly, the different stages of its life cycle, and how the trout feed on it. This information will help us know when, where, and how to fish during the hatch.

Trichoptera: Caddisflies

Trichoptera means "hair wing." More than two hundred species of caddisfly has been found in Montana waters. In the Yellowstone River there are ten major species of caddis and twenty-six minor species. The adults are often called *sedges*, and sometimes *moths* by the unknowing. The adults fly in a rapid and erratic manner. Sizes can vary from #8 to #22. The basic colors are olive, gray, tan, brown, green, and blackish. The adults live on the average of four weeks and tend to be crepuscular, or nocturnal, in nature. There are three ways in which caddis lay their eggs: 1, the adults hover (fluttering) just over the surface of the water; 2, the adults lie spent or at rest on the surface of the water; 3, the adults dive down to the bottom of the stream.

The caddisfly spends the majority of its life as an aquatic insect. There are a few species that produce two generations per year, but for the most part one generation per year is the rule. The caddis has a complete life cycle or metamorphosis, as egg, larva, pupa, and adult. Caddis eggs are of no importance to the angler. Caddis larvae, however, are found in forms that interest both the trout and the angler: cased, net-building, and free-swimming.

The cased caddis larvae are some of the most abundant forms found in the waters of the Yellowstone. The cases are made from small pieces of debris—sand grains, gravel, leaves, grasses, bark, twigs—and will generally blend in very well with the surrounding habitat. The head and thorax are the only parts of the insect to peek out of the case. Thorax colors will most often be olives, tans, or cream. The heads are most often blackish.

The net-building caddis larvae are not quite as available to the trout because they reside under and on rocks, boulders, and logs found on the river bottom. However, there are times when the trout will appear to be rooting in and around the bottom. Stomach samples have shown that these trout are indeed feeding on the net-building caddis larvae.

The free-living caddis larvae are predators always on the move looking for a meal, thus becoming meals for the trout. The larvae appear to be grublike organisms that either move about in search of food or build nets in rocks and other niches to trap food. The larvae appear to have short tails, with a long segmented abdomen, short thorax section and legs, and rather dark heads. The base abdomen colors can cover a wide range, from olives, tan, cream, gray, brown, and black to mottled variations. As the time for hatching draws near, the caddis go through an intermediate or pupal stage. Then it is time to hatch. This means a super abundant meal for the trout. Studies have shown that much of the trout's annual growth takes place during this time.

Now we are going to pass on some tips on how to fish the caddis hatch on the Yellowstone. We will discuss each stage of the hatch and what patterns and presentation techniques the angler will need.

Fishing the Caddis Hatch

There are three basic stages of the caddis life cycle that the angler must prepare for so that the proper patterns will be on hand to imitate the stages that are important to the trout, and thus the angler. These stages are nymph (larvae), pupa, and adult. Within the three basic stages there are twelve pattern types the angler may wish to have on hand while fishing during the caddis hatch.

1. Nymphs: cased caddis and free-living-caddis larvae
2. Pupas: deep caddis pupa, emerging caddis pupa, and stillborn/crippled caddis emerger
3. Adults: transitional caddis, crippled adults, fluttering adults, spent adults, at-rest adults, wet drowned adults, and diving adults

Caddis come in various sizes and colors, but we have found that with these patterns we can cover most of the caddis-fishing situations we encounter on the Yellowstone. During the spring caddis hatch we seldom find the trout super selective to color. If the size and silhouette are close and the presentation is right, then we have no major trouble taking trout during this hatch. However, this is not to say that the trout never become selective during the hatch and are always easy. There are times when everything must be right or it's no go. The reason we believe in carrying a diversity of patterns is to

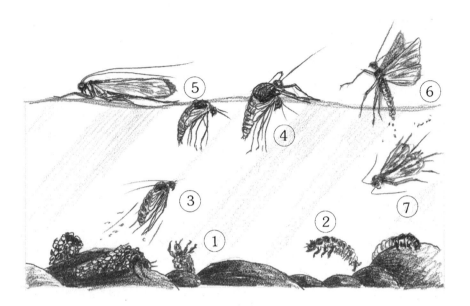

Stages of a caddisfly

1. Cased larvae	3. Emerging pupa	6. Egg-laying adult
2. Free-swimming larvae	4. Emerging adult	7. Diving adult
	5. Adult	

solve what we call "situational angling problems." Most of the time we just use the few favorites we like. However, when you come across situations where the trout are feeding on, say, stuck-in-the-shuck adults, if you don't have them, well, you find yourself frustrated. That is something we would rather avoid if possible.

The best all-around advice we can offer the angler is to be observant and creative, don't get stuck in a rut, and never base decisions on assumptions or hearsay. Just about the time you think you have the trout and the caddis hatch all figured out, they'll throw you a curve and knock all your theories into left field. We once heard someone say that all statements and theories regarding trout and fly fishing tend to be false at one time or another. This is especially true for anglers who are rigid in their thinking. They often find it hard to solve problems that defy the norm. There is no doubt in our minds that the activity surrounding the caddis emergence will not only control what the trout feed on, but how, when, and where they feed. Therefore, knowledge of this activity will play a major role in what methods the angler uses and the patterns he selects.

Much has been written about the speed of the emerging caddis pupa. The speed with which the caddis pupa rises to the surface during emergence varies between species, but the idea that the pupa blasts loose from the bottom of the stream and takes off like a guided missile is indeed silly. Stomach samplings have shown that trout feed heavily on the emerging pupa. Now, how could the trout capture such a speed demon? And what does this do to the accepted theory that trout feed on the most abundant and easiest-to-capture available food form? Remember that the trout's survival is based on energy spent versus energy ingested. Just think of the energy a trout would have to expend to capture the missilelike caddis pupa! It's almost funny when you think about it; therefore, we must rethink the theories on trout survival and behavior or assume that the caddis-pupa-missile theory is indeed off base.

Our own observations and studies have shown us that caddis pupa do not shoot off the bottom like a missile. This observation is reinforced by the findings of Gary LaFontaine in his excellent book *Caddisflies.* In *Caddisflies,* Gary states that "most all anglers seem to recognize the peak of the caddis hatch, when it happens. Though often times they are ill prepared for it and often find themselves frustrated and maybe even fishless." The keys to improving your skills as a caddis angler are observation and knowledge of both the insect and the trout. One must learn when to start looking for the hatch. Once you have determined that the hatch has started, you then can begin to fish hours before the actual emergence and the appearance of other anglers. Oftentimes the "prehatch" fishing can be better and produce larger trout than fishing right during the peak of the hatch.

Prehatch Caddis Action

Hours before the peak of the hatch, a few caddis will start emerging. These early risers are often ignored or missed by both the trout and the angler. This may be due to the limited numbers of emergers or because the trout are feeding on another food form that is more abundant. The angler often misses these early emergers due to a lack of observation. But as the numbers of emerging pupae increase, the trout will become keyed in on them. At first the trout will feed close to the bottom, where the greatest number of emerging pupae are noticed as they break free and begin their rise to the surface. This ascent to the surface is gradual as the pupa drifts along at the mercy of the currents. Keen observation over a long period of time has disclosed that during the pupa's rise to the surface there are several definite periods of hesitation where the ascent is halted and the pupa is at the mercy of the currents and appears to be struggling inside the pupal shuck. During these hesitation periods the pupae are most vulnerable, and the trout feed on them quite heavily.

During this time, we like to fish a Beadhead Caddis Pupa or Deep Sparkle Pupa imitation. We bounce these imitations along the bottom, often imparting just a touch of movement to imitate the pupa struggling inside the shuck. The trout will feed on these drifting, struggling pupae for hours before the main hatch, and for the angler standing on the banks of the Yellowstone it appears that nothing is happening and trout and insects are still in a state of inaction. This is the time the knowledgeable caddis angler will anticipate, taking advantage of an excellent angling opportunity and oftentimes having the river to himself.

As the Main Hatch Draws Closer

During this period, the observant angler will notice an increase in the numbers of emerging caddis. Generally the adult caddis will not ride on top of the water for long distances after hatching unless the air temperature has dropped and the day is damp. However, the emerging pupa will normally ride long distances in the surface film while struggling to escape the pupal shuck and become an adult. At this time the caddis is half on top of and half just under the film and is very vulnerable. The trout will prey on the caddis now with wild abandon.

During this period we have found that patterns like soft-hackles, K-Flash Emergers, and LaFontaine Sparkle Emergers are very effective. One of the easiest methods of fishing these types of patterns is to use the old wet-fly-swing method of fishing down and across. We will also use LaFontaine Sparkle Emergers, transitional caddis, and crippled caddis patterns. With these patterns we grease the leader and sometimes the head of the imitation and fish it half in and half on top of the film. We employ what we call the dead-drift struggle technique by fishing the imitation upstream in a dead-drift presentation and then using the rod tip to employ subtle movement to the fly to imitate the pupa struggling to break free.

Often we will fish right through the peak of the hatch, using various emergers and cripples. Many times anglers will switch to dry flies as the peak of the hatch occurs. This is because they see trout slashing and rolling on the surface, not realizing that the trout are feeding on emergers and not on adults. Sure, you can take fish on drys during this period, but you will take a lot more trout on emergers. The trout rises are slashing and violent because the caddis pupa is swimming and moving!

Dry flies such as Foam Skittering Caddis, Muddled Caddis, Goddard Caddis, and Elkhair Caddis often work best after the hatch or during the early afternoons as searching patterns. There is also a time during the mating flights and egg-laying flights that drys and diving-caddis imitations can be most effective.

As the Hatch Fades

As the hatch fades, we will often move to an area that offers a backwater or foam pool to fish. These areas tend to collect the stillborns, drowned adults, and crippled caddis. During this time the trout can be very selective to the type, size, shape, and color of the insect they are feeding on, and the angler must carefully observe what the trout are doing and may, in fact, have to treat each trout as an individual. Given a choice of several different food forms that are available in reasonable numbers, there is no law that says all trout must feed on the same insect. After careful observation, the angler can select the proper imitation and present it to the trout in an acceptable manner.

Oftentimes anglers head for home after the peak of the hatch is past, little realizing that they are leaving some excellent angling.

Generally the decision is based on, "Well, I don't see any surface activity, therefore the hatch and the fishing must be over." Nothing could be further from the truth. The trout will collect in the foam pools and back-eddies and continue to feed on these easy-to-capture forms of caddis for quite some time.

Egg-Laying Flights

This is the time when certain dry-fly patterns can be deadly if the angler is observant and realizes what is going on. However, few anglers use or know about diving-caddis patterns. This pattern style was developed by Gary Lafontaine, and with the addition of the bead head we feel it is deadly. Many caddis species dive into the river to lay their eggs. Seldom do they make it back to the surface. The diving caddis imitation can be lethal when fished both dead-drift and down and across. We will also fish these patterns upstream and impart some action to the fly. The takes are often very aggressive because the trout is chasing something that swims.

As the egg-laying flights taper off, we then switch and fish the patterns using a slightly up- and across-stream cast, and employing the Leisenring Lift. After the insect dives and lays eggs on the bottom, it then dies or tries to return to the surface, but it is subjected to the whims of the current, which will move it up and down in the water. Over the years we have found that the diving-caddis pattern accounts for most of the larger trout taken during this egg-laying period. If the caddis are falling spent on the water to lay their eggs, then we like the Foam Spent Caddis because it floats well and is easy to see.

Caddis fishing is fun and exciting, and the Yellowstone offers the angler caddis fishing for a large part of the season. The keys to being a successful caddis angler are few. Be observant, be willing to try new patterns and methods, and gain a knowledge of the hatch and the times of the hatch.

During the spring hatch, the actual emergence will take place around 1:00 P.M., however the angler can begin fishing deep caddis pupa by 11:00 A.M.. Remember that there is no super pattern that always works, nor is there any secret method. The keys to success are observation and a continued open mind and quest for knowledge.

We hope that in some small way we have helped to increase your understanding of caddis hatches and how to fish them on the Yellowstone. But most of all, remember—trout fishing is fun.

The following tables are based on a study Tom conducted over a six-year period. The results are interesting and clearly demonstrate why the angler visiting the Yellowstone River should be well versed in fishing the caddis hatches.

TABLE A: Aquatic Foods Consumed by 144 Brown Trout

Class of food organisms	Numbers found in 144 stomachs	Percentage of total
Cased caddis	870	43.51
Caddis larvae	159	7.96
Midge pupa	607	30.34
Stonefly nymphs	215	10.75
Mayfly nymphs	98	4.9
Sculpins	37	1.85
Total	1,999	99.96

This sampling was conducted during 1979, 1989, and 1991 on the Yellowstone River in the Livingston area. Each year the sampling was conducted during the period of March 1 to May 1 and July 10 to October 10. During each sampling period an equal number of brown trout was sampled. Over the course of the three-year study, the difference in the percentage points varied only 2.5 to 3.7 percent overall. The sampling was done with a stomach pump and all the trout were released. The sizes of the trout sampled were between 10 and 15 inches with an average size of 12.5 inches. This study, which covered a total time of six years, shows that the angler needs to have an ample supply of caddis imitations, because the trout in the Yellowstone River feed heavily on the aquatic caddis food forms.

The Mother's Day caddis hatch will generally start around April 25 and continue until late May. However, the annual runoff generally makes the river unfishable by May 10. Tom tried to conclude the study before the peak of the hatch arrived so the hatch would not distort the findings of the study. The study was wholly conducted on the Yellowstone River and the samplings were done at the same sites throughout the study. There was a total of five sampling sites, which shall remain nameless at this time.

TABLE B: Aquatic Foods Consumedby 144 Rainbow Trout

Class of food organisms	Numbers found in 144 stomachs	Percentage of total
Cased caddis	779	38.8
Midge pupa	701	34.92
Stonefly nymphs	299	14.90
Caddis larvae	111	5.5
Mayfly nymphs	99	4.91
Sculpins	11	.54
Other minnows	7	.34
Total	2,007	99.91

This sampling was conducted during the same periods as for the brown trout sampling, at the same stations and using the same methods. The only difference was in the years the study was conducted. The rainbow study ran during 1982, 1983, and 1984. The sizes of the trout sampled were between nine and fourteen inches with an average size of twelve inches.

TABLE C: Caddis Types Consumed by 50 Brown Trout

Stages of caddis	Numbers found in 50 stomachs	Percentage of total
Cased caddis	71	31.42
Caddis larvae	9	3.98
Caddis pupa	129	57.08
Caddis adults	17	7.52
Total	226	100.00

This study is based on the pumped stomach samplings of fifty brown trout during April 1 to May 15 in the years 1984, 1985, and 1986. The trout used for this study ranged between ten and fourteen inches and had an average size of 12.7 inches. The same sites were used as in the previous studies. The purpose of this study was to determine what portion of the trout's diet the various stages of the caddis made up during a major emergence cycle, and thus determining what stages the angler needs to concentrate on during the hatch.

TABLE D: Caddis Types Consumed by 50 Rainbow Trout

Stages of caddis	Numbers found in 50 stomachs	Percentage of total
Cased caddis	57	22.98
Caddis larvae	7	2.83
Caddis pupa	161	64.92
Caddis adults	23	9.27
Total	248	100.00

This study was conducted during the same time periods and the same years as was the brown trout study (Table C, above), and used the same methods. The trout used for this study ranged between ten and fifteen inches and had an average size of thirteen inches.

It is interesting to note the differences in the brown trout and rainbow trout preferences.

TABLE E: Comparison of Available Aquatic Food Forms

Types of food forms	Percentage found in collection area
Caddis	39.70
Midge	21.43
Stonefly	19.98
Mayfly	13.90
Sculpins	3.35
Other minnows	.75
Others	.89
Total	100.00

This study was conducted at each of the sites used in gathering the data for Tables A, B, C, and D. The data is based on a six-year collection period, all the years and sites are lumped together, and an average is used. However, in the categories listed in any of the sites or years there was a variance of only 3.87 percent.

The study area mentioned had three collection sites from Mallard's Rest to Ninth Street, and two collection sites from Ninth Street to Sheep Mountain. The results can only be applied to this section of the river during the time periods studied. Because the insect populations vary in different sections of the Yellowstone, anglers would be wrong to draw conclusions on other sections based on this study. The idea for these studies comes from the book *Trout Streams*, by Paul R. Needham, Ph.D. This work was done by Dr. Needham during the 1920s and 1930s to better understand stream management. This work, and other studies like it, will help anglers better understand the trout's world and its feeding behavior. This will help the the angler choose the proper patterns and the proper methods of presentation, thus furthering success.

For those of you who may choose to do a study on your home waters, set the goals of the study and the study area, and be consistent. If a single factor is off, the findings of the study may be inconclusive.

Locally Effective Patterns

BWO Para-Shuck

Hook:	Tiemco 101, sizes 14–22
Thread:	Olive
Shuck:	Olive-dyed grizzly-hackle tip
Body:	Olive brown dubbing
Wing:	Fluorescent red Antron body wool, tied as a post
Hackle:	Olive-dyed grizzly, parachute-style

Olive Soft-Hackle Beadhead Emerger

Hook:	Tiemco 2457, sizes 12–16
Thread:	Olive
Bead:	Gold
Tail:	Hungarian partridge soft-hackle fibers
Ribbing:	Lime Krystal Flash
Abdomen:	Pale olive dubbing
Thorax:	Dark olive brown dubbing
Hackle:	Hungarian partridge soft-hackle

Green Drake Nymph

Hook:	Tiemco 5262, sizes 8–14
Thread:	Brown
Tail:	Pheasant-tail barbs
Ribbing:	Copper wire
Abdomen	Peacock herl
Wing case:	Pheasant-tail section sprayed with Krylon
Thorax:	Peacock herl
Legs:	Pheasant-tail barbs alongside body

Tom's Dark Olive Skittering Caddis

Hooks:	Tiemco 101, sizes 10–20
Thread:	Olive
Rib:	Two or three strands of black Krystal Flash
Body:	Dubbed, #74 dark olive, Orvis super possum
Wing:	Natural whitetail body hair
Foam head:	Scintilla fly foam, dark green
Head:	Dubbed same as the body

Tom's Deep Olive K-Flash Caddis Emerger

Hook:	Tiemco 2457, sizes 10–18
Thread:	Brown
Bead:	Gold or silver
Shuck:	#65 medium olive/brown scintilla
Rib:	One or two strands of olive Krystal Flash
Body:	Dubbed, #65 medium olive/brown Scintilla
Hackle:	Brown Hungarian partridge, sparse
Collar:	Natural gray philo plume
Head:	Dubbed same as body
Antennae:	Two strands of olive Krystal Flash

Tom's Olive Foam Caddis Emerger

Hook:	Tiemco 2487, sizes 12–22
Thread:	Olive
Body extension:	Olive New Dubb
Thorax:	Olive sheared muskrat, dubbed
Wing:	Clump of brown Hungarian partridge fibers
Collar:	Starling feather
Head:	Dark green Scintilla fly foam

Other Effective Patterns

Besides all of the general attractor-type patterns, dry, wet, and streamers—or those listed in the text, the angler should also consider imitations from the following list.

Olive Krystal Midge Larva
Black and Olive Midge Pupa
Black Wire Midge Pupa
Beadhead Caddis Pupa Olive
Beadhead Caddis Larva Brown
CDC Drifting Cased Caddis Olive
CDC Olive and Black Caddis Pupa
Olive Slime Caddis Pupa
Sawyer PMD Pheasant Tail Nymph
Black Sawyer Pheasant Tail Nymph
Jacklin's March Brown Nymph
Olive Feather Duster Nymph

Nelson's Gray and Black Midge Emerger
New Dubb Gray Midge Emerger
Gray CDC Transitional Midge
Peacock Caddis
SRI Hi-Vis Tan Parachute Caddis
Olive Foam Skittering Caddis
Gray Foam Emerging Caddis
Harrop's Olive CDC Adult Caddis
Harrop's PMD Hairwing Dun
Harrop's CDC Tailwater PMD Dun
Quill Gordon
Baetis Stillborn/Spinner

7

Ninth Street
to Sheep Mountain

This twelve-or-so-mile section could be classified as the town stretch, because the river flows through Livingston. Many local and visiting anglers spend part of their time wading the upper reach near the Ninth Street access. There are many spots in which to wet a line within the town's borders, and this adds a certain charm to one of the country's fly-fishing centers. There have been many articles in print about anglers taking large fish as they float through Livingston, and this has helped create a legendary aura. The area is rich in western fly-fishing history, and as one fishes this section the names of many angling pioneers come to mind.

Livingston itself is a quaint western town with a laid-back atmosphere. This once-tough railroad town has evolved into a community rich in the visual arts, but it still retains vestiges of those rough-and-tumble days in the plethora of saloons found on Main Street. Angling tourism is a huge part of the local economy: fishermen from all over the world visit here. Some of the finest fly-fishing guides in the world operate from town, and there are literally thousands of guide trips a year in the area. The local fly shops offer anything and everything a visiting angler might need, and the town will cater to all the creature comforts. Two major airports nearby make trips in and out a snap, and there is plenty to do for the nonangling spouse or companion; Yellowstone National Park is but fifty miles away.

This section offers the angler anything from an hour wade-fishing to an extended float trip, and best of all, it's all within easy reach

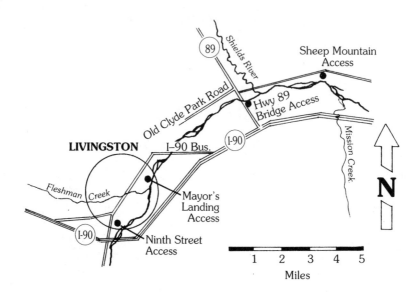

Ninth Street to Sheep Mountain

of town, if not in it. Large fish are still taken in this stretch, and, depending on the season, with some regularity.

Water Characteristics

As the river flows out of the narrows that define the edge of Paradise Valley and begins to braid, the landscape becomes more urban. Not that Livingston is a large city, but houses and commercial buildings become visible from the river. Compared to the splendid vista upstream, this section may seem a little dowdy, although by no means ugly. Many homes that border the river are tidy, the mountains are still visible, and the banks are generally clear of debris. People here take pride and a certain proprietary interest in the river's appearance.

The beginning of this section braids through part of town above the Ninth Street island. The island divides the river into a couple of

Winter fishing in the Ninth Street area.

smaller channels that are fishable by wading. The overpasses of the interstate detract from the aesthetics of this portion but by no means detract from the fishing. As the water levels begin to drop, the river's right channel may become too shallow to float a drift boat down without having to drag it across the skinny riffles. Those of you who float through this section from an upstream access would be well advised to take the river's right channel when the water is high. The left channel becomes extremely dangerous because it flows past some of the bridge abutments; many floaters have lost their boats and a few have lost their lives here. We stress extreme caution here; the danger comes fast and hard, and unless you are perfectly (and we do mean *perfectly*) set, the force of the water will force you into an abutment. Many experienced boat handlers get caught unawares here, and bad things do happen. In the summer of 1993 a family smashed up here. The children and wife were dumped into the water, from which they eventually were pulled out. But the husband was pinned to a piling by his drift boat. Luckily, a wrecker was called by another angler, and the boat was winched off him. He suffered only minor cuts and bruises; he and his family were fortunate, but his boat wasn't.

The channels eventually do come together about halfway through town to form a single river again. Here the river is wide and not conducive to wading from shore, especially from the west (or town) bank, at least until it flows toward the east side of town; there, the wading angler will find a few spots. The floating fisherman will find many places to pull over, get out, and wade.

This entire section has many bedrock formations, high rock banks, and cliffs. It also has every water type and characteristic imaginable, so there is something for everyone here. These formations are the single characteristic that differentiates this section from the upstream sections and they offer the angler a glimpse of the river farther downstream. Fish will often hold tight against these formations or in the little nooks and crannies cut into them. The floating angler has to bounce his offering off the rock face so it falls directly alongside the formation. The wading angler is pretty much out of luck here because the water is usually too deep to allow a wader to get into position to fish.

Another characteristic that becomes important to the fly fisherman is the side channels caused by gravel bars forming in the current. These are ever changing, and every year they are slightly different both in configuration and their placement in the river. The riffle corners of these bars are usually good spots from which to take a few fish, as are the quiet areas behind these mini-islands. A word of caution here: The gravel is generally pea-sized and very loose. It is extremely easy to lose one's footing, especially in the faster flows, and many anglers have taken an unwanted and potentially dangerous dunking by wading a little too deep. Drift boats have been known to drift loose from their anchorages because of the loose gravel. When it is windy—and this section can be very windy at times—it is a good idea to constantly check on your boat to make sure it is always securely anchored. It's not pleasant to watch your boat drift down the river while you're standing on a small island with

Out of the boat in the side channels.

fast water between you and the bank. It happens, probably more often than people are willing to admit.

As the river continues downstream from town it begins to braid
again. The main characteristic of the river here is that it is one large,
wide river with many smaller side channels. It does not braid here to
the extent of the upper section. These side channels often hold large
quantities of trout and are usually fishable earlier than the main stem.
Early in the season the main stem will be high and rolling with such
force that there isn't a "slower" bank to make good presentations to.
Unlike some of the upper sections where there are dominant banks
and slower banks, this section has many areas where both banks run
hard and fast. This makes fishing during the early part of the season
tough in this section, and many local anglers and guides will be upstream until the flows calm a bit. However, the side channels make
for some excellent fishing. They usually run slower, are shallower,
and in effect become "ministreams" in themselves. Some are no

longer than a few hundred yards but have very fishable water that can be covered adequately by a wading fisherman.

These side channels are best fished by floating to them, securing the boat, and wading. Early on in the season, especially if it is an angler's first time on this section, it is advisable not to float a side channel without scouting it out beforehand. We have witnessed boats caught or overturned by sweepers in these channels, and once you're in one there is no escape. These channels seem to claim a few boats every season. It makes for a very bad trip—exciting, maybe, but bad. There are enough channels in this stretch to make an early-season float worthwhile, especially if you know that the upper stretches will be crowded with floaters. Although the main stem of the river might seem devoid of any hatches, the side channels offer plenty of hatching insects. The fast water of the main river may carry hatching insects away so they are not visible to a floating angler, but the side channels have water character that is conducive to hatches. The water speed is slower, it is shallower, and very often partially protected from the wind.

Throughout the season these side channels continue to produce well. The trout seem to prefer to feed in them, even when the water gets on the skinny side in the fall. A theory is that the water types are to their liking, but it is more likely that they are used to seeing and feeding on the insects that hatch out there. They get accustomed to the hatches during the early season and continue throughout the seasons. These channels also act as food funnels. Some of the insects that hatch out in the main river drift down these narrower channels to the waiting fish. It would be very unwise to overlook these side channels when on this section—they have saved many a day for guides and their clients in the past. Actually, they have turned some mediocre days into super days.

There is a great deal of character to the river in this section: the twists and turns, high banks, riprap, bedrock formations, side channels, tailouts, pools, and riffles all make for interesting fishing. One of the other important features in this section is the abundance of riffle corners—the very edge between the riffle and the slow water alongside it. These corners form a vee, with the open end facing

Netting a fish along the riprap.

downstream. Many large fish are caught at the apex of such vees, or very close to it. The larger trout, especially browns, seem to lie in the shallow water, feeding on whatever the current may offer. Do not overlook these corners.

Most people tend to float the upstream sections in Paradise Valley and leave this stretch to the few "in the know," especially when the water is on the high and fast side. Eventually, over the course of the season, word gets out that the fishing here is super, and then more anglers frequent this section, but it is never very crowded. Quite a few of the local guides are not very familiar with it, so they opt for more familiar water, and this takes some of the pressure off. Also, many of the trips in this section are the kind where anglers stay in the boat and pound the banks. This leaves the side channels free for those of us who like to wade fish.

The weather affects this stretch much as it does the upper reaches. However, it does seem to be a tad bit windier here as a rule than upstream, and an easterly wind here can be a bear. With the exception of the Shields River, there are no major tributaries to muck up the water after a summer squall. The most that happens is that one bank is a little discolored for a short distance before it dissipates. The Shields can foul up the end of this section, but usually the problem is toward the end and only one bank is muddy. When one knows that the Shields is off-color, a shorter float to the 89 bridge could be made without sacrificing the quality of the fishing. The few miles from the 89 bridge to the Sheep Mountain access has some great water and excellent fishing, but why be confined to one bank or have to row in when the Shields muddies it up?

Accessibility

This is a very accessible stretch of water with four major and many minor locally known access points. We will concentrate on the major accesses—a visiting angler can always stop by one of the local fly shops and inquire about the local ones, those that are not on a map and not officially listed by fish and wildlife. For instance, a visiting fly fisher could always park at the end of Ninth Street Island and walk up to the many channels to fish. There is no official access point but it is commonly used by visitors and locals alike.

This stretch begins with the Ninth Street access, which is little more than a boat ramp in a little town park (Riverside Park). There are no signs directing one to the access site, which is unusual, because most other access points are well marked. As in any park there are picnic tables, some benches, and a small parking area. No overnight camping is allowed. Because this access is just upstream of the potentially dangerous Ninth Street Bridge, most of the locals use it as a downstream destination point from an upstream float. Walk-fishing is a little tough to do here because it's on the dominant side of the river—the water speed is fast and most of the banks are riprap. However, when the flows are low there is a riffle right in front of the park that can be fished.

About a mile downstream, at the other end of town, is the next major access point, Mayor's Landing. This is a major access, with a large concrete ramp that can handle a couple of boats launching at the same time. There is ample room to maneuver a trailer and plenty of parking areas. There are picnic tables with nearby barbecue grills and a handicapped-accessible outhouse. The local police make regular patrols through the area, so it is one of the safer access points in which to leave a vehicle. Many of the local guides have their clients leave their vehicles there because parking in town is less than perfect. There is no overnight camping allowed—this is a day-use-only area. The majority of fishermen using this section of river launch from this access point rather than from Ninth Street. There is limited walk-fishing from this point. Directly downstream there is some very wadeable water and a decent riffled area.

The next access point is about six river miles downstream and is usually the destination point for most boaters—it is the U.S. 89 bridge access. This area is strictly a day-use-only area, with no overnight camping allowed. There are no toilet facilities, but there are some high weeds nearby. The ramp itself is cut out from the riprap bank and a little on the narrow side. However, there is enough room to comfortably maneuver a boat and trailer. As one floats to this take-out, it appears to be tough to get to and a tad on the dangerous side, especially when the water is high. But it really isn't. As the water flows under the train trestle and highway bridge it slows considerably, so a boat can be safely maneuvered to the ramp. Many local fly fisherman use this access from which to walk both upstream and down; a few will hike a considerable distance upstream and fish back. There is a great deal of fishable water that can be reached from this point.

The last access point on this stretch is Sheep Mountain, a few miles downstream of the U.S. 89 bridge. For those of you who like to camp, here is a place that fits your needs, although it is on the primitive side. There is a handicapped-accessible outhouse, picnic tables, and a dirt road winding through the riverside vegetation with some obvious places to set up a tent or camper. There is no electricity available, so if creature comforts are what you're after, perhaps a different area should be explored. There is a fourteen-day limit on camping. The boat ramp is dirt, actually only a cut in the bank. It could be a little tough maneuvering a vehicle and trailer there because the quarters are a bit tight. This is an area where a walking fisherman can reach the river and fish some interesting water upstream and down.

In general, most of the access points on the entire river are in good shape, convenient to get to, and spaced so a visiting angler can tailor a trip to suit his needs. There are very good shuttle services available in town, and because these access points are so near town the cost of a shuttle is extremely reasonable. It is a rare event when one of these shuttle services screws up. This section of river offers the angler points to set out walk fishing, float trips of various lengths, an easy vehicle move, and some incredible fishing, all within a few minutes from the creature comforts of town.

The Fish

A fair amount is known by the state fish and wildlife agency about this stretch of river because it is and has been a traditional electrofishing section. Electrofishing is the politically correct term for the outdated "shocking." There are relatively high populations of trout in this section, with more than three thousand per mile of seven inches or greater. These numbers are variable year to year, because these are fish that are about one and a half years old, and any poor spawning year or years will significantly reflect lower populations. The populations of fish greater than ten inches are more stable. Seventy percent of the fish in this section of river are rainbows, thirty percent are brown trout, and zero percent are cutthroats. Statistically, there are no (at best one to two percent) cutthroats, even though they seem to make up a decent portion of an angler's daily catch. Currently the department of fish and wildlife, when electrofishing, handle approximately fifteen hundred fish per day, but only about twenty-five are cutthroat trout. When we did the research for this section is was a mild surprise to find the cutthroat populations so low, especially because we catch fair numbers of them over the course of a season. There are days when it seems that the majority of fish caught here are cutthroats. Most likely, their feeding habits make them seem more abundant than they actually are.

Historically, cutthroats have been hammered. They have been severely overpressured because they were considered to be the best-tasting trout and have been selectively culled by fishermen for the table. Poor water-management practices have led to the dewatering of cutthroat spawning streams—the majority of tributaries are bone-dry where they meet the main river during the irrigation season, which happens to coincide with the cutts' spawning season. Although there are three spring creeks directly upstream of this section that are used by other species of trout for spawning, the cutthroats make little use of them. They seem to prefer the colder water of the mountain streams rather than the warmer spring-creek water. Fish have a tendency to drift downstream because there is very little water suitable for reproduction directly upstream. These are perhaps the most important reasons for the low population of cutthroats in this portion of river.

But they are making a comeback because of some regulation changes and through efforts of local Trout Unlimited chapters. Catch-and-release for all cutts was established in 1988, but because this section is starting from virtually a zero population, it will take some time for them to establish themselves as viable. Montana Department of Fish, Wildlife and Parks has also developed a management plan that will help bring back the numbers. The Joe Brooks Chapter of Trout Unlimited has completed the Fleshman Creek Reclamation Project, which will establish a viable cutthroat spawning tributary. All these efforts should enable the cutthroat trout to reestablish itself here and add to the enjoyment of anglers. Even so, the cutthroat population will more than likely never be as high as thirty percent of the entire trout population here because the water types in this section aren't as suitable for them as it is in other sections. Cutts prefer slower water types that are rocky and fairly deep. Although there are areas that suit cutts, particularly in the lower reaches of the section, most of the water is not optimum cutt habitat.

There is a high percentage of rainbow trout in this section primarily because the water types are very suitable to them. Major spawning sites are immediately upstream in the form of the three spring creeks, and some positive changes in spring-creek management have allowed for more successful rainbow spawning. This has been reflected in the downstream populations. The fish and wildlife department has identified very few main-channel or side-channel spawning sites for rainbows in the main river. That is not to say that they don't use the main stem to spawn but rather that the majority of spawning seems to occur in the spring creeks.

Large rainbows, fish greater than twenty inches, are somewhat unusual in this stretch for reasons that are more than likely genetic. These fish are relatively short-lived fish—few seem to live past six years. Once they reach spawning age their growth rate slows, so it's unusual when a five-pound rainbow is caught. There *are* some big rainbows in this section, but they are rare.

Historically, a diverse assortment of rainbow species were stocked into the river system, and nearly one hundred percent of the rainbows here are hybridized with cutthroats. This has been so for so many years that fish can be observed spawning in the spring creeks from January through April. Their gene pool is so diverse that, possibly, as time goes by (hundreds of years) they may evolve into a separate species (the Yellowstone Rainbow) and spawn at the same time each year. The "leaking" of hatchery fish from private hatcheries over the years has also contributed to the genetic confusion. Nineteen fifty-eight was the last year fish were officially stocked in the river, so all the fish are now wild trout.

The brown trout is perhaps the fish that most eastern anglers associate with the Yellowstone River, and especially so in this stretch, because many stories have been written in the past about the town and the brown. The Yellowstone has a reputation for having good brown-trout fishing, and deservedly so. Even though the brown population is only thirty percent of the total trout population, it stays relatively constant over the years. The populations of cutthroats and rainbows can fluctuate wildly over the years, but brown trout populations remain stable. The water types in this section are very suitable to brown trout, and there are excellent habitat and food sources. A brown will generally live to be ten years old, so there are significant

A nice rainbow taken from this section of the river.

numbers of large fish—eighteen- to twenty-inch fish, with many considerably larger. An interesting side note: 1980 saw a tremendous number of large fish taken downstream of the sewage treatment plant. Since the discharged water has become treated and the nitrates have been cleaned out, the numbers of large fish have declined.

There are other species of fish in this section of river, and they include the suckers (long-nose, red horse, and mountain), carp, an occasional ling, a variety of minnows (long-nose dace, sculpins), which can be a significant food source for trout, and the ever-present whitefish. The whitefish is actually considered to be a native gamefish. The state fish and wildlife agency has very little information about whitefish populations in this section, but it feels it needs to know more because everything in the river system is linked. The agency feels there is zero correlation between populations of whitefish and trout because their preferred habitats are different. Trout water is not necessarily whitefish water, and trout are more aggressive and territorial—they will push whitefish out of their territory. Many fishermen will most likely disagree with this, because it seems that, when trout fishing, all one catches sometimes are whitefish.

The fish and wildlife agency tries to manage this section, as others, as a healthy system. The fishing ethic has significantly changed primarily through education to the point where special regulations like slot limits are probably not needed any more. Catch-and-release has become the norm for most fishermen. Fish are still killed, but not in significant enough numbers to create a change in the population. More and more fishermen don't take fish and certainly don't take their limits on a daily basis. A move in the direction away from meat fishing has enhanced this ethic.

The Yellowstone River is a changing, healthy, and dynamic system; however, there are some threats to the river. Most are not fishing-related but are due to human population increases over the years. There needs to be wise use of water and an effort to stop the dewatering of the tributaries. Wise land use is also needed, although it may be too late for that. As land is subdivided, changes take place, such as increases in nutrients from drain fields leaching into the river and changes in bank ecology because of the cutting of streamside vegetation. The clearing of trees and brush for homes, trails, and boat ramps all have a negative impact on the river. All this can change the river ecologically, and it certainly doesn't help it esthetically. The saving grace is that the headwaters and about 150 miles of the river are in Yellowstone National Park, which should help preserve the entire system.

Seasonal Changes: The Fishing

This section is subject to all the usual ravages of Montana weather, and it also marks the beginning of one of the windier stretches of river. Maybe the wind really doesn't blow any harder here than anywhere else—it just seems that way, probably because the river begins an easterly turn here. If the wind comes out of an easterly quarter it seems that a floating angler has to fight to keep his boat in position. The fisherman casting from a boat has to constantly mend line upstream because the wind will usually blow the lighter leader, tippet, and fly sections upstream above the heavier fly line. The fly line in its downstream position will pull the fly away from the banks too quickly and cause an unnatural drag. The angler who doesn't constantly make upstream mends will have few strikes and a relative fishless day.

On the other hand, if the wind is blowing very hard from a westerly quarter, the oarsman will have to constantly back-row to slow the boat down. The wind can literally push the boat downstream faster than the current speed, and the fisherman will have trouble getting a natural drift. There have been occasions for us when the wind blew so hard that it was almost impossible to keep the boat from being blown onto the bank. One has to be on the ball and make sure there is plenty of time to maneuver, especially in critical spots, when it is very windy.

With the exception of the wind, this section experiences similar seasonal changes to the upper sections. The hatches are slightly different, as are the optimum times to fish. One thing that makes it different is its proximity to town—this makes it easy to fish for an hour or so in the winter months or take a quick after-work float in the summer months. It is a very convenient section to fish.

Hatch Chart for Ninth Street to Sheep Mountain

Stoneflies
Salmon fly
(*Pteronarcys californica*)   Size: #2–#6   June 25 to July 10
Golden stone
(*Calineuria californica*)   Size: #4–#8   June 25 to July 15
Yellow sally
(*Isoperla mormona*)   Size: #14–#16   July 1 to July 30
Small golden stone
(*Hesperoperla pacifica*)   Size: #6–#10   July 1 to July 20
Little olive stone
(*Alloperla signata*)   Size: #14–#16   August 10 to August 20
Giant western golden stone
(*Claassenia sabulosa*)   Size: #2–#6   August 1 to September 10

Caddisflies
Early grannom
(*Brachycentrus occidentalis*) Size: #12–#16   April 25 to May 20
Spotted sedge
(*Hydropsyche cockerelli*)   Size: #12–#16   August 15 to October 20
Little brown sedge
(*Lepidostoma veleda*)   Size: #14–#18   July 10 to August 10
American grannom
(*Brachycentrus americanus*) Size: #12–#16   July 10 to August 30
Long horn sedge
(*Oecetis avara*)   Size: #12–#16   June 25 to August 1
Spotted sedge
(*Hydropsyche occidentalis*) Size: #10–#12   June 15 to July 20
Plain brown sedge
(*Lepidostoma pluviale*)   Size: #14–#18   July 1 to July 31

Mayflies
Western green drake
(*Drunella Grandis*)   Size: #10–#12   June 25 to July 15
Western march brown
(*Rhithrogena morrisoni*)   Size: #14–#16   April 15 to May 15
Pale morning dun
(*Ephemerella inermis*)   Size: #16–#20   July 5 to August 15

Western black quill		
(*Rhithrogena undulata*)	Size: #12–#14	July 1 to August 15
Western yellow drake		
(*Heptagenia elegantula*)	Size: #14–#16	July 20 to August 20
Giant western red quill		
(*Ephemerella hecuba*)	Size: #10–#12	August 25 to September 25
Gray drake		
(*Siphlonurus occidentalis*)	Size: #10–#12	September 1 to September 20
Blue-winged olive		
(*Baetis tricaudatus*)	Size: #18–#20	March 10 to April 20, September 15 to November 10
Trico (*Tricorythodes minutus*)	Size: #18–#22	August 15 to October 10

Terrestrials

Grasshoppers (Acrididae)	Size: #8–#14	July 20 to October 15
Crickets (Gryllidae)	Size: #12–#14	August 1 to September 30
Black ants (Formicidae)	Size: #16–#22	July 15 to September 30
Cinnamon ants (Formicidae)	Size: #18–#20	August 20 to September 20
Black beetle (Coleoptera)	Size: #12–#18	July 15 to August 15

Other Important Hatches and Food Forms

Midge (Chironomidae)	Size: #16–#24	February 15 to April 20, September 20 to November 10

Minnows

Mottled sculpin		
(*Cottus bairdi*)	Size: #2–#8	All year
Whitefish minnow		
(*Prosopium williamsoni*)	Size: #2–#10	All year
Long-nose dace minnow		
(*Rhinichthys cataractae*)	Size: #2–#10	All year
Long-nose sucker minnow		
(*Catostomus catostomus*)	Size: #2–#10	All year
Mountain sucker		
(*Catostomus platyrhynchus*)	Size: #2–#10	All year

Winter: Mid-November to February

The weather is the single largest factor the angler has to consider when fishing during the winter. As an example, by November 23, 1993, we had experienced a cold front sweeping down from the Gulf of Alaska that sent the temperature plunging to ten degrees below zero. Within a very few days the Yellowstone was frozen over and unfishable. However, during some years the weather can be moderate and the angler can enjoy some very decent fishing. During this time the brown trout are still spawning; therefore, streamers and nymphs can be productive. For those who wish to fish dry flies there is some limited action on late-season midges. The best dry-fly action will be found in the foam pools, back-eddies, and quieter waters. It is a time when there is very little competition on the water because many local folks are out chasing elk, deer, partridge, ducks, and pheasants.

December brings us the holiday season, and we all seem to be too busy to do much serious fishing. Any fishing that we might wish to do will of course depend on the weather. If there has been moderate weather, one can always find a few hardy souls bouncing a nymph or streamer deep through a pool or perhaps working a riffle. There are still a few brown trout in the spawning mode during the early part of the month, but that quickly fades.

By January we once again turn our attention to the river and hope that the weather will moderate so we can spend a few days fishing. If the weather cooperates, the fishing will mostly be nymphing because the low water temperatures make the trout pretty sluggish. Suggested patterns are Prince Nymph, Zug Bug, Brownstone Nymph, Rubber-Legged Hare's Ear Nymph, Tom's Fox Squirrel Stone Nymph, Burlap Nymph, Troth's Stone, and Whitlock's Red Fox Squirrel Nymph, all in #8 to #12.

February is an odd month here in Montana because the weather can vary so radically. During some years the cold of January carries over into February, and the fishing can be limited. However, during 1987 the average daily temperature was thirty-seven degrees with a record-setting high of seventy-three and many fifty-degree days. Once again in 1990, February was a warmer month than March with many days in the forties. During February of 1992 the weather was great, with many days ranging between forty and fifty degrees. During these warmer periods the midge hatches are exceptional on this section of the Yellowstone. Therefore, if you are going to be in the area during the month of February, call one of the fly shops— you might find the weather very agreeable and the fishing very good.

Some of the various strains of rainbow trout will begin spawning at this time, and most are preparing to. An interesting note is that, beginning at this time, the rainbows seem to move into the faster water higher up in the riffles, where it is shallower. Maybe they are seeking more oxygenated water for some reason related to spawning. This is just a guess, but it is worth prospecting this type of water because many fish can be caught there and almost all of them will be rainbows.

A word of caution. During the winter months we seldom float the river, because storms can move in quickly, and once you shove off in the boat you are committed—it is very difficult to cut a trip short if the weather turns miserable. If you do decide to float, make sure you are well prepared, with plenty of extra warm clothing, good raingear, and maybe something to start a fire with. Also, before you start doing any floating you need to be sure that the section you are going to float is ice-free. Coming around a bend and finding out that the next pool is ice-choked and impassable can lead to lots of fun.

The temperature of the water can have a decided effect on the feeding activity of the trout, and a clear understanding of those effects will assist the angler in knowing how the trout react during the various seasons. The single most important factor in understanding how water temperatures affect the trout and how they will then feed is not just a knowledge of the water temperature on the day you are fishing but also a knowledge of what the water temperatures have been running. We know that the optimum water temperatures for trout activity levels are between forty-five degrees and sixty-eight degrees. During this optimum period the average healthy trout will digest its food within a nine- to eleven-hour period. Once the water temperatures rise above seventy or drop below forty-five degrees, the metabolism of the trout slows down, meaning more time is required for the trout to digest its food. Over a period of several years we have studied this function of water temperature as related to trout metabolic rates and have formed the following conclusions.

The effects of water temperature on the metabolic rates of the trout are relative to the stream being discussed. For example, here on the Yellowstone River from January 6 to February 15, 1991, the average water temperature was thirty-three degrees. During this time the trout's activity level was very low. To be even moderately successful anglers had to present the imitation right to the trout. In other words, they had to hit them right in the mouth with it because the trout were not very willing to move. However, from February 16 to February 25 there was a slow warming of the water temperature from thirty-three to forty-two degrees. By the time the temperatures reached forty-two degrees, trout activity levels had increased considerably. The temperature held at forty-two degrees for twenty or so days. By the ninth day there was a drop in trout activity levels. The levels did not increase again until the water temperature increased to forty-six degrees. Thus, we concluded that the trout's activity levels will rise for short periods as the water temperatures rise until the optimum range is reached. Therefore, the angler needs to obtain information on water-temperature variation during the winter season to know how to properly present imitations. Our studies have also shown that this will vary from river to river around the state. Therefore, what holds true on the Yellowstone may not be true during the same time on the Big Horn or Madison Rivers.

The Yellowstone River from the boundary at Yellowstone National Park to the Montana border is open to fishing all year, and the winter months provide the angler with fishing opportunities. However, the angler who plans on doing a lot of winter fishing and who would like to survive should plan on dressing in layers. You can always take off a layer if you become too warm, but it's hard to put it on if it's home in the closet. If you are dressed too lightly and get caught in a storm you can suffer needlessly before getting under shelter. Remember to bring a warm hat and fishing gloves. Also, a small hand towel for drying off your hands after handling fish is good. We also carry a couple of the chemical hand-warmers, just in case it gets too cold.

Fishing alone at any time isn't a great idea, and in the winter this is even more true, but we often do so. Therefore, in the hopes of keeping you safer, we offer the following suggestions. Always wear a wader belt, and if you must fish alone, you should wear a personal flotation device. For security in wading, wear stream cleats or something similar. The cleats grab the slippery rocks and help you remain upright. During the summer when the angler takes a spill, generally the most damage is done to the ego. But during the winter a spill can mean . . . well, you get the picture.

During the winter months from mid-November to early March we don't venture too far from the vehicle, and we don't float. Once you get in a boat you are committed. If something were to happen, like getting caught in a storm or taking a spill, you could find yourself in serious trouble. With all the angling opportunities available in winter, anglers can fish close to their vehicles and still have fun and be safe.

Finally, we carry a little survival package in the backs of our vests. These items are double-bagged in zip-lock bags and take up very little space. The survival kit contains waterproof matches, a Bic lighter, two chocolate bars, a space blanket, a section of folded newspaper, two pads of 00 fine steel wool, and a small knife. With these items you can start a fire very quickly, and that just might help you survive a spill in the frigid waters or any other circumstances that can develop. Remember that fishing is supposed to be fun, not dangerous. If you are looking for adventure with an element of danger, try skydiving or driving in downtown L.A. during rush hour.

During the winter months anglers will spend a good deal of time nymphing. Let's take a closer look at some of the reasons we do and the methods that we use.

As we were doing the research for this text we came across an interesting quote from George Washington Bethune, who served as the editor of the first American edition of Isaac Walton's *Compleat Angler*, published in 1847. The quote is interesting, because Bethune has a thoroughly modern view of what many anglers today still fail to recognize, that "a lot of things work a lot of the time, and that some may work more than others, but none seem to work all the time." Even in today's high-tech world there are no secret patterns or methods that work all the time. Therefore, the only way an angler can hope to be effective most of the time is either to be lucky or to be knowledgeable. No angler should discount luck, for there are those days, as one our friends says, when "I'd rather be lucky than good." But for those of you who do a great deal of fishing on a number of different waters, the only way to be effective day after day is to be knowledgeable about the trout, the available food forms, the different patterns and how to present them properly.

We usually break down our nymph-pattern types into categories for easier classification: imitations, searching patterns (rough imitations), and attractors. Speaking of attractors, when reading *American Fly Fishing—A History* by Paul Schullery, we ran across another interesting quote from Austin Hogan, who has this to say about attractors: "All flies are designed to attract and so the word attractor . . . is ambiguous and entirely without meaning." How a pattern is classed would depend, at times, on how it is being used. For instance, during late June a Girdle Bug could be classed as a rough imitation (imitative) of the salmon fly nymph. During early August this same pattern could be used as a searching pattern, alone or in conjunction with another fly. During September this very same pattern might be employed as an attractor, in hopes that the movement of the rubber legs or the retrieve being used would attract a trout and lure it into striking. Now you might think that all of this is confusing, and it is—for the beginner. But the more you understand the patterns and when and why you are us ing them, the more effective you will be as an angler.

Using well-known nymph patterns, we will demonstrate when and why you might use a pattern as it relates to the aforementioned categories. Those who state that fly fishing should be kept simple have obviously not spent much time fishing on rivers like the Yellowstone. The fishing pressure and quality of available food forms there demands that the angler have the right patterns and present them in the proper manner. Most anglers accept the fact that there are times when the trout can become very selective to a certain dry fly. This normally occurs during a hatching situation, but many of these same anglers fail to realize that the trout can be just as selective to certain nymph forms. Maybe even more so, because they see the nymphs much more clearly—the nymph is in their world and not distorted by the surface of the water and its refraction of light.

When working selective trout, the nymphal imitation has to be correct in design, shape, color, and size, and the angler needs to be able to present the imitation in a natural manner at the depth in which the trout is feeding. A couple of examples of imitative patterns that we use here on the Yellowstone are the Hare's Ear and the Sawyer-style Pheasant Tail. Both can be tied in several different colors and shapes to represent many of the small stoneflies and mayflies found on this river. In short, imitative patterns are used to work trout that are feeding heavily on a specific nymphal form.

Now there are times when the trout don't seem to be feeding heavily on anything. Then what? You will often encounter this situation when fishing during the winter months on the Yellowstone. Then the angler can kick-screen or pump the stomach of a caught fish and determine what the one or two most predominant food forms are and, employing the use of one or two imitations, use them as searching patterns by covering the water. In this case you are showing the trout something it is used to feeding on, and you are looking for those feeders of opportunity.

Searching patterns may be any imitative or roughly suggestive pattern style. Often there may be several different nymphal food forms available to the trout, and we are then unsure what the trout are feeding on, whether it be a specific individual form or perhaps several different types. There appears to be no selective feeding and no steady feeding rhythm. Examples of good searching imitations are Whitlock's Red Fox Squirrel Nymph and the Rubber-Legged Hare's Ear Nymph. They can be tied in many different shapes and colors. Are they mayfly, stonefly, caddis, or scud imitations? In a rough, suggestive way, they kinda look like any and all of those food forms. When using searching patterns we most often employ the use of two or more patterns and will cover the water carefully, looking for feeders of opportunity. We will change patterns and sizes and work different water depths until we find a combination that is working. Once we start taking trout, we then pump their stomachs, looking for a preferred food form.

There are times when we will employ attractor patterns. First, we will use an attractor pattern if we have tried imitative patterns and searching patterns and had no success. Sometimes we use an attractor pattern in conjunction with an imitative pattern. We have all had those days when, regardless of how much knowledge we have of the river, nothing seems to produce. On these days we employ an attractor pattern such as a Girdle Bug, Sparkle Bugger, Yellow-Bellied Sapsucker, or a Black Sparkle Nymph. We will generally use one or two of these patterns and fish them at various depths, using both dead-drift and active-retrieve methods. Manipulated in this manner, they may entice a trout into striking. Besides, at this point, what have you got to lose? You sure won't catch any fewer trout. We will often employ the use of an attractor pattern in conjunction with a streamer, crayfish, or leech imitation. This allows us to use an imitative pattern to search with, while at the same time employing an attractor pattern that may help induce a strike. Attractor patterns are flies that really don't look like anything the trout feeds on yet the combination of material in the water seems to attract the trout.

The tackle you use to fish nymphs with will depend on the type of water you are fishing, the size and weight of the patterns being used, and, to some degree, the weather, or more to the point, the wind. We often hear and read how this rod or that rod is an all-around rod. If you can only have one rod, we would suggest an eight- to nine-foot rod for a 6-weight line. We would also suggest that you have a floating line, an intermediate sinking line, and a sinking tip. One line will not allow you to cover all the presentation methods properly. Now, if you can have more than one rod, and we each have several, we suggest a seven-and-a-half- to eight-foot for a 4-weight for fishing small nymphs and fine tippets. Often all you will need is a floating line, though we also use the intermediate slow-sinking a good deal of the time for our winter nymphing.

For much of our general fishing we use the 6-weight system, and we do use various types of lines. For fishing big nymphs and for fishing even medium-sized nymphs under windy conditions we suggest an eight-and-a-half- to nine-foot rod for an 8-weight line. You want the heavier rod and line to help to move the larger imitations or you may have an encounter of the wrong kind. With an 8-weight system we strongly urge you to have a good selection of fly lines. You need the various lines if you are going to be able to present the imitation at the proper depth and keep it there for the longest period possible.

One of the reasons for choosing the 8-weight system over others is that it lets you take advantage of various sinking lines and their sink rates. Throughout the season in certain water types on this section, you are going to need a very fast sink rate if you want to get the fly down to the proper level. We suggest the following lines for the 8-weight system: floating; intermediate sinking; sinking tips, type II and IV; sinking shooting head type IV; and uniform sink line type III. This system will also allow you to fish any section of the river, from the bottom to the top, successfully.

Winter is always an interesting time to fly-fish. Many problems have to be dealt with that don't come into play during the other seasons, but it nearly always seems to be worth it. Sometimes it is a miniadventure that helps break the monotony and shake out those cabin-fever blues. Other times it is a pleasant way of spending a few hours outdoors.

Spring: March to Runoff

During a normal March, whatever that is, many things start to happen on the Yellowstone in this section. Besides the midge hatches, which can be very heavy at times, we will start to see the blue-winged olives by mid- to late March, depending on the weather cycles. During March the rainbows start to seriously move and gather for spawning. The water temperatures are hovering in the mid- to low forties, and the trout are fairly active. The weather can be a real mixed bag, with some warm days, some cold days, and snow showers, but seldom are we cabin-bound for more than a day or two. As we get toward the end of March the cased caddis and free-swimming caddis larvae will become very active and the trout will start feeding on them heavily.

The majority of fishing will still be nymph fishing, but the patterns used will be more specific and imitative. Look to the higher sections of the riffles for good rainbow action and the quieter sections of water for the isolated dry-fly action. The blue-winged olives are very often hatching toward the afternoon, when the water temperature begins to rise slightly.

April can have still have some up and down weather days, but mostly the weather is pretty decent. The fishing is excellent; the rainbows will finish their spawning during the month. Midges and blue-winged olives will continue to hatch early in the month, although the midges will start to taper off by midmonth and the best of the blue-winged olive hatches will be over by the end of the month. However around the tenth of April the western march browns will start to appear and will continue till runoff. These are a riffle insect, and the best dry action is always found on the flats below the riffles or in the glides below the riffle corners.

Around the twenty-fifth of April the famous Yellowstone caddis hatch starts, and it carries on into May. At this point we would like to take a moment to set the record straight concerning the caddis hatch on the Yellowstone. During recent years much has been written about this hatch; unfortunately, much of the information is incorrect. First, this hatch has been mistakenly called the Mother's Day caddis hatch. Each year we receive many letters and phones calls from anglers wishing to come out around Mother's Day and fish. Generally, by Mother's Day the river is unfishable. The caddis hatch on the Yellowstone starts around the twenty-fifth of April and continues on into May, long after the river is no longer fishable due to rising and discolored water. The name "Mother's Day caddis hatch" was coined during the 1970s by Dave Kumlien of Bozeman, Montana. Dave owns Montana Troutfitters and used the term "Mother's Day caddis" in regard to the Madison River from Bear Trap Canyon to Three Forks. The caddis hatch normally starts on that stream right around Mother's Day. Well, someone got his facts wrong, and the story was told, retold, and the rest is history.

If you have never fished on the Yellowstone during the caddis hatch, you owe it to yourself to do so. For most anglers, the first experience with the caddis hatch brings the statement "Wow, I didn't know that the Yellowstone held so many trout!" The hatch and the activity levels of the trout are both very impressive. There are so many caddis on the water and in the air that some anglers can have an allergic reaction to the powder on their wings—it happens every year. Some of the back-eddies are literally covered with thick layers of caddis that are inches deep; it is totally awesome.

Fishing with adult patterns, emerger patterns, and even deep emergers brings good results. One technique that has worked well for us is to float a dry adult with a beadhead emerger trailing about eighteen inches behind it. In the morning, before all the surface activity fires up, nymph with deep emergers, larva and pupa patterns, for some good action. Toward the late afternoon, when there are billions of insects flying around and some of you have trouble breathing, look to some of the quieter pockets of water for steadily rising fish. There are afternoons when every fish in the river is feeding on the surface, but there are many days when the rising fish are somewhat isolated, even though there are bugs everywhere. When a pocket of fish is discovered, spend some time fishing to them because the next pocket may be a distance away.

The weather is seldom a problem, though we still suggest that you pack a warm jacket and bring a rain jacket, because both late April and early May can be rainy. As for the fishing, well that can be summed up in three words: *caddis and super!* However, the annual spring runoff is about to begin, and during a normal year the Yellowstone becomes unfishable around May 10 to 12. Some years the river goes out the first of May, and every now and then the river doesn't go out until late May. So if you are planning on coming to fish the Yellowstone in May, call first. There are times when either the fishing is great or the river is gone.

During the springtime period we start to float this section of the Yellowstone, and seldom do we float the entire section at once. When the fishing is super, most people want to spend more time fishing than floating, so short floats are recommended. There is so much good water to cover that an angler is fortunate to have so many access points in this section that enable him to tailor the length of the float depending on where most of the insects are hatching. The caddis hatch will start downstream and travel upriver. The speed at which the hatch travels upstream will depend on the weather cycles. If the bugs have already made their way to the upper reach of this section, it would be counterproductive to float the entire section.

The walking fishers will have good opportunities to get in on this hatch, because there are many places to reach the river. Visiting anglers should inquire at the fly shops for information about some of the local accesses. Although floating anglers have a greater opportunity to find mass quantities of rising fish, the walking fisher can cover the water better—he doesn't have the worry about getting somewhere to nag at him. Very often the evenings will find fish working hard in the quieter waters on spent insects. The float fisherman may have to pass them up so he can get off the water before it gets too dark; not so for the walker.

Early Summer: June and July

For the majority of June the Yellowstone is high and unfishable. Somewhere around the twentieth to the twenty-fifth the river will start to drop and clear. During this time the salmon flies first appear in Livingston. When these large insects start to emerge they get the attention of all the trout, and all the fly fishers, as well. As the hatch travels up the river, so do the anglers, leaving the Livingston-to-Sheep-Mountain section and, for the most part, not returning until late July. The old excuse is that "the banks are still too high and fast and the angler cannot get a good presentation." Many anglers feel it is tough to fish this section during this time, but that is because not too many are familiar with it. They fish as they would farther upstream, and catch few fish. Their technique is what fails them—dominant banks cannot be fished because the water is too fast to either hold fish or make decent presentations, so a change in tactics is in order. A change to the slower side of the river, when there is one, will often make a difference, and a switch to the side channels will definitely make a difference.

The salmon fly hatch is not very heavy on this stretch of water, and it is fairly brief. However, these trout can be found feeding on the green drakes, pale morning duns, and caddis that are found in this section. The green drakes seem to be making a comeback on this section; as each year passes their numbers seem to increase. This is fast becoming the major hatch of the early summer. Look to the middle of the afternoon for excellent dry-fly action. By mid-July the golden stones and yellow sallys are also hatching in good numbers, and the anglers who choose to fish this section will not find many other anglers doing so until late July. Anglers who tell you that certain sections of the river will fish better at certain times of the year are correct. However, they don't always have the right reasons. Often, they have had no experience on that particular section during the time they are talking about.

By mid-July the trout has many different food forms available, and it's now that they start to get a little finicky. They become selective to the available insects and, often, various stages of those insects. It pays to be prepared with a good selection of flies. A visit to the fly shops will provide you with up-to-date information about what is happening and what is working. This can arm you with the information necessary to make informed decisions about how you will fish. A float fisherman in mid-July can almost always catch some fish by throwing junk (the large attractor patterns) against the banks, but the angler well armed with knowledge and prepared with the proper patterns will do much better.

Riffle corners are extremely productive spots to fish at this time. During nonhatch periods a Trude or Stimulator with a beadhead emerger trailer will more often than not nail some fish in these spots. This combination also works well when prospecting for fish as one floats downstream. When specific insects are hatching more imitative patterns are usually necessary to have a good day.

There always seems to be something hatching on this stretch of water. An angler has to be observant and cover some water on most days to find the hatch because it may not be very obvious. This section has few fishermen, some very good fishing, and it all can be had in or near town.

Late Summer: August to Mid-September

August is often referred to as the hopper month. The hopper fishing on this section of the Yellowstone rates as some of the best in the world. However, there are also many important hatches and other available food forms to be found during this time. During August and on into September you will find hatches of the giant western red quill, western yellow drake, and spotted sedge, along with the little sister sedge. The angler will also encounter the little olive stonefly, giant western golden stone, and lots of hoppers, beetles, and ants.

A four-pound brown taken from this section of the river.

The hopper fishing can be described as fantastic. There are times when fish come from everywhere in the river to inhale a hopper, so make sure that at least one of your flies is a hopper pattern, or that at least someone in the boat is fishing with one. The optimum time of day is in the afternoon, when the wind picks up and begins blowing the naturals into the water. When hopper season is in full force the afternoons are still better, but fish can be had with hoppers anytime during the day then. A technique we employ is to begin the day fishing the morning with two flies: some sort of small attractor (Trude, Stimulator, Wulff) and a hopper, or even a hopper with a slightly weighted nymph as a trailer. As the day wears on and it becomes obvious that the fish are taking the hopper pattern, we might switch to two different hoppers—one large and one small (or one that is a low-water type or parachute type, or even one that rides slightly submerged). This way it can be determined which pattern is hot. If it happens to be one of those super days, then only one pattern is needed. Fish these tight to the banks, but don't overlook the middle of the river because fish can and do—especially when they are keying on hoppers—rise from great depths for a mouthful of hopper. An oversized pattern will very often bring the extraordinary fish up from its hidey hole.

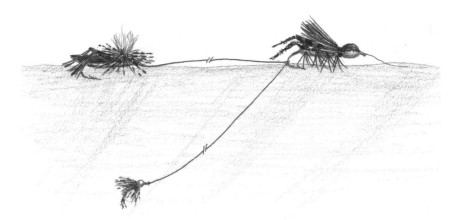

Hopper and dropper set-ups

Start the day (morning) using an attractor dry (hopper) and a weighted nymph. Then, switch to two different style hoppers, and then to the effective hopper.

During this time the river has dropped and become well defined. Finding the riffles, flats, pools, and runs are much easier. Finding the current lines off the banks is also easier, and this makes for some excellent float fishing. How well the side channels continue to fish depends on the water flows for that year.

As September draws near, we start to look in the back-eddies for trout that are sipping ants. Often it is hard to spot the riseforms, but once they are found the challenge can be exceptional. Seldom do anglers think of using 6X tippets when fishing the Yellowstone, but when working over trout that are sipping ants in a back-eddy you will soon find the 6X is not the exception but the rule.

There is a virtual plethora of food sources available in the late summer: varieties of mayflies, caddis, stoneflies, and terrestrials. One of the challenges a fly fisher has to meet is identifying what the fish are feeding on. In the course of an average day's float, tactics and strategies have to be altered to optimize one's chances of consistently taking fish. Sure, a guy could float and throw the same pattern all day long and still catch fish, but for us a major portion of this sport is finding, meeting, and fishing the hatches. It makes it all that much more rewarding. This section of the river can challenge the fly fisherman who plays by those rules.

Fall: Mid-September to Mid-November

The hopper fishing on this section of river can continue way into October, depending on the weather cycles. Hoppers are tough, and it takes an extended period of cold weather to kill them off. During late September the angler will encounter flights of flying red ants. The trout are very fond of them and feed heavily on them. During late September the angler will also see the gray drake and the return of the blue-winged olives and midges, both of which can last until mid-November. The dry-fly fishing is almost an afternoon event because the water cools at night and it isn't until the afternoon that it starts to warm again. By October the brown trout are starting to move off the banks and collect in the pools as they start on their annual spawning run. For us this means streamers and the chances of taking a truly large, trophy-sized brown trout. Often, we are using

Hi-Speed Hi-D shooting heads to cover the pools. The speed of the retrieve will be dictated by the water temperature—the colder the water the slower the retrieve.

In most years the weather in October is pretty decent, though you *can* get snowed on. However, every now and then we get an October where winter comes early and shuts down the fishing. This happened during October 1991. During the year the winds shifted to the north during the third week and we received several heavy snows. This, along with two weeks of cold temperatures pretty well shut down the fishing on the Yellowstone. It did, however, make for a great big-game hunting season.

In most years winter doesn't come until mid-November, and the fall is the time for chasing brown trout with streamers and nymphs. Now, don't come to fish with visions of large brown trout swimming at your feet and mobbing you, because that will not happen. Trophy trout fishing is demanding, and you spend a lot of time fishing and little time actually catching. This is a game for the patient, for the angler with stamina. Throwing shooting heads all day long requires a special person—it isn't for everyone. However, the rewards can be great, and if a trophy fish is what you're after, this is the way to catch one.

All in all, an angler could fish an entire season on this stretch of water and come away very satisfied. Obviously, there is no need to have to fish this section all the time when there is so much other good water to fish in the river, but a guy can do real well here anytime.

Locally Effective Patterns

Extended-Body Moose-Hair Drake (Gray)

Hook:	Tiemco 100, sizes 10–14
Thread:	Dark gray
Tails:	Two moose hairs, left unclipped from body
Abdomen:	Moose body hair
Wing:	Moose body hair as a post and clipped to shape
Thorax:	Dark gray dubbing
Hackle:	Grizzly, parachute-style

Gray Gnat

Hook:	Tiemco 101, sizes 18–26
Thread:	Gray
Shuck:	Grizzly-hackle tip
Body:	Gray dubbing
Hackle:	Grizzly, palmered
Wing:	White Z-lon fibers

Tri-Winged Caddis

Hook:	Tiemco 100, sizes 12–16
Thread:	Tan
Body:	Amber dubbing
Wings:	Medium brown deer hair, tied in at the rear third, middle, and front of hook shank

Tom's Tan Foam Spent Caddis

Hook:	Tiemco 101, sizes 10–20
Thread:	Tan
Rib:	One to three strands of pearl Krystal Flash
Body:	Dubbed, #68 tan Super Possum
Wing:	Natural whitetail body hair, tied spent
Foam head:	Scintilla fly foam, yellow
Head:	Dubbed same as the body

Olive CDC Biot Foam Caddis Emerger

Hook:	Tiemco 2487, sizes 10–20
Thread:	Brown
Shuck:	Rusty olive caddis/emerger dubbing, upstream
Abdomen:	Olive turkey biot
Underbody:	Upstream caddis/emerger dubbing, #15 yellow olive
Thorax:	Upstream caddis/emerger dubbing, #15 yellow olive
Legs:	Olive Hungarian partridge, sparse
Foam head:	Olive dry-cell foam
Wings:	Two natural CDC tips, short
Head:	Upstream caddis/emerger dubbing, rusty olive
Antennae:	Two brown turkey-hackle fibers

Yellowstone Black & Olive Caddis Surface Emerger

Hook:	Tiemco 2487, sizes 10–20
Thread:	Black
Shuck:	Dubbed, Rich olive #16 Scintilla
Rib:	Two strands of black Krystal Flash
Body:	Dubbed, Rich olive #16 Scintilla
Wing:	Natural costal deer hair
Hackle:	Brownish gray Hungarian partridge
Collar:	Olive grizzly philo plume
Antennae:	Two strands of black Krystal Flash
Head:	Black muskrat fur

Other Effective Patterns

Besides all of the general attractor-type patterns—dry, wet, and streamers—or those listed in the text, the angler should also consider imitations from the following list:

Beadhead Muskrat Nymph
Parker's Beadhead Golden Stone
Parker's Beadhead Firefox
Beadhead Caddis Pupa Olive
Partridge and Yellow Soft-Hackle
Starling and Hurl Soft-Hackle
Rod's Beadhead Pheasant Tail
Dark Gray Deep Sparkle Pupa
J.B.'s Black and Olive Caddis Pupa
Tom's Olive K-Flash Soft-Hackle
LaFontaine's Brown and Green
  Diving Caddis

Matthew's Tan Sparkle Caddis
Tan New Dubb Elkhair Caddis
SRI Olive Hi-Vis Para-Caddis
Tom's Extended-Body Green Drake
Tom's Extended-Body Yellow Drake
Multi-Purpose Midge Adult
Foam Hi-Vis Black Ant
Irresistible Yellow Stimulator
California Trude
SRI Green Hopper
Henry's Fork Cricket

8

Sheep Mountain
to Big Timber

Lewis and Clark called the beginning of this stretch "the big bend" because the river makes a swing here to an east-west orientation. The thirty or so miles to Big Timber have some historical significance, because Clark was supposed to have camped here at the "Big Timbers" in 1806. As he passed the mouths of Big Timber Creek and the Boulder River he called them "Rivers Across." The "big timbers" name apparently didn't stick, because a small community sprang up here called Dornix, which means small round stones. Later the name was changed to Big Timber, and the historical significance thus survived.

As we proceed in our downstream journey we begin to notice a marked decline in the number of boats and fishermen on the water. As we continue farther and farther down, the fishing pressure definitely declines. Interestingly, this section and the sections farther downstream are almost the forgotten waters of the Yellowstone. Anglers know they're there and that there are good fish in them but seem to "forget" to explore and fish them. This isn't to say that this section isn't fished and floated, that's not true. But compared to the upper river, this section doesn't see near the number of fishermen.

As an example, Wayne Marlow, who runs a shuttle service that we use, told us that prior to 1994 he only averaged about five shuttles a year from Springdale down. Considering the hundreds of shuttles he must do over the course of a season, this is extremely light traffic. Of course, he isn't the only one who runs shuttles, but we are reasonably sure others haven't had many calls for this area.

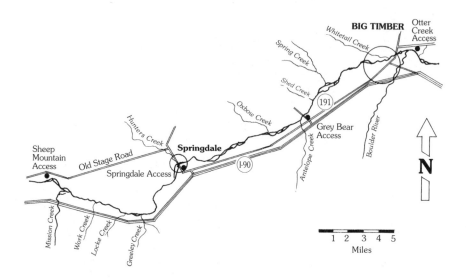

Sheep Mountain to Big Timber

The year 1994 saw more anglers on this stretch of water than did any of the preceding years because it was an extremely low-water year. The upper sections of the river were fishing poorly, and other nearby rivers also fished poorly, so anglers, and especially guides, sought water where the fishing was better. This lower section soon was discovered, or rediscovered in some cases. There was simply more water here than upriver, and less pressure—more tributaries add to the flows. Although this section received more pressure then than it probably ever had, it was still not crowded compared to the upper reaches.

The farther one gets down this section, the less use it gets from guides, especially the guides who come over from Bozeman. It is just a little too far for a day's fishing and all that entails. There is a fly shop and guide service in Big Timber, but nothing on the scale of the Paradise Valley section.

When the fishing is decent on the upper river, this section is almost completely ignored, much to our delight. The opportunity to have a great day on the water is enhanced by not seeing too many other fishermen. Even during the 1994 season there were many days on this stretch where we were the only fishermen on it, at least that we could see. So it is with mixed emotions that we write about this stretch and tell it like it is. What it is is good water, good scenery, good fish, and good fishing.

The river works its way toward Big Timber and flows between the Crazy Mountains to the north and the Absarokas to the south. Although not as spectacular-appearing as where they loom over the Paradise Valley, these mountains still add a very scenic backdrop to a day on the water. There are numerous ranches that line the river's banks. Hay fields and herds of grazing cattle attest to the agricultural nature of the area. The river is lined with cottonwoods as it begins to broaden and begin, ever so slightly, to change character. No longer does it rush out of the park and tumble down toward Livingston. It begins to appear to glide its way east, the precursor to the prairie river it will eventually become. It does have moments when it resembles the fast freestone mountain river of its upper sections, and a floater has to be on his toes. It's easy to become lulled by the slower, calmer stretches, only to get a shot of adrenaline as the river makes a sharp bend with a distinct change in elevation. There are a few places that build waves high enough to endanger a drift boat if the oarsman happens to fall asleep, and other places, when the water is high, that will test one's skills at the oars.

Access sites are farther apart down here, so a day on the water can be a little longer than on other sections. Anglers tend to float longer distances between stops to get out of the boat to fish good-looking water. When fish are rising the temptation is to stop and fish them, but somewhere during the float there is the nagging thought about making up time in order to get off the river before dark or at a certain time. There is so much water to be fished here that a guy doesn't have sufficient time to fish it thoroughly when longer distances have to be covered.

That's the downside of this stretch. The upside is that the fishing is usually good enough to warrant the extended days. Of course, an angler based in Livingston or the Paradise Valley has to add the extra time it takes to get on and off the river if he decides to float near Big Timber. The Big Timber stretch is forty-five miles from

Typical landscape and water in this section of the river.

Livingston; but then again, Gardiner happens to be fifty-five miles away. The distance probably accounts for the lack of fishing pressure.

Water Characteristics

The character of the water begins to change as the runs and pools get longer. There is also less braiding in this thirty-mile stretch, at least less of the major braiding found directly upstream. From the Sheep Mountain access down a short distance there are some good channelized areas that should be worked. Then the river takes a straight shot of a few miles with some fairly decent banks to cast to. There are also some minor channels upstream of the Springdale Bridge that can have some good action. Like the upper river, these channels will very often have areas that are sheltered from the wind, and any insect hatching will stay on the surface before being blown away.

The wind can be a bear on this stretch, especially if it blows from

Floating and fishing the banks.

an eastern quarter. There has been many a time when we didn't think we'd make it off the river and had to exert ourselves way beyond what we planned to do. The wind does mess with the fishing, especially if there is a hatch on, because it becomes difficult to make proper presentations to rising fish from the boat. An upstream wind is always hard to contend with because making the necessary mends to control the drift is difficult.

There are some good banks as the river makes some bends on its way to Springdale that hold good numbers of large browns. If the wind does make fishing the surface just too much of a pain, don't hesitate to switch to a sink tip and big streamer-type pattern, because some of these fish are quite large. The lower river is noted for having fish that are larger than the upper river. It would be fair to say that the fish we catch on this entire stretch are consistently larger on an average than in the valley. Also, when it is hopper season, this section is hard to beat for the action it provides.

From Springdale down, the river again makes a subtle change

because there are some rather bizarre bedrock formations along this section. There is one stretch in particular that has the quality of a rapids, and one has to constantly be on guard and make adjustments in the drift line. The bedrock looms up and forces the water every which way. Some of the formations resemble docks or old pier stanchions—very weird. There is a good deal of riffle corner water in this section and even more pocket-type water created by the bedrock formations. Some sections are relatively shallow, and getting through them without chipping the bottom of a boat is tricky, especially when the water levels drop or in a low-water year. But these sections hold a good number of fish because behind each formation is a deep pocket that holds fish, and all the converging currents and current edges bring food by these pockets for the trout to feast on.

Mixed with these bedrock formations are gravel bars of the kind that change from year to year as the runoff water shifts them around. Some of these gravel bars hold all kinds of fish, and they tend to add character to the water in the form of current edges and such. There are also some excellent riprap banks that hold good quantities of trout—make sure that you work them. In between the interesting water are some good glides where the water is deep and fairly slow. In the afternoons when the bugs are about, one can be fairly certain that there will be some cutthroats rising there.

The river twists and turns on its way to the Grey Bear access, creating a number of the inside corners that nymph fishermen really seem to like. Another feature common to this entire stretch is high rock walls with bedrock shelves extending out in the river. There are some big drop-offs along these ledges. They are often hard to detect because the water is slow and quiet and doesn't give a clue about what's under it. Trout will sometimes cruise these ledges, and a well-placed fly will be rewarded.

The Grey Bear access in Big Timber has all of the aforementioned characteristics with the addition of some very high banks and boulder-strewn shorelines. These probably are the most consistent places to take trout from, whether there are fish rising along them or not. They are excellent holding areas, and food gets funneled by the trout. There are more minor braided areas in this stretch than

Fishing off a gravel bar.

upstream. Some of the banks seem to be consistently shallow, especially on the nondominant side of the river, but suddenly there is a major pocket, or for that matter a minor pocket, that always holds a few fish. Look for any changes in color as you float these shallow banks.

Speaking of shallow banks, don't overlook them for big trout. Once we were floating and had quit fishing because the bank didn't look very productive, only to see a very large (twenty-six inches plus) trout lying tight against the bank in less than a foot of water—and this was in the bright sun of midday. This has happened often enough that we now hesitate to quit fishing even if it doesn't seem productive. One never knows—does one?

When the water is high, the nondominant banks are obviously the banks to fish, and there are times, even when the water is low, when they can be extremely productive. On late-summer evenings these slow shallow banks often have some relatively large brown trout cruising in search of a goodie or two. Many times we have been surprised by hooking one of these fish because we were too lazy to row across the river to the good-looking bank. Being rewarded for laziness ranks high on our "Good Things To Do" list, it also gives us a chance to fish water we normally wouldn't.

As you float into Big Timber, check out the high bank on the south side of the river and all the springs that seep or pour into the river. There is a fair number of springs along this stretch that dump clear cold water into the river. In the dog days of August, especially when the water temperatures rise, these springs will hold fish and should be worked.

This entire stretch has different water characteristics than do the Paradise Valley sections. Those of you who visit the Yellowstone and seem to always wind up fishing the valley owe it to yourselves to give this lower section a shot. We're almost certain you'll find the fishing good, the water interesting, and the experience rewarding.

Accessibility

Accesses tend to be farther apart and not as numerous in this lower section of river. Although we started at the Sheep Mountain access in this section, we hardly ever use that access, for a couple of reasons. First, it can be difficult to get a rig down to the water because the turnaround is constricted; usually there is someone camped in a spot that makes it almost impossible to turn around. The other reason is that the people who run the shuttle services don't care for this access. To get anywhere downstream they have to take the gravel road down to the access, then back to the U.S. 89 bridge, and then back downstream. However, this access does cut some distance off a float to Springdale, and when the wind is howling this becomes a very good thing. Most of the locals who float this stretch usually put in at the U.S. 89 bridge access.

The first access point down from Sheep Mountain isn't an official access point, but it is used by those who know where it is. It's call the Pig Farm access. It is little more than a cut in the willow-lined bank, and if you don't know where it is exactly or happen to see other boats tied up there it's really easy to miss. It is a couple of miles down from Sheep Mountain, and many locals use it to end a float from Mayor's Landing in Livingston, or for a short evening float from the U.S. 89 bridge, or to cut the distance to Springdale. Inquire at the local shops for directions, because it is a little out of the way.

The next access down is a real access point, the Springdale Bridge access. It has a good ramp, allows camping, and has a handicapped-accessible rest-room facility. It is difficult to miss because it's right after the bridge. It is about ten miles from the Sheep Mountain access. The next in line is another ten miles downriver: Grey Bear access. (All these accesses are off the interstate, so one has to pay attention to the exit signs. It is a good idea to check a map before trying to locate these accesses.) Grey Bear also has a handicapped-accessible rest room, a dirt ramp, and camping is allowed in a camping area adjacent to the access. There is also a bridge immediately before the access, so it is difficult to miss as one floats downstream.

The last access point on this stretch is at Big Timber—actually a little way past Big Timber. There is about a mile of floating left when you float under the bridge at Big Timber. This access is called the Otter Creek access, and it is on the north side of the river. It has a concrete ramp, handicapped-accessible rest rooms, and camping is allowed. There are shuttle services in Livingston that will go down as far as Big Timber, and there is also a service in Big Timber (inquire at the local fly shop). It's a tad cheaper because it's closer.

The Fish

The hatchery at Big Timber kept this area well stocked with trout before the late 1960s. Currently, there are still very good numbers of trout in this section, though not as much as in the Livingston stretch. As we move downstream we find that the total numbers of trout decrease, but the water becomes such that they tend to concentrate in specific areas. The population mix works out to about fifty percent rainbows, thirty percent brown trout, and twenty percent cutthroat trout. There is suitable habitat for all species of trout in this section of river.

Many of the rainbow run up to the spring creeks to spawn, and some even make it up to the Shields River and its tributaries. Because they tend to drift downstream from the spawning grounds, this area is still within their reach. There is a fair amount of rainbow water—the faster, more riffly water—down here for them to use. The populations are healthy and the fish tend to run larger than farther upstream.

Brown trout find suitable habitat here and plenty of gravel in the main stem to spawn in. There is a minor run of fish up into the Shields River and some of the other tributaries along the way. This can be a section of river in which to snag a really good fish.

The cutthroats fare better down here also because there is more habitat to their liking. Also, the Boulder River is at the lower reach and is used, to an extent, for spawning purposes, and there are a couple of other creeks the cutthroat use to spawn in the Springdale area. The cutthroats in this section also appear to run larger than their brethren upstream.

Down toward Big Timber two other species make rare appearances: the goldeye and the burbot. The goldeye (*Hiodon alosoides*) is often called the skipjack, shiner, or shad. It is a member of the mooneye family, is native to Montana, and is really more common much farther downstream, where the river becomes a warmwater fishery. The burbot (*Lota lota*) is commonly called the ling or ling cod. It is a member of the codfish family, and is also a native of Montana. These fish are found in this stretch, but rarely, and are clues to what we can expect much farther downstream.

Hatch Chart for Sheep Mountain to Big Timber

Stoneflies

Golden stone
  (*Calineuria californica*)   Size: #4–#8   June 15 to July 1
Yellow sally
  (*Isoperla mormona*)   Size: #14–#16   July 10 to August 15

Giant western golden stone
  (*Claassenia sabulosa*)   Size: #2–#6   August 1 to September 10

Caddisflies

Early grannom
  (*Brachycentrus occidentalis*) Size: #12–#16   April 20 to May 20
Spotted sedge
  (*Hydropsyche cockerelli*)   Size: #12–#16   August 15 to October 20
Little brown sedge
  (*Lepidostoma veleda*)   Size: #14–#18   July 15 to August 15
American grannom
  (*Brachycentrus americanus*)   Size: #12–#16   July 10 to August 30
Long horn sedge
  (*Oecetis avara*)   Size: #12–#16   July 15 to August 20
Spotted sedge
  (*Hydropsyche occidentalis*)   Size: #10–#12   June 25 to July 25
Plain brown sedge
  (*Lepidostoma pluviale*)   Size: #14–#18   July 1 to July 31

Mayflies

Western green drake
  (*Drunella grandis*)   Size: #10–#12   June 25 to July 15
Western march brown
  (*Rhithrogena morrisoni*)   Size: #14–#16   April 15 to May 15
Pale morning dun
  (*Ephemerella inermis*)   Size: #16–#20   July 20 to August 25
Western black quill
  (*Rhithrogena undulata*)   Size: #12–#14   July 15 to August 15
Western yellow drake
  (*Heptagenia elegantula*)   Size: #14–#16   July 20 to September 20
Gray drake
  (*Siphlonurus occidentalis*)   Size: #10–#12   September 1 to September 25
Giant western red quill
  (*Ephemerella hecuba*)   Size: #10–#12   August 25 to September 20
Blue-winged olive
  (*Baetis tricaudatus*)   Size: #18–#20   March10 to April 20,
                                                    September 15 to November 10
Trico (*Tricorythodes minutus*) Size: #18–#22   August 15 to October 10

Terrestrials

Grasshoppers (Acrididae)   Size: #8–#14   July 20 to October 15
Crickets (Gryllidae)   Size: #12–#14   August 1 to September 30
Black ants (Formicidae)   Size: #16–#22   July 15 to September 30

| Cinnamon ants (Formicidae) | Size: #18–#20 | August 20 to September 20 |
| Black beetle (Coleoptera) | Size: #12–#18 | July 15 to August 15 |

Other Important Hatches and Food Forms

Midge (Chironomidae)	Size: #16–#24	February 15 to April 20
	Size: #18–#22	September 20 to November 10
Leeches (Hirudinea)	Size: #2–#10	July 15 to October 15
Snails (Gastropoda)	Size: #12	August 1 to September 15
Damselfly nymphs (Zygoptera)	Size: #8–#14	July 20 to September 1
Dragonfly nymphs (Odonata)	Size: #6–#10	July 15 to September 1

Minnows

Mottled sculpin		
(*Cottus bairdi*)	Size: #2–#8	All year
Whitefish minnow		
(*Prosopium williamsoni*)	Size: #2–#10	All year
Long-nose dace minnow		
(*Rhinichthys cataractae*)	Size: #2–#10	All year
Long-nose sucker minnow		
(*Catostomus catostomus*)	Size: #2–#10	All year
Mountain sucker		
(*Catostomus platyrhynchus*)	Size: #2–#10	All year

Seasonal Change: The Fishing

Regardless of the season, the angler must be observant in this section of the river. Why? Because the water types are so varied that the angler who is in a rush or who just can't read the water is going to miss half of the fishing this section has to offer. This is one of the reasons this section hasn't been as popular as the upper sections. Each time we push the limits of the Yellowstone by exploring the next section down, we find that it takes a while to learn the water and the moods of the river in that section. That is, perhaps, the Yellowstone's greatest gift to anglers: the river makes you learn how to read water; that is, if you wish to be successful.

To learn this stretch of the river you must take the time to break it down into shorter sections to learn each section and how it changes seasonally. Take, for example, the section of river from the Pig Farm to the Springdale Bridge. For several miles the river seems to glide along in sections that maintain a fairly uniform width and depth, or so it seems. The angler who started fishing this section would enjoy excellent float fishing where the banks could be worked. In a normal year this would hold up until late July. As the water dropped, the angler might only find a few areas that continued to fish well. However, because of the bedrock ledges and fingers in this section, if the angler were to carefully look over the water out in the middle of the river, he would see some shallow and then some darker areas. These darker areas are the channels and trenches among the bedrock ledges and fingers. These areas hold plenty of fish.

Once when we were floating and fishing these areas, a boat of fishermen came and demanded to know what we were doing fishing out in the center of the Yellowstone. Having observed where they had been fishing, we replied, "Catching trout. Why are you fishing on the banks that are not deep enough to hold trout?" We were later told that they had been advised to fish the banks, that this was a good hopper section. This is true. However, the trout need a certain amount of water and cover in order to be on the banks. Therefore, be observant; know the habits of trout and what they require and don't waste your time on unproductive water. Fish where the trout will be. In a low-water year, this is even more true. We had a few low-water years in 1988 and again last 1994. This is a great time to fish the Yellowstone. During a low-water year you can learn where the ledges and bedrock formations are located. You learn what can change in high water and what will not. This information will be of great value to you as you continue to fish the river.

Winter: Mid-November to February

Once again, as we move away from the towns, we find that this section of the river receives very little fishing pressure during the winter. As always, the weather will be the single greatest factor affecting how often we are able to fish during this time. During a cold winter this section of the river can really ice up and the fishing can be nonexistent on certain sections. Many changes in the river can happen during periods of ice. However, for those who do venture afield, all of the access sites fish very well during the winter months.

Within walking distance of all the access sites there are riffle corners that offer nymphing opportunities. Good patterns for the winter months are Prince Nymph, Golden Stone Nymph, Peeking Caddis Nymph, Whitlock's Fox Squirrel Nymph. A word of caution: Do not attempt to float this section during the winter unless you are absolutely sure the river is open and free of ice. Coming around a blind corner and finding that the river is iced up can ruin a person's whole day!

In mid- to late February there is some very fine midge fishing in this section of the river. One of our friends, Jim Woodhull, who is an avid fly fisherman, has a spot in this section where he loves to fish the midge hatches. We once caught him in this secret spot, which up to that time we had considered our own and, well, we finally swore him to secrecy not to reveal its location. The one thing you will notice here during the winter is a lack of anglers. You will seldom have to share the water during the winter months.

Tactics for Midge Fishing on the Yellowstone

It was a beautiful Montana afternoon in late February. The sky was semiovercast and the snow-covered peaks glistened in the background. The air temperature had crept up to the mid-thirties and the day was calm. The Yellowstone was in standard winter form, which is to say that it was low and very clear. We checked and found the water temperature to be thirty-eight degrees. When we arrived at the river there were just a few trout starting to dimple and bulge, feeding on the midge pupae that were trapped in the foam-slicked back-eddy. With each passing minute the number of feeding trout increased as the intensity of the midge hatch grew. With hands that were trembling from excitement we geared up as quickly as possible, which means that it took twice as long as normal. Maybe it was the helpful comments we were making to each other! When we were finally ready we carefully approached the tail of our favorite back-eddy and proceeded to observe how the trout were feeding. After determining that they were sucking down midge pupae trapped in the surface film, Rod insisted that Tom take the first fish. He quickly grabbed his camera, found a place on the bank to his liking, and began offering kind words of encouragement, something about casting like a duck with a broken arm, and so forth. However, trying to ignore his verbal assistance, Tom proceeded to place his first cast so that the fly would come right down the very edge of the currents and be carried right into the back-eddy and the feeding lane of the trout. Tom saw the leader hesitate and he reacted, with verbal assistance from Rod. Now, we would like to tell you that the water exploded with silvery brilliance as a healthy rainbow made a hard run for the heavier currents and deeper water of the main river; that Tom was able to subdue the trout through superior skill and finally that he was able to slip the net under this trout of tremendous proportions. But, alas, that wouldn't be true, for in his excitement Tom had lifted the rod perhaps a trifle too fast and hard and had felt a heavy surge, and then the line went slack as he broke off a trout of modest size. During this whole episode Rod was busily clicking the shutter, and Tom knows that those photos are definitely going to cost him dearly.

Somewhere on the Yellowstone during almost every month of the year there is a major midge hatch in progress. It seems that just a few short years ago all the angler needed to successfully fish a midge hatch was a Copper Nymph, a Griffith Gnat, and perhaps a simple midge pupa imitation. Today that is not the case. The flies mentioned will sometimes produce, but often the angler finds that other patterns must be used if the trout are going to be fooled. The single most important tool the angler can employ while fishing midging trout is the ability to observe the entire situation and properly use this information when choosing imitations, methods of approach, and presentation.

Before we delve deeper into patterns and presentation methods, we should first have a better understanding of the trout and how it feeds on midges, along with a basic understanding of the life cycle of the midge. One of the most important factors the angler must consider when working over midging trout is that the trout's very survival is based on energy spent versus energy taken in. Thus, the trout will most often eat what is abundant and easiest to capture. This means that midge worms, pupae, stillborns, drowned adults, and semi-emerged midges will often draw the trout's attention, because they require little energy to capture, unlike the adults that are hovering and skittering over the water.

In heavier currents the trout will most often stake out a feeding lane where the currents bring the food right to its position. In slower-water situations the trout can often be found cruising and feeding on the move. At times the puzzle is easy to solve, and so the angler is fast into the trout. But more often that not the puzzle is difficult and many variables must be considered before the trout can be fooled. The key to this problem-solving is the angler's ability to observe.

In many midging situations the trout can choose from midge worms, midge pupae that are floating at various depths, stillborns, drowned adults, semiemerged adults, and adults. Now with this mix the angler can find success if each trout is treated as an individual. This is a logical move. Many studies have shown that trout do indeed have individual characteristics, and with many types of food forms available during a midge emergence it is logical to assume that different trout will feed on different food forms. Therefore, it is very important for the angler to have a complete selection of midge patterns and to pick out an individual trout and carefully observe how it is feeding and on what food forms. Once the angler has determined all this, the proper approach and presentation method can then be considered.

Now we know that all this sounds very complex, but in all reality it is the most logical and least frustrating way for an angler to proceed. Furthermore, as angling pressure increases, we find that the most successful anglers are those who pay attention to detail and solve problems in a logical and determined manner.

Understanding Midges

To clear up any confusion and set the record straight we need to have a statement of definitions. When speaking of midges we are referring to an insect that closely resembles the pesky mosquito but doesn't bite. As a matter of fact, the midge and mosquito are cousins. In truth, midges are a species by themselves and not to be confused with other species in the order of Diptera. Diptera is formed from the Greek words *di* meaning "two," and *ptera*, meaning wing. Dipterans are highly specialized two-winged flies that include such common insects as the housefly, mosquito, cranefly, horsefly, and blackfly. Nice group, huh? The family of Diptera we are interested in is the Tentepedaidae and the genus is *Chironomus*. We see no useful reason for the angler to try to identify individual species of midges, but to each his own. On the Yellowstone River there are approximately fifteen species of midge. From the angler's point of view the best scientific name might be *Littlus small bugus*.

Midges, like the caddisfly, go through a complete metamorphosis, consisting of the stages egg, larva (worm), pupa, and adult. Although the adult midges are never aquatic, the egg, larva, and pupa spend their entire existence in an aquatic environment, and thus are very available to the trout. Some midges require as long as a year to mature, but in many cases only a few weeks are needed. Some species on the Yellowstone hatch out several generations per year. For the unknowing, the locals often refer to the midges as "snowflies," because they speckle the snow along the banks of the river during the winter emergence cycle. So don't be fooled; the snowfly isn't some secret hatch—it is just the midge.

The larvae are wormlike and dwell on the bottom, clinging to rocks or other bottom obstructions as well as inhabiting weed beds. The larvae will vary in size from two to twelve millimeters or from #12 to #28 in hook size. However, the best sizes for the Yellowstone are #14 to #18. The most effective colors are olive, red, and brown.

It is when the midge larva pupates and prepares to hatch that it becomes most available to the trout. The midge pupa leaves the bottom and slowly drifts along with the currents, working its way toward the surface film to hatch. From the time it breaks loose from the bottom until it flies away as an adult, the midge is very, very vulnerable, and the trout will often feed heavily on it. During this emergence activity the pupa is at the mercy of the currents and will often be concentrated in back-eddies, deep quiet pools, major current lines along the edges of riprap banks, and along the edges of whirlpools. The trout will feed on these pupae from the bottom up to the surface film.

Once the midge pupae make it to the surface film, they hang vertically and start to move inside their exoskeletons in order to break free and emerge. The trout will feed on various forms of this emerging pupa. As with the surface emergence of any aquatic insect, there are stillborns as well as adults that are defeated and drowned in the surface film due to waves, currents, wind, or genetic imperfections.

There are times the trout will feed on the hatched adults. Often when the air is cooler, the adults will emerge and ride the water surface for a considerable distance before flying off. At other times the midge adults seem to cluster or ball up while on the surface during mating. It is during these happenings that the Griffith Gnat is so very deadly.

Anglers should keep these various forms of the midge in mind when observing what the trout are feeding on. Don't jump to conclusions.

Tackle for the Midge Fisher

This is a good question, because everyone seems to have his own favorite. We can only tell you what we prefer and why. Our two favorite rods for midge fishing are the Orvis One Weight and the newer Orvis Power Matrix eight-foot four-inch 4-weight. Both rods offer what we call "feel," and when you are fishing 6X and 7X tippets, you need to be able to feel the trout and how much pressure you are applying. These rods are fishing tools and not high-tech casting tools—the two do not always mix. Some of you might question the use of the One Weight on a river like the Yellowstone, which is noted for wind. Well, the One Weight has a lot more guts than you might imagine; furthermore, there are angling situations where a super-delicate presentation is needed.

We prefer reels with good smooth drag systems that are capable of holding one hundred yards of backing. Every now and then you will hook a fish that just explodes and heads for the main currents, then you will be glad for the one hundred yards of backing.

When thinking of midge fishing, most anglers assume that the only line needed is a DT or WF floating line. This isn't the case; on the Yellowstone we have found ourselves using slow-sinking Stillwater Stealth Lines as well as sink tips on occasion. The leaders used in midge fishing will vary depending on the type of line being used. Therefore, we suggest that you carry a complete kit of your favored leader material, because many of the leaders you will need are not available, and you must tie them yourself. We prefer to use Umpqua or Orvis SSS leader material. But we also believe that the material of today is so much better than it was ten years ago that if you have a leader material that you are happy with—use it! The trout will act as the ultimate judge.

Moving Water, Locating Trout, and Presentation Methods

In the Yellowstone there is a midge hatch occurring somewhere throughout most of the year. In a large river like this the angler must first find the water that will hold the midging trout. Look for the foam-slick corners, back-eddies, current pockets along the riprap banks, riffle corners with strong leading-edge current lines, flats, and the tailouts of long, slow pools. These are the places where the trout will gather to feed on the midges. Because some of these hatches occur in the cooler months of the year, the actual hatching often takes place during the warmest time of the day, which is most often the afternoon. We like to arrive on the river around 1:00 P.M. Two of our personal favorite places to work for midging trout are back-eddies and current pockets along riprap banks. Here on the Yellowstone you can often find both areas in close proximity to each other on certain sections of the river.

Along the riprap banks the trout hang in the current pockets, which are often right along the shore. They feel safe because these pockets are themselves deep or are bordering on deep water that offers the needed security. Anglers will generally have to approach on foot; anchoring a boat within casting distance of midging trout can indeed be tricky. We prefer approaching the trout in these pockets by carefully working our way upstream. Once the angler is in position to observe the trout, then what they are feeding on can be determined and the proper pattern selected. We often find that these pocket trout will be feeding on midge pupae. However, you need to carefully watch the riseforms to determine at what depth they are feeding. We often see anglers assuming that the takes are in the film, only to be frustrated when the trout ignore their offerings. In reality, the trout are feeding on pupa that drift three to six inches under the film.

The next trick is to use the cast that will allow you to present the imitation without spooking the feeding trout; this is usually accomplished with a reach cast or hook cast. You want to place the fly and leader along the edge of the main current so that the current will sweep the imitation into the pocket and the waiting trout in a natural manner. Once this presentation method is mastered, the angler can work right up a bank and pick off several trout. This method is based on a careful approach and the angler's ability to see the feeding trout. The cast is often done with nothing more than four to eight feet of fly line and the leader. For some, seeing the strike can be tough; we suggest that you watch for the hesitation of the leader and the movement of the trout. Another method is to fish the pupa behind a white Griffith Gnat or Parachute Adams and let the dry fly be your indicator.

Back-eddies are another of our favorite places for fishing to midging trout. They offer the trout excellent feeding opportunities and shelter at the same time, for most of them are fairly deep. In other words, this would be a prime feeding lie. The main river currents bring the drifting midge pupae and other midge forms swirling into the back-eddy, where the trout can capture them with little or no effort. The most important thing for the angler to remember when approaching a back-eddy is that the currents are running opposite from that of the main river. Approach from the wrong direction and you will spook the trout! Because a back-eddy is a prime feeding lie, you will find that it can and will hold some larger trout.

We approach the tail of the back-eddy and quietly observe to determine what form of the midge the majority of the trout are feeding on. Once we have selected the imitation, we can employ the proper presentation methods. Often we find that the trout will be heavily feeding on midge pupae or drowned adults in a back-eddy situation. One of the methods that we employ for fishing back-eddies is to use a long, fourteen-foot, leader, which we will dress with floatant so it won't sink and cause drag problems. How close to the imitation that floatant is applied will depend on the type of imitation and the depth it is being fished. Fishing in back-eddies may require some longer casts of thirty feet or so; however, we do not like to use indicators because often even the smallest and most delicate indicator will spook the feeding fish or cause drag problems. Rather, with the greased leader we watch for the hesitation in the leader track or tighten on the riseform. We also start by working the trout farthest back, then work our way up to the next fish in line. We cast up above the trout using a reach cast or hook cast so the fly and leader, not the line, sails over the trout. When we see the hesitation in the leader or the riseform, we *gently* lift and tighten. Do not strike! If you do, you will soon be tying on a new fly.

Another method we have found very effective is to fish a riffle that empties into a deep slow pool or medium-deep flat. For this method we use a Stillwater Stealth or uniform sink type 1 full-sinking line and a tapered six-foot leader. Often we are using a two-fly cast while employing this method. With a sink rate of only 1.25 inches per second, the speed of the current generally keeps this line off the bottom. This allows the angler to present midge pupae and drowned adult imitations in the middle water. Larger trout will often move into the riffle water to midge, because the broken water offers cover from predators. We cast slightly up and across, allowing the imitations to dead-drift, keeping a taut but not tight line.

Seldom have we seen an angler fishing riffles during a midge hatch, but when you think about it, fishing the riffles is very logical. The midges are at the mercy of the currents and surely they get swept through riffles, and we all know the riffles are oftentimes prime feeding lies for the trout. The uniform sinking line or Stillwater Stealth line allows you to present the imitations at the proper depth, speed, and angle with the least amount of drag. Here again, you will feel the take rather than see it.

Another method we often employ before the peak of the midge emergence or after the hatch is over is to fish through slow pools with midge pupae or drowned adult imitations. To do this we use a sink tip type 1 line. This line has a sink rate of 1.25 inches per second, and the use of the sink tip allows for some added line control. For this method we use a ten- or twelve-foot leader. What's that? Did we

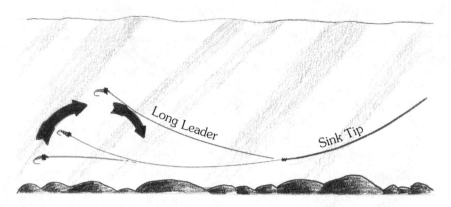

False-starting midge pupa

The long leader allows the fly to rise and fall with the current.

hear some groans and other words of wonder? Yes, we said a ten- or twelve-foot leader knowing full well that the fly and leader will ride up in the water from the depth the line is traveling. Remember that we have often said that the angle of presentation is important for angler success. This is such a case, where the sink tip line and long leader will allow us to present the imitation at the proper angle and in the most natural manner. The sink tip will allow the angler to mend the line on the water to keep pace with the drift of the leader and the sinking portion of the line. Make the cast slightly up and across. The line tip sinks, but the leader and fly are above it. As the line continues to sink, the leader and fly are slowly drawn deeper. This creates the *illusion* of the midge pupa false-starting by rising from the bottom and falling back, or of the midge drifting with the currents—which by the way, is never in a straight line. It is, in fact, an erratic up-and-down motion. In the case of the drowned adults, the currents draw these morsels down deeper.

Problem-Solving on Flat Water

Flat water can offer the angler some very perplexing challenges. For working flat water we choose to only use floating lines because the water isn't deep and we are working visible feeding trout. Oftentimes during a very heavy emergence the trout will move into a flat to feed. Due to the intensity of the hatch and the sheer number of midge forms available to the trout, the angler must determine what form of the midge the trout is feeding on. A careful approach must be planned and the imitation presented in the proper manner. The key to successful midging on flat, clear water is *observation*. The angler must get as close as possible to the feeding trout; remember that you must not let the fish see you and that you must move quietly enough that your movement through the water doesn't send out ripples that spook the fish. Once you have gained a suitable observation station, then you can determine what form of the midge the trout is feeding on. If there are several trout working in the area, you may need to treat each trout as an individual. There is no rule that says all trout must be eating the same stage of the midge at the same time.

A technique for maximizing the fishing opportunities is to fish two stages at the same time. We very often will fish a pupa imitation in conjunction with a dry. Not only does this cover two stages nicely, but the dry fly aids in detecting a strike on the pupa—it works much as a strike indicator would. Fishing these tiny patterns can tax anyone's eyesight, so another fishing aid when fishing adult patterns is to fish two flies—one large enough that you can see it on the water and the other the size that you should be fishing. By watching the larger fly it should be easy to notice a strike on the smaller, even if you don't see the small fly strike when you see a swirl near it.

This is some of the finest and most challenging fishing the angler can encounter, and success is not always measured by how many are landed! The Yellowstone offers the angler some of the finest midge fishing opportunities found anywhere, although few anglers who visit the river are aware of these hatches.

Spring: March to Runoff

During March the angler can enjoy some excellent nymphing, although the fishing is not all just nymphing. There will also be some midge hatches, and toward mid-March the blue-winged olives will arrive. This section of river has some super blue-winged olive hatches. For the most part, you will still be by yourself a great deal of the time. As we move into April we see good western march brown hatches, and by mid-April we start to see the early grannom. Even now, in the midst of plenty, anglers don't appear in numbers. All of the fishing is still focused upriver. It is remarkable, as if the river ends at the U.S. 89 bridge. But that is okay, we don't mind. Soon the annual runoff is on us, and we will be off the river until it clears.

Early Summer: June and July

Due to the entry of the Shield's River, Mission Creek, and normal runoff, the Yellowstone in this stretch is not clear enough to fish until about the fourth of July. It may be a little earlier in a low-water year, and in a wet year we may not be able to return to this section until mid-July. Other than a few fishing guides from Big Timber and a very few other anglers in the know, we often have this section of river all to ourselves until the last week of July. Even then the traffic will not be heavy.

When we first return to the river we like to have a rod rigged up with a sink tip and a streamer-nymph combination fished about ten inches apart. Using a short leader, we will work the banks with this rig, moving some very nice trout in the process. The speed of the strip is governed by the speed of the current; if you are not occasionally feeling the bottom, slow down. However, if you are getting stuck with every cast, speed up the retrieve slightly.

During July, anglers who find their way downstream to this section will encounter good hatches of little brown sedge, American grannom, long horn sedge, spotted sedge, and plain brown sedge. Besides the caddis, anglers can also encounter some excellent hatches of western black quill, western yellow drake, and by late July the pale morning duns should appear. Remember, these are not river-wide hatches; rather, they are local in nature, and anglers will have to be looking for them.

Late Summer: August to Mid-September

It is in the late-summer season where you will see the most traffic on this section of the river. However, it never rivals that which can be found upriver. In August, many of the caddis hatches continue, and anglers will also see the start of the Tricos. However, there are two major hatches during August that cast a shadow over everything else. These are the appearance of the giant western golden stone and of the grasshoppers. Now, the hoppers are not really a hatch, because they are landborn insects. However, every August for the past twenty years this stretch has provided some of the best hopper fishing on the river, and, frankly, in the entire state of Montana. Due to the profiles of both the giant western golden stones and the hoppers, one is really never sure what the trout are taking the imitations for, but take them they do.

During this time of the year we like to fish a Foam Hopper or a Dave's Hopper and use an Olive Gray Beadhead Caddis about three inches behind the imitation as a dropper. By now the water levels have dropped and anglers should pay special attention to where the fishing is done; the trout will move off the banks as the water levels drop. In this section the angler needs to be looking for water that will offer the trout both cover and food. In other words, be looking for those prime lies.

For floating anglers, the handling and placement of the boat is critical. The oarsman should keep the boat parallel to the area being fished and row against the current to slow down when needed. Every year we see hundreds of boats on the river, but few anglers seem to know what the straight wooden sticks that protrude from the sides of the boat are used for. Don Williams, longtime fishing guide in the Livingston area, is perhaps one of the finest oarsmen on the river. If you follow Don down the river you notice that he doesn't cock the boat but rather sideslips it to keep his position. If you are a novice with a boat, practice before you attempt much of the Yellowstone.

September brings a few more hatches as well as the continuation of the hopper fishing. During September, anglers can encounter good hatches of gray drakes and the giant western red quill. These are both large mayflies, and you will have no trouble seeing them if you encounter the hatch.

Autumn streamer fishing has good results: a fine brown.

Fall: Mid-September to Mid-November

This is a great time to be on this section of the river—not only is it scenic but you will generally find that you have much of the river to yourself. During September the hopper fishing will continue—in 1993 we were able to fish hoppers right up to the seventh day of November. Also, you will see the return of the blue-winged olives as well as the midge hatches. During September the savvy angler can find some excellent fishing with ants on this section of the river. Look for the back-eddies, swirl currents, and slow glides for this ant action.

During the fall the brown trout start to move and gather for the fall spawning run, and the angler who wishes to take a bigger brown trout can do so in this section. However, to catch brown trout you have to be fishing for them. During this time of year you will not take many large browns on the surface—you must go down after them.

Locally Effective Patterns

Kiwi

Hook:	Tiemco 100, sizes 10–16
Thread:	Gray
Tail:	Grizzly and brown hackle fibers, mixed
Body:	Deer hair, spun and trimmed to shape
Wing:	White calf tail, tied as post
Hackle:	Grizzly and brown, mixed

Rod's Hopper

Hook:	Tiemco 2302, sizes 4–12
Thread:	Lime green
Body:	Yellow closed-cell foam wound on hook shank
Hackle:	Brown, palmered
Underwing:	Turkey quill section
Legs:	Yellow grizzly-hackle stem, clipped and knotted
Head:	Yellow closed-cell foam wound on hook shank
Wing:	Yellow-olive deer hair, tied half-bullet-head style
Spot:	Fluorescent red

PT Soft-Hackle Beadhead Emerger

Hook:	Tiemco 2457, sizes 12–18
Bead:	Gold
Thread:	Brown
Tail:	Pheasant-tail fibers
Ribbing:	Lime green Krystal Flash
Abdomen:	Pheasant-tail fibers
Thorax:	Peacock herl
Hackle:	Hungarian partridge soft-hackle

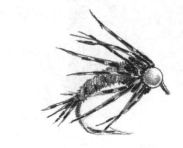

New Dubb Midge Adult Gray

Hook:	Tiemco 2487, sizes 14–22
Thread:	Black
Body extension:	Gray New Dubb
Hackle:	Two grizzly, undersized

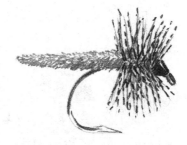

Travis Black Para-Midge Adult

Hook:	Tiemco 2487, sizes 14–22
Body extension and wing post:	Black New Dubb
Thorax:	Black muskrat fur, dubbed
Hackle:	Black, parachute-style

Gray Para-Emerging Midge

Hook:	Tiemco 100, sizes 16–24
Thread:	Black
Abdomen:	Moose mane, bleached and dyed gray
Wing post:	White Antron body wool
Thorax:	Black muskrat fur, dubbed
Hackle:	Black, parachute-style, undersized

Even whitefish take the fly (this whitefish was caught on one of Tom's patterns).

Other Effective Patterns

Besides all of the general attractor-type patterns—dry, wet, and streamers—or those listed in the text, anglers should also consider imitations from the following list.

Dave's Hopper
Whit Hopper
Yellow Foam Hopper
Bullet-Head Hopper
SRI Yellow Hopper
Gartside Pheasant Hopper
Schroeder's Parachute Hopper
Jacklin's Hopper
SRI Hi-Vis Cricket
Natural Mouserat
Madam X
Turck's Tan Tarantula
Western Yellow Drake
Gray Drake
SRI Irresistible Yellow Stimulator
MMA's Super Foam Trude

J.B.'s Tan Caddis Pupa
Olive Sparkle Soft-Hackle
Beadhead Olive Rabbit Emerger
Rod's Beadhead Amber Emerger
Rod's Beadhead Olive Emerger
Beadhead Fox Squirrel Nymph
Tom's Gray-Olive Beadhead Flymph
Lepage's Beadhead Olive Nymph
Olive Bunny Bug Streamer
Drowned Mouserat
Western Lite Spruce Feather Streamer
Yellow Marabou Muddler
Dark Olive Bead-A-Bugger
Partridge and Orange Soft-Hackle
SRI Black Squirrel Nymph

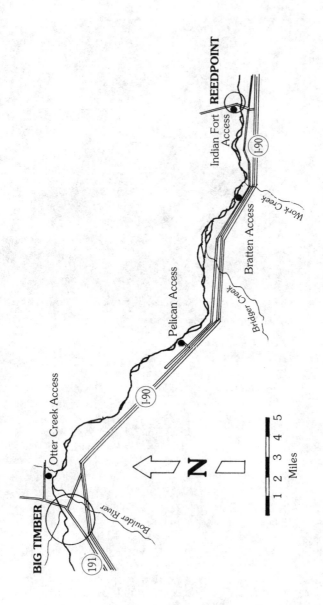

Big Timber to Reedpoint

9

Big Timber to Reedpoint

Chief Red Cloud, a Lakota Indian, was supposed to have hunted with his warriors in the area of the "big timbers." The Lakota apparently made life a little uncomfortable for the early white men who came seeking gold in Paradise Valley. Imagine, if you will, while floating down this stretch of river, coming around a bend and being confronted by a hunting party of hostile Lakota warriors—warriors who felt they had proprietorial rights to the land and took offense to infringements upon those rights. As it turns out, they had every reason to feel indignation at what they surely thought was criminal trespass. It isn't too difficult to imagine what it must have been like in those bygone days while floating the river today. The landscape and the soothing effects of the river lend themselves to this kind of reverie.

The Lakota had the right idea about using Big Timber as a staging area for their sporting activities, and many visiting anglers should take a hint. Big Timber is a small western town with all the flavor of days gone by—old historic hotels, taverns, and a cowboy spirit. Quaint as it may seem, it has all the amenities of a larger town, some of which may be even better. The Grand Hotel has one of the finest restaurants in the state, if not the West, and the rooms have been renovated to turn-of-the-century elegance. It is quite the place to stay and dine or toss back a few in the saloon. Rub shoulders with the "beautiful" people, because this has evolved into an area many famous movie, television, and artistic celebrities have chosen to call home, if only on a part-time basis.

There is a fly shop and guide service in town as well as a shuttle service. Eateries abound, as do other forms of lodging, and there are a couple of unusual taverns that should be appreciated. Using Big Timber as home base has some advantages: access to this section of river isn't time-consuming; there is other water besides the Yellowstone, like the Boulder River, to explore and fish; and there are all kinds of scenic and historical jaunts to take when not fishing. But fishing is why you're here, so let's get to it.

This stretch of the river is the beginning of a transitional area between the brawling mountain river upstream and the slow warmwater fishery farther on downstream. It has been said that this portion of river is the most underused quality fishery in the state of Montana. The angling pressure does decrease as one moves farther downstream. It is the kind of water that has a fish in every spot that looks like it should hold a fish. That's the neat aspect of this section—because it is so big and underfished, the fish are not used to seeing many flies and are willing to take a properly placed imitation. There is a fair amount of people who spin-fish this section, but not a heck of a lot of fly fishermen. This is a section where one can expect to see a jet sled or two. Annoying as they are, they are there to share the water, and we'll all have to live with it.

The scenery begins to change as we get away from the mountains and into rolling hills. The floats are along ranch bottoms, and herds of cattle can be seen grazing in the fields. Interestingly, many of the islands have good deer populations all along the entire river, as does this section, but this lower portion has a noticeable shift in the species of deer. Most of the upstream islands abound with white-tailed deer, some of them quite large and heavily antlered, but this portion seems to have mostly mule deer bounding around. There are all kinds of wildlife along the banks, and if you're lucky enough to come across some of the river otters, stop and enjoy their antics. This section takes on the appearance of a waterfowl sanctuary in the autumn as it teems with assorted ducks and geese. A late afternoon or early-evening float in the fall, when the light is low and rich, with geese flying overhead and deer sneaking out for a drink of river water, is as rewarding an experience as anyone is likely to have. All this with good fishing and relative solitude. What more can a guy ask for?

Water Characteristics

This is the section where the river changes, but not in an overt way. It isn't noticeable at first, and it's not until you're on it for a while that the changes become apparent. The riffles are longer than the ones farther upstream, as are the pools, which are much deeper. The river's width is broader here as it slowly becomes a wide expanse. The changes are slow and gradual; a person floating the entire river would only notice these changes if he thought about them. More and more tributaries empty their contents into the Yellowstone, increasing its flow and making it a much larger river than the upstream portions. Because these tributaries have become numerous, this section becomes fishable much later than the upstream parts because early-summer flows are quite heavy and powerful. This is a section of river that is far more suitable to the floating angler than the wading angler because the main channel is much broader and many of the sections are long rolling stretches. That doesn't mean the river is unwadeable. It is very wadeable in spots, especially where the river braids around the numerous islands, but the distances between this area become greater and greater as we go downstream. There are few access points, and they are spaced a distance apart. Most of the land bordering the river is private and hard to reach.

The water does, however, have a fair amount of character, but there are longer distances between these productive areas. Everything seems to be stretched out down here, with very long riffles, glides, and deep, slow pools. The river does twist and turn along its course, and many islands force it to braid, especially down toward Reedpoint. These braided areas have all the water types any fly fisherman needs for any style of fishing. The inside bends, current edges, converging currents, runs, and small pools created in these channels are a joy to fish. There are excellent banks to cast to, and some really unusual rock formations with springs seeping out of

Typical bankside formations in this stretch of the river.

them along the way. Also, there are many places that have submerged gravel bars running quite a distance midstream, reminiscent
of the Buffalo Ford area in Yellowstone National Park. When there
is a hatch on, many trout will move to these bars to sip insects off
the surface. It almost seems a bit weird to anchor so far out in the
river and get out to wade to these feeding fish.

Some of the shelving-rock formations in the river are just under
the surface, and floating anglers have to be alert for them. (It is a bit
surprising to have your boat bottom out when you're not expecting
it.) These formations can usually be found on outside bends of the
river. Usually they're not dangerous, but if a boat happens to be side-
ways and the current strong, there is a good chance of being
swamped. Heads up.

The fly fisherman who likes to throw shooting heads will love the
long deep pools found in this stretch. It does have some fabulous
streamer water that holds some truly large trout. The best thing

about these pools is that you can have them all to yourself and know for sure that the trout are not used to seeing streamers on a daily basis. Because of the lack of fishing pressure and their depth, these pools can fish well at any time of the season, not just during the fall when we are accustomed to fishing streamers. It's nice to have that kind of almost naive fishing available—it tends to add to the overall quality of the area.

In many places there are long slow glides that challenge the dry-fly enthusiast. When a hatch is on, the trout line up where current tongues funnel insects to them and seem easy targets to the floating angler. Those funneling current tongues wreak havoc on a drag-free presentation, and some thoughtful mending or approach angles need to be mentally worked out before a cast is made. It is often nearly impossible to approach these fish from the bank because they are fairly spooky and some of the banks are just too deep to allow an angler to wade into position for a good presentation. A floating fisherman needs to be as stealthy as any spring-creek fisherman lest the trout be put down by bow waves, unusual noises, or sloppy casts. It is quite challenging and extremely rewarding when a hook-up finally does happen. One would think that, in an area that doesn't see many fishermen and where the fish haven't been pressured to any extent, they would not be as wary as they are. Once these fish are put down they usually stay down, at least longer than we are willing to wait.

Accessibility

Access is somewhat limited on this twenty-five-or-so-mile section of river, unlike many of the upstream portions. However, the access sites do break the river into relatively even sections, allowing floaters to customize to a degree or to cover this entire section in equal parts. The wading fisher will only be able to access the river at these sites, and that limits his ability to cover water. Wading to the opposite side of the river is nearly impossible, and this again limits the walking fisherman. This wide expanse of river is more suitable to the floating angler, who has the mobility to cover any bank or area that looks good.

The first access downriver from the Otter Creek site is about twelve miles away, a short way past the tiny town of Greycliff. It is called the Pelican access. This and the other accesses are off a service road that runs along the south side of the river, paralleling the interstate. Pelican has rest-room facilities, allows camping, and has a good concrete ramp to launch from. There are no tables or barbecue grills. In very low water, a floating angler has to get out of the boat and walk it to the ramp because the water is just too shallow. This is not the case in normal-flow years.

Another eight miles downriver is the Bratten access site. Eight miles is a comfortable distance to float and fish because it allows an angler time to get out and wade to good water or cover rising fish without having to worry about making time up somewhere else in the float. This site was apparently named after a member of George Rogers Clark's party, a private who served as a blacksmith and hunter. This site does have handicapped-accessible rest rooms, allows camping, and has a decent ramp to launch from.

The next access down is the Indian Fort access, which was probably named after some of the old Indian-built log fortifications that Clark noted in his journals. It's about five miles down from the Bratten access and is the end of the road for this section. This five miles may seem like a relatively short float, but it has some of the most interesting water in this stretch. Before the river reaches Reedpoint and the Indian Fort access, it travels through some braided channels. These channels are worth the time and effort to stop and fish because there is everything one needs in water types. An entire day could be spent in these channels alone. A wading fisher could hike back upstream to these channels and have all the fishing desired.

The Indian Fort access has a good concrete ramp facility, allows camping, and has rest rooms. Most people who float to Reedpoint bypass this access and continue to an unofficial access near the bridge that crosses the river. A large, sandy, gently sloping bank is all there is, but it's suitable for taking out a drift boat or other craft. The reason for this extended float is that there is a good riprap bank

that extends down from the Indian Fort access and a very good riffle that one would miss by taking out at Indian Fort. This riprap bank
is always good for a few last fish before taking out, and the riffle
should be stopped at and fished, especially if no one else is there.

Although there are limited access sites on this section of river,
they are enough to fully cover the water. The wading angler may
have a tougher time here than on other sections, but he still can
have plenty of good fishing. He just won't be able to cover the water as he may want to. With longer distances between good holding
water, the wading fisherman will just have to work a little harder and
walk a little farther. However, we have been at these access points
when fish have been actively rising right in front of the ramp.

The Fish

This is a section that begins to see a decline in trout populations,
and that will continue as we float even farther down the river. The
good news is that, even though this section doesn't have the average trout per mile that the upper stretches have, they are concentrated in the water that has the character we normally associate with
holding fish. The long stretches of water that look unproductive are,
in reality, unproductive. That doesn't mean they shouldn't be fished,
because some of this deep, slow, gliding water holds some monster
brown trout that cruise around like submarines. Here a trophy fish
(five pounds or better) can make a fly fisher's day. Of course, one
may fish these sections hard with no results, but then again one may
get lucky and nail an extremely good wallhanger.

Most of the trout in this section are brown trout, but there still
are good numbers of rainbows and cutthroats. The habitat is ideally
suited to brown trout, and especially large brown trout. The population breakdown is probably like the immediate upper section: fifty
percent browns, thirty percent rainbows, and twenty percent cutthroats. We will begin to lose the cutthroats as we move farther
down the river, but they are doing all right in this stretch. There is
enough good habitat for rainbows, especially in the long riffles and

Gary Borger with a carp taken on a fly.

channels, where there are all kinds of different water. These rainbows seem to be consistently larger than the ones farther upstream. As a matter of fact, it would be fair to say that most all the fish caught down in this stretch of river are on the average consistently larger than those farther up. The really nice thing is that these fish are underfished and will readily take a fly that's properly presented.

The burbot and goldeye begin to appear a little more often; however, the fly fisherman would more than likely not see any in this section. The common carp makes an appearance down here and increases in number the farther down we get. A good-sized carp on a fly rod is a blast, and we hardly ever pass up the opportunity to fish for them when we have the chance. It's one of those addictions we are often afflicted with.

It is easy to see that the river is about to change as we float closer to Billings.

Hatch Chart for Big Timber to Reedpoint

Stoneflies
Yellow sally
(*Isoperla mormona*)   Size: #14–#16   July 10 to August 15
Olive/brown stone
(*Isogenus tostonus*)   Size: #10–#12   July 1 to August 15
Olive stone
(*Isogenus elongatus*)   Size: #12–#14   July 15 to August 15
Little olive stone
(*Alloperla signata*)   Size: #14–#16   August 10 to August 20
Giant western golden stone
(*Claassenia sabulosa*)   Size: #2–#6   August 1 to September 10

Caddisflies
Early grannom
(*Brachycentrus occidentalis*) Size: #12–#16   April 15 to May 15
Spotted sedge
(*Hydropsyche cockerelli*)   Size: #12–#16   August 15 to October 20
Little brown sedge
(*Lepidostoma veleda*)   Size: #14–#18   July 10 to August 10
American grannom
(*Brachycentrus americanus*) Size: #12–#16   July 10 to August 30

Long horn sedge
  (*Oecetis avara*)   Size: #12–#16   July 1 to August 1
Spotted sedge
  (*Hydropsyche occidentalis*) Size: #10–#12   June 25 to July 25
Plain brown sedge
  (*Lepidostoma pluviale*)   Size: #14–#18   July 1 to July 31
Little sister sedge
  (*Cheumatopsyche campyla*) Size: #14–#16   July 20 to September 15

Mayflies
Western green drake
  (*Drunella grandis*)   Size: #10–#12   June 25 to July 15
Western march brown
  (*Rhithrogena morrisoni*)   Size: #14–#16   April 15 to May 15
Pale morning dun
  (*Ephemerella inermis*)   Size: #16–#20   July 20 to September 1
Western black quill
  (*Rhithrogena undulata*)   Size: #12–#14   July 10 to August 15
Western yellow drake
  (*Heptagenia elegantula*) Size: #14–#16   July 20 to September 20
Blue-winged olive
  (*Baetis tricaudatus*)   Size: #18–#20   March 10 to April 20,
                                     September 15 to November 10
Trico (*Tricorythodes minutus*) Size: #18–#22   August 15 to October 10
White fly
  (*Ephoron album*)   Size: #12–#14   August 20 to October 15
Ghost fly
  (*Traverella albertana*)   Size: #10–#12   August 15 to October 15

Terrestrials
Grasshoppers (Acrididae)   Size: #8–#14   July 20 to October 15
Crickets (Gryllidae)   Size: #12–#14   August 1 to September 30
Black ants (Formicidae)   Size: #16–#22   July 15 to September 30
Cinnamon ants (Formicidae) Size: #18–#20   August 20 to September 20
Black beetle (Coleoptera)   Size: #12–#18   July 15 to August 15

Other Important Hatches and Food Forms
Midge (Chironomidae)   Size: #16–#24   February 15 to April 20,
                                     September 20 to November 10
Leeches (Hirudinea)   Size: #2–#10   July 15 to October 1
Snails (Gastropoda)   Size: #12   August 15 to September 30
Damselfly nymphs (Zygoptera) Size: #8–#14   July 20 to September 1
Dragonfly nymphs (Odonata) Size: #6–#10   July 20 to September 1

Minnows

Mottled sculpin		
(*Cottus bairdi*)	Size: 2–8	All year
Whitefish minnow		
(*Prosopium williamsoni*)	Size: 2–10	All year
Long-nose dace minnow		
(*Rhinichthys cataractae*)	Size: 2–10	All year
Long-nose sucker minnow		
(*Catostomus catostomus*)	Size: 2–10	All year
Mountain sucker minnow		
(*Catostomus platyrhynchus*)	Size: 2–10	All year

Seasonal Changes: The Fishing

The fishing in this stretch is excellent; however, due to the number of tributaries entering the river, this section is rarely fishable until mid-July. On the plus side, the hatches here continue into October, allowing good dry-fly fishing long after it has ended or tapered off on some of the upper sections. The Trico, yellow drakes, white fly, and ghost fly hatches have to be seen to be believed. This is perhaps some of the finest hatch fishing on the river. This section of river is little known and receives very little attention from fly fishers.

Winter: Mid-November to February

This section of the river sees very little activity during the winter months with the exception of the odd local angler who wanders into one of the access sites. During late November anglers can still find a few fish working midges and maybe even a few blue-winged olives. The nymphing can be fair during this same time period. During December and January the fishing is at the mercy of the weather and this section rarely sees an angler then. During February there are always a few warm days, and those who venture out to the access site can enjoy some good nymphing opportunities and encounter a few midges. If the warm spell in February is too extensive, the river can actually rise and discolor slightly.

Fishing the Trico spinner fall in the area between Bratten and Reedpoint.

Spring: March to Runoff

Even in the spring, most anglers ignore this section of the river. During March anglers will encounter heavy midge hatches as well as the blue-winged olives. During this time the nymphing and streamer fishing can be very good. In April we see hatches of western march browns and early grannom caddis. We can tell you that we have spent days on this section of river during the spring and have had the river to ourselves or have seen just a few anglers scattered at the access points. The river will go out due to the annual runoff around May 10 and will be high and unfishable until sometime in July.

Early Summer: June and July

June is a total wash; seldom is this section of the river fishable during the month. As a matter of fact, we generally find that this section of river doesn't become fishable until about mid-July. This is due to everything that happens upriver, in addition to tributary streams.

All these streams have to drop and clear before the Yellowstone will. However, once the angler can make it back to the river there are plenty of hatches and lots of activity. During the last half of July the angler can encounter yellow sally stones, medium olive/brown stones, olive stones, and little olive stones. There are also lots of caddis, starting with the little brown sedge, American grannom, long horn sedge, spotted sedge, plain brown sedge, and little sister sedge. What this means to the angler is that dry-nymph combinations are deadly. We like to fish a Stimulator-type fly that will imitate either caddis or stoneflies, and then we fish a beadhead caddis emerger about three feet behind the dry.

Due to the river conditions we generally miss the green drakes; however, the angler will encounter hatches of the western black quill along with the start of the pale morning dun and the western yellow drakes. As you can see, the angler wishing to spend a few days here in late July will have plenty to keep him occupied.

Late Summer: August to Mid-September

This is the time where this section of river will receive the greatest number of anglers, and that's not saying much. In August, anglers will see many of the caddis hatches continue, as well as the western yellow drake and the pale morning dun hatches. Due to the limited number of days we get to spend on this section, we would not be surprised to find that there are hatches we know nothing about. During this time the angler will also see the giant western golden stone and of course the hoppers. By mid-August the Tricos appear. Mid–August until mid-September is as good as it gets. Our favorite section to fish the Tricos is the Bratten-to-Reedpoint stretch. In this section there are plenty of flats and channels and the fishing just doesn't come any better.

Now after reading this, you might think that it is all dry-fly fishing on this section of the river. Nothing could be further from the truth. The nymph and streamer fishing can be done at any time of the season with good results. When fishing dry flies, you will mostly take rainbows, cutthroats, and smaller browns. If you want big browns, you need to be fishing for them. On occasion we have fished big dry mice imitations right at dark on this section and had some scary encounters with larger browns. During the day the angler who will use streamers can generally move a couple of nice fish.

Fall: Mid-September to Mid-November

The fall is a great time to fish this section of the river. The crowds of summer have left. You often find during the week that you will have the river to yourself. On weekends you see a few more spin fishers, but it is never crowded. During mid- to late September the Trico hatches continue and the blue-winged olives return. However the two most notable species are the white fly and the ghost fly. These are larger mayflies, and when they hatch in numbers, everything is up feeding on them. Later in the fall the midges return as other hatches taper off and disappear for the year. Also, fall means that the brown trout are starting to spawn, and the talk often brings to mind large flies and big fish. But each year we meet many anglers who are frustrated and fishless simply because they are fishing the imitation in the wrong places, using tackle that doesn't allow for a proper presentation.

There are many times of the year when streamers are effective, but the angler must understand why the trout take streamers and where and how to effectively present them. Gaining an understanding of the trout, tackle, and presentation methods needed for successful streamer fishing takes focus and organization. Therefore, we will explain how we use the "Formula for Success" to master the angling skills and gain the knowledge necessary to be successful streamer-fly fishers throughout the year.

Research

The angler who desires to become a more knowledgeable and skilled streamer-fly fisher should first research the topic by reviewing books, videos, and magazine articles dealing with streamer fishing. Talk with fly shops, guides, and angling friends who successfully fish streamers with an eye toward learning what tackle, patterns, and presentation methods are used with success. Then you can properly prepare and obtain the tackle and patterns and can practice and master any presentation skills needed.

For those looking for information on streamer fishing, we suggest you review 3M's *Fly Fishing For Trout*, with Gary Borger. There is also a section on streamer fishing in 3M's *Advanced Strategies for Selective Trout,* with Doug Swisher. In this video, pay close attention to the line control and mending Doug uses to control the angle and plane of the presentation.

If you need to review a certain casting method, we suggest reviewing 3M's *Basic Fly Casting* or *Advanced Fly Casting,* with Doug Swisher. We also suggest that the prospective streamer-fly fisher review 3M's *Fly Fishing for Pacific Steelhead* and *Advanced Fly Fishing for Pacific Steelhead,* with Lani Waller. These two tapes hold a wealth of information that can be applied to streamer fishing for spawning trout; for instance, properly fighting larger fish, mending and line control used in fishing various lines, and some of the water-reading techniques will apply to streamer fishing.

Once the angler has gained a basic knowledge of the tackle, patterns, and presentation method used, then it is time to study the trout.

The Trout

The study of the trout has to be broken down into species; each species will move to the streamer differently. The brown trout is the most important species in this section of the river for streamer fishing; therefore, we will concentrate on them and just briefly discuss rainbows and cutthroat trout. Now, there is no sense in listing the scientific name for the brown trout as the taxonomy group will more than likely change it next year. Therefore, to avoid confusion we will just refer to it as "brown trout."

During the greater part of the year a brown trout will establish a territory, in which it will live and feed. It will aggressively defend this area against all comers. This is one of the reasons the trout takes the streamer. Due to the streamer's minnowlike shape, the brown attacks because it is defending the home stand. Brown trout are very predacious and feed actively on aquatic insects, terrestrials, minnows, crayfish, and even smaller trout if they are unwary! The brown trout prefers the shaded banks, undercut banks, and deep pools and tends to prefer overcast to bright days when surface-feeding. Territories are established based on the size and strength of the trout. Therefore, the fast water will generally hold the largest trout. So it is very important that the prospective streamer-fly fisher learns how to read water and understand where the trout will be.

The habits of the brown trout and the various reasons why streamers are taken remain fairly constant throughout the year, except during the spawning season. At this time the browns will leave their territories and start to gather in the deep pools to migrate to their spawning area. This gathering will start as much as sixty days prior to the actual spawning. During this migration period the browns will continue to feed. Although they won't expend much energy to chase a minnow, they seldom turn down an easy meal. This makes line control, fly speed, angle and depth of presentation very important to the angler. During the two- to three-week period prior to and during actual spawning, the brown's food intake drops to almost zero. But during this time streamers are still very effective because the browns become very protective of their redds.

Brown trout spawn in the Yellowstone River, and in this section they will start to move and gather by the third week of September.

The rainbow trout do limited spawning in the main stem of the Yellowstone—they are primarily tributary spawners. The rainbow trout is not as aggressive or as territorial as the brown. *Bows* are in fact very efficient insect eaters and don't search for the larger food forms as often as do the browns. This is not to say that they don't or won't eat minnows, but often this will depend on the other food sources available. During the spawning period they go through the same cycle as do browns and at that time can become very aggressive. Larger rainbows will opportunistically follow other species of spawning fish to feed on the eggs. Rainbows are spring spawners: their spawning takes place from mid-March to the first of May.

Of all the trout, cutthroats seem to feed on minnows the least, but there are times when a few can be taken. We have always found that white streamer imitations can be very effective on cutthroats during the first half of September. Often it is the larger cutthroat an angler will pick up on streamers. During the fall, as the insect activity declines, the cutthroat will become very aggressive and feed on minnow life forms. They, like all trout, become very aggressive during their spawning cycle, which takes place from mid-May through June. The cutthroats here on this section of the Yellowstone are entirely tributary spawners, and do not use the main river at all.

Once the angler has established an understanding of how, why, and where the various species of trout are feeding on minnows, proper selection of tackle, patterns, and presentation methods can be made for the angling situation at hand, thus ensuring a greater success rate.

During the summer season the trout are back to holding and feeding in established territories and are behaving in a normal manner. During this time of the year we believe trout take streamers for three main reasons: *hunger, anger, and curiosity.* The first step in solving this riddle is observation on the part of the angler: observing a situation and being able to select the right tackle, pattern, and presentation methods to move the trout.

One of the methods we have used with a great deal of success is called the "downstream flutter." This method is used to fish through an area that holds some fairly large boulders that offer cover. We are most often using a floating line when fishing this method. We cast downstream and let the fly swing in behind the boulder and keep working back and forth in the current pocket. We will put on a copper sleeve about four inches above the fly and then work the rod tip up and down. The additional weight and the movement of the rod tip will imitate the dancing and darting of the natural minnow. Be careful—the strikes can be very savage.

Another method that we use in the summer is the direct result of observation. One afternoon while dry-fly fishing, we noticed several minnows darting and skipping across the surface in the tail of the pool we were working. We never saw what was causing this commotion, but we realized that minnows were being chased by a larger trout. We selected a small unweighted Muddler Minnow and soaked it for a minute or two before using it. This allowed the fly to sink three or four inches under the film, and then we could skitter it on the surface by simply raising the rod tip while stripping in the line. We were able to take several nice rainbows with this method. These trout were chasing a school of

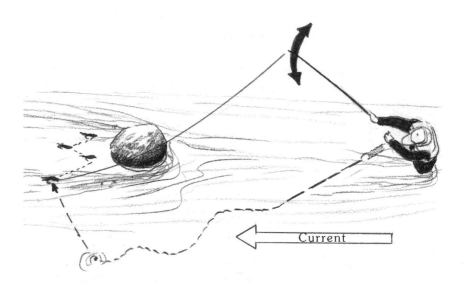

Downstream flutter

1. Cast to side of boulder;
2. Allow the fly to swing in behind the rock;
3. Raise and lower the rod so the fly works back and forth behind the rock.

minnows they had herded into the tail of the pool. We have also used this method employing various types of uniform sink lines.

Here on the Yellowstone the sculpin minnow, which looks like a baby bullhead, is one of the prime foods for larger brown trout. Sculpins, unlike most fish, have no swim bladder, so when they get swept away by the current they will dead-drift along until the current brings them close to the bottom, and then they will dart behind a rock or other obstruction. In deep slow pools they will dart six to ten inches, then rest. Often we have taken browns using sculpin imitations in many different water types by employing a dead-drift technique or a dead-drift-and-dart technique. The key is choosing the right type of fly line that allows you to present the fly at the proper depth and angle.

Fall Fishing with Shooting Heads

As the water temperatures begin to drop and the days begin to grow shorter, the brown trout will leave their established territories

Playing a trout.

and start to collect in the pools and runs in preparation for the annual spawning run. To effectively cover the water in these areas the angler should use full-sinking shooting-taper fly lines. We prefer the Wet Cel Hi-Speed Hi-D lines, in 9-, 10-, or 11-weight, depending on the flows. The rods used are powerful casting tools—our favorite is the Orvis Power Matrix 9010 (nine feet for 10-weight). The reel should have a good smooth drag system and be capable of holding at least 150 yards of backing and 200 feet of Amnesia shooting line. The shooting tapers allow the angler to thoroughly cover the water with both the distance of the cast and the depth of the presentation.

These brown trout are holding in deep water, and the angler must get the imitation down to their level and keep it there. Because the browns are moving, they can, and will, be found in all sections of the pool. The angler must learn how to recognize the pool and be prepared to thoroughly cover the water.

The method that we use is to start at the head of the pool and work all the way through to the tail. By the end of the second pool you will have a good idea where the trout will be holding in the pools on that day. For the rest of the day, spend your time working the most productive sections. The actual fishing method is to start at the head of the pool and cast across and slightly up, mend the shooting line immediately, drop the rod tip, follow the progress of the drift, and begin the retrieve. We suggest that you work the imitation back until the butt of the shooting taper is at the tip of the rod, then move down five paces and do it again, until you have covered the pool.

The two casting techniques the angler must master to effectively fish the tapers are the single and double hauls. These casting methods allow the angler to generate line speed that allows for longer casts, which means the angler can cover as much of the pool as possible. The speed of the retrieve will depend on the water temperature, depth of the water, and speed of the current. There is no set of rules to follow, but here are a few guidelines that work for us.

When the water temperature is between fifty and fifty-eight degrees, we will use a fairly active retrieve. As the water temperature drops to the forty-two- to fifty-degree range we will slow the retrieve down to a crawl. Once the water temperature drops below forty-two, we will dead-drift the imitation and bounce the rod tip to impart a small amount of movement to the imitation.

There is a small group of hard-core shooting-head anglers on the Yellowstone. This type of fishing isn't for everyone. However, there are anglers, like Jay Swartzwelter, of Boulder, Colorado, who have traveled to fish the Yellowstone during the fall for over twenty-five years, seldom missing a year. Why? Because of the scenic beauty of the river, the uncrowded fishing conditions, and the lure of trophy trout.

Locally Effective Patterns

Translucent Beadhead Emerger

Hook:	Tiemco 2457, sizes 12–16
Bead:	Gold
Thread:	Olive
Tail:	Hungarian partridge soft-hackle fibers
Abdomen:	Lime green Krystal Flash as underwrapping; light blue dun larva lace (midge lace) wrapped over Krystal Flash
Thorax:	Olive-brown dubbing
Wing:	White Z-lon
Hackle:	Hungarian partridge soft-hackle

PR Big-Eyed Bugger

Hook:	Tiemco 5263, sizes 2–10
Eyes:	Chromed-lead eyes
Thread:	Brown
Tail:	Brown marabou over yellow marabou
Body:	Brown Krystal Chenille
Hackle:	Brown and yellow, palmered
Legs:	Two pairs yellow rubber legs

Krystal X Trude

Hook:	Tiemco 2312, sizes 10–18
Thread:	Brown
Tail:	Golden pheasant tips
Body:	Peacock herl
Underwing:	White calf tail
Wing:	Pearl Krystal Flash
Hackle:	Brown
Legs:	White rubber legs

Tom's Lite Spruce Streamer

Hook:	Tiemco 9394, sizes 2–8
Thread:	Hot red
Body:	Red Ultra Chenille
Wings:	Four silver badger hackles, matched two per side
First topping:	Six strands of pearl Krystal Flash
Second topping:	Black marabou
Cheeks:	Jungle cock (optional)
Collar:	Two or three silver badger hackles

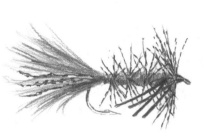

Tom's Black Sparkle Sap-Sucker

Hook:	Tiemco 5262, sizes 2–8
Thread:	Black
Tails:	Black marabou with three strands of black Krystal Flash per side
Body:	Black Krystal Chenille
Legs:	Eight black rubber strands, four per side, in two groups of two
Hackle:	Grizzly dyed black, palmered

Tom's Black Girdle Bugger

Hook:	Tiemco 700, sizes 1/0–8
Thread:	Black
Tails:	Black marabou, with one strand of white tied in on each side
Rib:	Two or three strands of pearl Krystal Flash
Legs:	Six strands of white rubber, three per side
Body:	Black chenille
Wings:	Black marabou
Topping:	Three strands of pearl Krystal Flash
Collar:	Grizzly hackle, dyed black

Other Effective Patterns

Besides all of the general attractor-type patterns—dry, wet, and streamers—or those listed in the text, anglers should also consider imitations from the following list:

Olive Sawyer Pheasant Tail Nymph
Black Sawyer Pheasant Tail Nymph
Brown Mottled Sculpin Bugger
Brown Diving Woolly Bugger
Whit's Olive Damsel Nymph
Brown Diving Damsel Nymph
Tom's Olive Beadhead Damsel
Whit's Brown Dragon Nymph
Yellow-Bellied Sapsucker
Copper Sparkle Bugger
Olive Yellowstone Sculpin
Black Super Collider
Gray Sparkle Sculpin
Olive Zonker
Whit Gold Multicolored Marabou Muddler
Whit's Hare Water Pup Olive

Harrop's CDC Trico Nymph
Trico Para-Nymph Emerger
Harrop's Trico Hairwing Dun
Tom's Trico Stillborn/Spinner
CDC Trico Spinner
Western Yellow Drake
Western Gray Drake
Yellow Foam Hopper
Dave's Hopper
Mouserat
Yellow Sally
White Wulff
White Drake
Brown Bunny Bug
Clouser's Deep Minnow

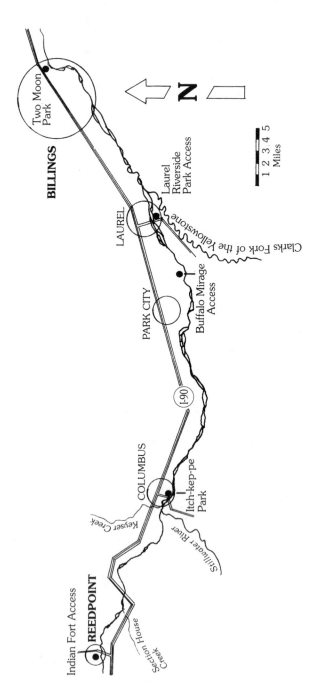

Reedpoint to Billings

10

Reedpoint to Billings

While it would be fair to say that the section of river upstream of Reedpoint is the forgotten fishery, it would also be fair to say that the section between Reedpoint and Billings is the unexplored fishery. Sure, anglers have been fishing this section since white men first appeared here, but little is really known when it comes to the fly fishing. Insects appear here that are not found on the upper stretches, as do other species of fish, and yet fly fishing is not the main item down here. When one thinks of fly fishing the Yellowstone River one thinks of large brown trout and the Yellowstone cutthroat sipping insects off the surface in a large, clear, brawling mountain river—not of walleye, sauger, carp, and catfish.

This is an unexplored fishery for many reasons, but mostly because it is a sixty-six-mile stretch with very limited access. The stretch from Reedpoint to Columbus covers twenty-one miles—that's a very long way just to float, let alone fish properly. There may be anglers who either live along the river or have some private access and really know and understand a small piece of water, but it is difficult for the average Joe to get to learn this stretch on an intimate basis. The stretches of water on the upper river are easier to fish and learn because the distances are relatively short and they are convenient to access, so anglers fish there often and with diligence. It is another story down here. Without the ability to use the fishery repeatedly and spend the necessary time on the water, it is very tough for any one person to "know" this water. Anglers who have a bad day on this section, for whatever reason, very often are reluctant to come back, even though it may have been one of those days when the fish just weren't active. Those of us who fly fish tend to fish the areas we know and have had success. We're all for exploration unless it severely cuts into our fishing—a trip here or there seems to be adequate. Most people who fly fish just do not have the time to spend exploring. Guides tend to stick with areas they know because it's in their best interests to get their clients into fish, and they have little free time for exploration.

This sixty-six-mile section is really two different sections, with the confluence of the Clark's Fork a watery dividing line. The upper reach is still a transition zone with an emphasis on trout, while the lower reach from the Clark's Fork down is really the beginning of the warmwater fishery that typifies the rest of the river. The beginning not because the water turns murky or slows to a snail's pace but rather because the number of other fish species begins to increase. The mouth of the Big Horn River, downstream of Billings, is really the actual beginning of the warmwater fishery. We have separated this stretch because of the variety of fish that can be caught from the Clark's Fork down, not because it lacks trout.

The first fifty-two miles of this section is still an excellent trout fishery and contains some absolute hogs—rainbows as large as twelve pounds and brown trout in the nine-pound class have been reported. Although the trout do not appear in the same numbers as in the upper river, they appear in numbers enough to satisfy any fly fisherman. Even in the stretch from the Clark's Fork down, trout appear in enough numbers that an angler could wade-fish within the city of Billings and still "limit out," if he so desired. We have been hearing reports of an increase in the trout populations in the Billings area, but this may be due in part to an increase in fly fishers actually fishing for trout down there.

This entire stretch of water enables the fly fisher to "push the envelope" of what he may be accustomed to. It's a place to explore not only the water but the life within it and the fishing opportunities and techniques, not just for trout but for other species as well. A variety of insects hatch here that don't appear on the upper sections, but the average fly fisherman knows little about them. Here is the opportunity to spend time pushing the envelope of learning. There are species of fish that also don't appear on the upper river. How many anglers actually fly-fish for walleye? Some of our friends do and love it. What about carp or catfish? We realize that we may be pushing the envelope of your tolerance, but the fact is that this section of river offers opportunities that are relatively rare in our river systems. How often can a guy find a flat with bugs hatching and a variety of fish species feeding on them?

Water Characteristics

This huge section of river has all the water characteristics anyone could want, and some are even on a grand scale. As we have moved downriver, more tributaries have emptied more water into the system and created a rather large river. This section sees a few rapids that can test the skills of a novice oarsman, so care should be taken. Diversion dams become an occasional hazard and need to be avoided. There are some rather sharp bends in the river that can force a boat against rocks, especially when the flows are high and powerful. This section can be deceptive because the flows are so powerful yet appear to be mild. A fair amount of additional water has entered the system through the tributaries, some of which are rivers in their own right and not just trickle streams. Consider that the average stream flow at Billings toward the end of June approaches the twenty thousand cubic feet per second mark—that's a lot of water. The end of July sees about ten thousand cfs and September sees about thirty-five hundred cfs. This kind of water should not be underestimated when floating or wading; it's a power that should be respected.

This entire section has a number of islands, and in some areas some complex braiding through those islands. This makes for some excellent water characteristics, with current edges, inside bends, converging currents, and pockets. One could literally spend months fishing all the available channels and still not cover them all. Their presence not only makes for good fishing opportunities but also poses a threat in the form of hazards. It's not a good thing to decide to float down a narrow channel only to find it obstructed. Drift boats have been known to be capsized by these obstructions. At the very least, it can ruin a perfectly good day to have to drag your boat up and over an obstruction or to have to walk it back to the head of a channel. If you are unfamiliar with this section, stick to the channel you think is the main stem; then, you can anchor or tie your boat up and walk to the side channels and fish. Speaking of which, we both have seen our drift boats begin to float away from us even though we thought they were secured along the shore. It is not a pleasant sight. If at all possible, tie your boat to something secure, such as a tree, because a good gust of wind may be all that is needed to force the boat into the water to float away by itself. Dropping anchor may not be enough to hold the boat in place, and once the heavy current catches it, well, you can figure out the rest.

This section has a number of riprap banks with those little hidey-hole pockets that fish hang out in. There are long banks with fair-sized boulders that also act as holding areas for trout. Some of these banks are in sections with bluffs overlooking the river. There are very long riffled areas and equally long pools, some of which are fairly deep, at least deeper than the average fly fisherman can reach without specialized gear. Some of these pools and runs are excellent water for the streamer fisherman to throw shooting heads into, and they can hold some monstrous trout.

The force of the water during runoff shifts much of the bottom around in certain areas and continually creates new gravel bars from year to year. These gravel bars are excellent places to find a trout or two, especially in the quieter water at the downstream end of the bar where the currents converge. Fish often hold along the bars where there might be a drop-off of sorts. We have taken many a good fish within inches of a gravel bar as fast water raced by it—there is an edge of slower water immediately along these bars. Some of them, especially the ones with very fast water angling away from them, have back-eddies that move at a considerable speed up the river, and they also usually hold fish right alongside. It is almost a sure bet that there will be a decent fish right in the corner pocket, where the fast water meets the bar and begins to angle away.

All the channels and riffles found along this stretch make for some good fishing in the riffle corners. Because there is so much water in this section, if an angler just fished the riffle corners and nothing else he would probably have a super day of fishing. It's the nature of trout to hang out in these riffle corners; food is constantly swept by them, and they can hold along the slower edges, picking off whatever fancies them. There is a good number of riffle corners, ranging from the very small in some of the channels to very large in the big riffles. Try using an attractor dry fly and hang a small beadhead-style nymph off it in these corners—it just may make a believer out of you.

The mouths of the many tributaries are also places that can hold quantities of trout. Besides the many creeks that flow into the Yellowstone, there are a couple of rivers: the Stillwater and the Clark's Fork. The Stillwater is used by the rainbow trout during spawning in the early spring. Good numbers of rainbows make their way up into the Stillwater at this time and eventually move back to the Yellowstone. The angler who has the opportunity to fish the river in the spring can cash in on the rainbows heading to or coming from the Stillwater; excellent fishing can be had until runoff begins. Of course, there will be those days when the weather doesn't cooperate at this time of year, but that's why television was invented.

Because of the heavy water flows, the fishing may start a little later down here than it does upstream, but that's not bad. When you count the number of drift boats floating down some of the upper sections, you may welcome the opportunity to fish some of this unexplored water. Take a few days, maybe even take your time and camp out along the way, and expand your experience a bit. There are good water and good fish. What else do we need?

Accessibility

Compared to the upper river, access is a bit of a problem down here because the distances that need to be covered are so great. It would take days to float this entire stretch—sixty-six miles is a long way by anyone's standard. The low flows of the fall or early spring add

more time to a day on the water, thus some good sections must be by-
passed. However, there are some stretches where short floats are feasible. Then there is the fact that boats with motors are allowed down
here. Although we may not be in favor of jet sleds, some of the local
fly fishermen use them to their advantage. They provide transportation to specific areas and a means of quickly getting through water that
may be unproductive. How we have often wished for a jet sled when
the wind howled from an easterly quarter. No kidding—on a twenty-
mile float with an in-your-face wind, it's all you can do just to get downriver, let alone attempt to fish. Of all the sections we have covered so
far, this is the only section where we, grudgingly, can see the feasibil-
ity of jet sleds and accept them for what they can do.

There are many unofficial access areas along this stretch that are
not mapped—a good bet would be to stop in at the few fly shops in
Billings or Columbus and ask for directions. Many of these are on
private property, and even though the landowners may not mind occasional use by a local, they may resent publicity and close their access off to everyone. There are also many bridges crossing the river
that are used as unofficial access points. Although you may not be
able to launch your boat at these bridges, you can use them to reach
the river and wade fish. We will cover all the official fishing access
sites in this section.

The first access site downriver from Reedpoint is Itch-Kep-Pe Park
in Columbus. This is the longest single stretch of river, at twenty-one
miles, that doesn't have a major access site in between. There is, however, a chance to reach the river where Sectionhouse Creek dumps
into the Yellowstone, about seven miles down from Reedpoint, but this
is not an official fishing access. Itch-Kep-Pe Park is a town park and
has all the facilities of a town park. There are many camping sites with
picnic tables and barbecue pits, and camping is allowed for up to ten
days at a time. There are handicapped-accessible rest rooms, and
fresh water is available. There is a concrete ramp to launch from about
one-half mile down from the main camping area, where there are additional spaces to camp in. All this is on the outskirts of the small community of Columbus. This section is best covered in a two-day float if
you are going to stop and fish.

The next access site down from Columbus is called Buffalo Mirage (Sportsmen's Park), located between Park City and Laurel. It's another long stretch of river at about twenty miles. This is the tricky stretch for the oarsman, with rapids and diversion dams to contend with. This section is also heavily channelized. Buffalo Mirage has a boat ramp of sorts, allows camping and has restroom facilities.

Another six (yes, we did say only six) miles downriver is the Laurel Riverside Park access. This is water that can easily be covered in a day's float or even in a half-day float if stopping and fishing is kept to a minimum. This is another of those full-blown town sites with pavilions and a caretaker. Camping is allowed on a daily fee basis for up to fourteen days. There are handicapped-accessible rest-room facilities, tables, and barbecues. The ramp is in excellent condition and is concrete. It is on this stretch of river where we really notice a change not so much in the character of the river but in the responsibilities of the river. Until this point the river supported many agricultural concerns and will continue to do so, but here is where we see its industrial responsibility as the first oil refinery appears. The river loses some of the scenic wonder—oil tanks and a labyrinth of piping somehow don't have the same appeal as mountains and hills.

Billings is our last stop on the Yellowstone, and as any city, it is full of areas from which to reach the river—a full seven miles of it as it flows along the city. Riverfront Park, Coulson Park, East Bridge, and Two Moon Park are some of the available access points. It is fairly obvious that the river here tilts toward industrial uses, and for that reason we will finish our downstream journey of the Yellowstone at the boat ramp of the first major fishing access in Billings: South Hills. This is a sixteen-mile float that sees the Clark's Fork add to the flows as it enters the Yellowstone a few miles downstream of Laurel.

The Fish

This is a section that has a mélange of fish species, especially in the lower reaches below the confluence with the Clark's Fork. Above this confluence the emphasis is on the trout fishery. There are some other species that can be taken in some impressive sizes; for instance, burbot from seven to twelve pounds. The total number of trout continues to decline as one floats through this entire stretch, and we lose the cutthroat because of the change in habitat. Rainbows are also supposed to be lost, especially from the Clark's Fork downstream, because of the warming of the water. They are a species that is less tolerant to warm water than are brown trout, but many anglers have experienced good catches of rainbow right in the city of Billings. It seems as if they are holding their own there, and may even be on the increase—but this is speculation on our part based on anglers' reports.

Rainbows have some decent habitat to live in, but much of that is concentrated in the fast aerated water of the long riffles and rapids. They have some good spawning habitat in the Stillwater River. Recent angling reports state that the Stillwater becomes a super fishery in the month of March, when the rainbows from the Yellowstone make their way into this smaller river. The sections of river near the Stillwater will have decent numbers of rainbows, and some rather large ones.

This is typical brown trout habitat; as a matter of fact, brown trout will remain in the river as far downstream as nearly to the North Dakota border. They are very tolerant of the warmer water of the downstream sections. Some huge brown trout have been reported in this stretch of river, but that shouldn't surprise anyone, because the habitat is ideal for the hogs. The addition of other species of fish and baitfish add a little variety to their diets and pounds on their skeletons.

From the mouth of the Clark's Fork downstream, some other species of gamefish appear, as do some of the baitfishes. Notably, we will see some catfish, sauger, pike, and an occasional largemouth bass. Some of the areas farther downstream have had introductions of smallmouth bass, which every so often will make an appearance in the lower reaches of this stretch. We don't necessarily think that these other species degrade the fishing opportunities, quite the contrary. It makes for an interesting day on the water to be able to catch a variety of species on a fly.

If you decide to give the lower river below Billings a try, expect

A goldeye taken on a fly.

to find a very wide variety of fish—and the wider it becomes the farther down one gets. Northern pike, freshwater drum, smallmouth bass, green sunfish, white and black crappie, yellow and black bullhead, channel catfish, and yellow perch are but some of the fish available. Even farther downstream you will encounter some prehistoric giants like the shovelnose sturgeon, pallid sturgeon, and the paddlefish. The cold, clear water of the mountainous upper river is now a slower, wider, warmer prairie river as it flows out of Montana.

Seasonal Changes: The Fishing

Much of the information we have on this section comes from interviewing local anglers in the area. Though we have fished this area, we would by no definition consider ourselves to be experts on this lower section.

Due to the number of tributaries that empty into the Yellowstone, this section of the river is rarely fishable until late July, at least for the fly fisher. The hatch chart for this section will be different from the others. With this chart we will only list the hatches we have been involved with, collected, and identified. However, we would like to point out that someone who has the interest would have a field day collecting, identifying, and charting the hatches on this section of the river. Furthermore, we would be very interested in receiving that information.

Hatch Chart for Reedpoint to Billings

Mayflies

Blue-winged olives
  (*Baetis tricaudatus*
  & others)   Sizes: #16–#22   March 10 to April 10,
                                             September 15 to November 15

Western yellow drake
  (*Heptagenia elegantula*) Sizes: #14–#16   August 1 to September 25
Tricos
  (*Tricorythodes minutus*) Sizes: #18–#22   August 15 to October 15
White fly (*Ephoron album*) Sizes: #12–#14   August 20 to October 15
Ghost fly
  (*Traverella albertana*)   Sizes: #10–#12   August 20 to October 20

Other Important Hatches and Food Forms

Midge (Chironomidae)   Sizes: #16–#24   March 10 to April 10,
                                            September 15 to November 15
Leeches (Hirudinea)   Sizes: #2–#10   August 1 to October 1
Grasshoppers (Acrididae) Sizes: #6–#14   August 1 to October 10

Caddisflies

Little sister sedge
  (*Cheumatopsyche campyla*) Sizes: #14–#16   August 1 to September 25

There are various minnows in this section that can be important to the angler. Somewhere between Reedpoint and Columbus we lose the sculpin minnows, due to changes in the habitat.

The chart lists the hatches we know about and have fished. However, we will also list some of the other insects we have collected and identified from this section; whether they are present in sufficient numbers to be of interest to the fish remains to be seen. The hatching dates are also unknown at this time. These insects are listed by scientific name only:

Mayflies
Paraleptophlebia heteronea
Paraleptophlebia bicornuta
Ephemerella margarita
Baetis parvus
Rhithrogena undulata
Brachycercus prudens

Caddisflies
Psychomyia flavida
Arctopsyche inermis
Brachycentrus occidentalis
Lepidostoma veleda
Hydropsyche oslari
Glossosoma velona

Stoneflies
Alloperla pallidula
Nemoura cinctipes
Alloperla signata
Isoperla mormona
Arcynopteryx parallela
Brachyptera nigripennis
Isogenus tostonus
Pteronacella badia
Isogenus elongatus
Isoperla patricia

Winter: Mid-November to February
Due to the storms of winter and the length of these sections, fishing at this time is done mostly at the access sites. During November nymphing in the riffle water can be good, and anglers may still find a few fish eating midges.

Spring: March to Runoff
During the month of March anglers will encounter some very heavy midge hatches on certain sections of this stretch of river. Anglers will also find the nymphing off the mouth of the Stillwater to

be exceptional. The rainbow trout use the Stillwater River as a spawning tributary and will be gathering in the Yellowstone in preparation for the annual spawning run. During March you will also find good blue-winged olive action.

Early Summer: June and July

In a normal year the fly fisher will be able to fish this section of river until late July. We have floated from Reedpoint to Columbus during low-water years around the twentieth of July. We had our best fishing by using big attractor-style dry flies, and with sink tips and double streamer-nymph combinations fished into the bank. During a normal year we expect the angler will encounter some good caddis and smaller stonefly hatches.

Late Summer: August to Mid-September

It is during this time that we have the most experience on this section of river. During August the hopper fishing can be good. We have always found that, regardless of the time of the year, streamers and leeches will bring results—and not just trout. During late August and on into September anglers will encounter western yellow drakes, Tricos, the white fly, and the ghost fly. We have seen and fished good hatches of western yellow drakes and Tricos (the stories we could tell about selective goldeye!). However, it is the incredible hatches of the ghost fly and the white fly that bring up every fish in the river—this is something you have to see to believe. More than once we tarried too long in one spot during the hatch and didn't bring the boat in until way after dark. (Which is something we don't recommend doing unless you know the river very, very well or have owl vision, as Tom does.)

Fall: Mid-September to Mid-November

Once again anglers will see the ghost fly and white fly hatches, and once again every fish in the river will be up. During the late fall, anglers will also encounter the return of the blue-winged olive and midge hatches. A technique that we often use when fishing the fall *Baetis* hatch incorporates the use of two flies and two fishing methods in the same drift. Attach a BWO dry of your choice to the end of your tippet,

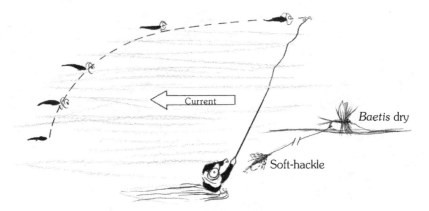

Current

Baetis dry

Soft-hackle

Wet-fly swing (Baetis dry and soft-hackle)

1. Cast up to rising fish, making sure to obtain a drag-free float;
2. Allow the fly to swing across the current in front of downstream rising fish.

then hang a small soft-hackle off it about eighteen to twenty-four inches away. Make your presentation to a fish or general area as you would make a dry-fly presentation and fish the dry as you normally would, with a drag-free drift. However, when the dry starts to drag, usually the signal to pick up and recast, allow it to continue to float downstream. Here the soft-hackle comes into play—by allowing this set-up to continue on its way we, are fishing the soft-hackle in the old wet-fly style. Strikes will come as the soft-hackle swings through the current. After the line has straightened out below you, you can make a new cast. A drawback of this technique is that the fish are positioned downstream of you, and when you attempt to set the hook you can pull it out of the fish's mouth or away from the fish. You'll receive many more strikes than solid hook-ups. Instead of striking, all you need do is simply tighten the line. This is an excellent technique for working flats and tailouts.

Also, during the fall anglers can fish a series of nymphs and streamers with sinking lines or shooting heads with excellent results. There are some truly large trout down in this section of river. The angler looking for that "fish of a lifetime" might consider spending some time down here streamer-fishing the large pools common to this area. You never know—besides, it's kind of fun when some other species of fish whacks your offering.

For us this section of river is a fair drive, and it is "pushing the envelope." However, we have never fished here and been disappointed. The mystery and allure of this unexplored section of the Yellowstone is something we find hard to resist. It concludes our journey down the river, and we hope that you will find this book as interesting to read as we did to write.

Locally Effective Patterns

Baetis Soft-Hackle

Hook:	Tiemco 101, sizes 14–20
Thread:	Olive
Ribbing:	Fine copper wire
Abdomen:	Olive thread
Thorax:	Olive-brown dubbing
Hackle:	Hungarian partridge soft-hackle

Whitey

Hook:	Tiemco 100, sizes 10–16
Thread:	White
Tails:	Two white deer hairs, unclipped from the body
Abdomen:	White deer hair
Wing:	White deer hair, ends of the body hair, upright as a post
Thorax:	Light gray dubbing
Hackle:	Grizzly, parachute-style

PR Double Bunny

Hook: Tiemco 5263, sizes 1/0–8
Thread: Brown
Body: Brown rabbit strip over
          yellow rabbit strip
Sides: Five or six strands of
          orange Krystal Flash
          laid along the body
          where the lateral line
          would be
Eyes: Doll eyes, glued on

Tom's Trico Spinner

Hook: Tiemco 101, sizes 18–22
Thread: Black
Tails: Three moose body hairs, split
Abdomen: Natural dark moose mane,
          soaked and wrapped
Wings: White hackle, wrapped
          tightly in the wing area,
          one size larger
Thorax: Sheared black muskrat
          dubbing, used in a crisscross
          manner to form the wings

Tom's Trico Para-Nymph Emerger

Hook: Tiemco 100, sizes 18–22
Thread: Olive
Tails: Three to five olive
          pheasant-tail fiber
Rib: Fine copper wire,
          reverse-wrap
Abdomen: Olive pheasant-tail fibers
Wing case
  and post: Orvis Sparkle Wing
          #60 clear
Thorax: Light olive sheared
          muskrat dubbing
Hackle: Black, parachute-style,
          one size under

Tom's Ghost Fly

Hook: Tiemco 101, sizes 10–12
Thread: Cream
Body
extension: .017 Maxima monofilament
Tails: Cream micro Fibetts
Rib: One or two strands of pearl
            Krystal Flash
Abdomen   Scintilla dubbing #12 honey
            cream and Scintilla dubbing
            #40 transparent white,
            mixed evenly
Wing post: Cream Antron body wool
Thorax: Dubbed same as abdomen
Hackle: Cream, parachute-style

Other Effective Patterns

White Drake
Ghost Fly
Trico Spinner
Whit Hopper
Royal Wulff
White Wulff
Mouserat
Blue-Winged Olive Parachute
Griffith Gnat

Gartside Olive Soft-Hackle Streamer
Black Sparkle Sapsucker
Olive-Eyed Bunny Bug
Whit's Purple Hare Water Pup
Western Feather Streamer Olive
Whit's Silver Multi-Colored Marabou
Drowned Mouserat
Byford's White Zonker
Lite Spruce Streamer
Black Stone Rubber Legs

11

The Best of the River

We are often asked where and when we fish over the course of the season. What follows is a month-by-month account of where we would fish if we had our druthers for an average year. Obviously, there are many variables, such as water flows, weather patterns, and so on, that are very different from year to year and will affect our choices. We will offer our opinions of the best places to fish over the course of what could be considered an average year. Some months offer a wide variety of opportunities, so we will offer only our mutually agreed upon first two choices. Yes, we have had some minor discussions, and we each have reluctantly compromised on occasion in an attempt to offer you accurate selections. Here they are:

January

January is a month where we are hoping the temperature of winter moderates so we can go fish. However, there are winters when all we can do is sit around and watch the NFL play-offs and the Super Bowl. In those years when the weather cooperates we find ourselves in the Ninth Street island back-channels fishing nymphs.

February

There is rarely a February where we don't get a warming trend. This will bring us out of the tying room looking for the midge hatches. One of our favorite areas to fish the midge hatches is in the

Pine Creek channels. They have flats, back-eddies, and good riffle water for nymphing if we happen to miss the midges.

March

March brings us more days to fish as the weather moderates. However, be careful—winter hasn't totally gone. March brings a continuation of the midge hatches as well as the start of the blue-winged olives. Also during March the nymphing activity picks up. For this action we like the Mayor's-Landing-to-89-bridge section. There are excellent flats to work during the hatches and plenty of good riffle corners.

April

The month of April will find us somewhere between Mallard's Rest and Carter's Bridge. Early in the month the annual rainbow spawning run is underway, and the fishing off the mouth of the three local spring creeks can be awesome. You also have a continuation of the blue-winged olives and midges, and this section has plenty of back-eddies, riprap banks, and flats to work. By mid-April the western march browns will appear. It is best to fish these insects below riffles, and this section has many. By late April the caddis hatch starts, and there is then no better section than this to be on.

May

We will take what we can get during May and finish the caddis on the Mallard's-Rest-to-Carter's-Bridge section. Generally the river goes out and becomes unfishable around the tenth of May due to the annual runoff. Now we go find another river!

June

Through much of June the river is still unfishable and you will find us fishing other waters. However, by late June the river starts to

drop and the salmon fly hatch begins. During late June you can normally find us on the Gardiner-to-Yankee-Jim section chasing the salmon flies. During this same time we will have an eye out for the green drakes.

July

This is a tough month to decide where to fish because so much of the river fishes very well during the month. Early July could still find us in the Gardiner-to-Yankee-Jim section fishing the salmon fly hatch. We might also be found chasing the hatch up the Black Canyon. However, we always spend a few days this time of year between Yankee Jim and Emigrant fishing the many hatches this area offers. After mid-July we would prefer to be on the Yellowstone above Yellowstone Falls. This section of the river has some truly incredible hatches and fishing opportunities.

August

During August you can always find us in the Sheep-Mountain-to-Big-Timber or Big-Timber-to-Reedpoint sections. The big attraction is the *super* hopper fishing these sections offer. There are some other good hatches that we like to fish in these sections, but the hopper fishing is the headliner!

September

September is another month where we divide up our time. Early September might find us on the river above Yellowstone Falls, stalking individual fish and challenging the selectivity of the cutthroats. Midmonth will often find us fishing close to Reedpoint, where we can fish the Trico hatches in the morning and work the streamer pools in the afternoon.

October

October means spawning brown trout, and we will divide our time between the Grey-Bear-to-Otter-Creek and Mallard's-Rest-to-Carter's-Bridge sections. It is in these two sections that our favorite streamer pools are located. Often we take time off from fishing the streamers to work a midge or blue-winged olive hatch along one of the riprap banks or below the mouths of the spring creeks. However, we will always save a couple of days to travel down to the lower river and fish the ghost fly hatch.

November

On a year-in-year-out basis, this is the month of wind, along with the first real storms of winter. During November we may wander the river, spending a day wherever our mood takes us. In very early November we may spend a day on the river above Yellowstone Falls to close out the season in the park, knowing that it will be many months before we can return to this favorite water. Mid-November may find us fishing a midge hatch around LaDuke Hot Spring or fishing streamers and big nymphs through some of our favorite streamer pools. Late in November, weather permitting, you might find us working the Pine Creek channels or nymphing in the Ninth Street side channels.

December

Once again weather is the determining factor. Some years find us sitting behind the fly-tying table creating patterns for the next season. As for other anglers, December brings lots of other events that take our time. Rod is normally found at the drawing table plying his craft as an outstanding illustrator. Tom has no such talents, so he spends his time figuring out how he can talk Rod into another book. Merry Christmas!

APPENDIX A
List of Insects by Common Name

American grannom . . . . *Brachycentrus americanus*
Ants (black, cinnamon) . . . . Formicidae
Aquatic worms . . . . Annelida
Black beetle . . . . Coleoptera
Blue-winged olive . . . . *Baetis tricaudatus*
Cranefly larva . . . . Tipulidae
Crickets . . . . Gryllidae
Damselfly . . . . Zygoptera
Dragonflies . . . . Odonata
Early grannom . . . . *Brachycentrus occidentalis*
Ghost fly . . . . *Traverella albertana*
Giant western red quill . . . . *Ephemerella hecuba*
Giant western golden stone . . . . *Claassenia sabulosa*
Golden stone . . . . *Calineuria californica*
Grasshoppers . . . . Acrididae
Gray drake . . . . *Siphlonurus occidentalis*
Green sedge . . . . *Rhyacophila bifila*
Leeches . . . . Hirudinea
Little olive stones . . . . *Alloperla* species
Little sister sedge . . . . *Cheumatopsyche campyla*
Little brown sedge . . . . *Lepidostoma veleda*
Little olive stone . . . . *Alloperla signata*
Little western weedy-water sedge   *Amiocentrus aspilus*
Long horn sedge . . . . *Oecetis avara*
Mahogany dun . . . . *Paraleptophlebia bicornuta*
Midge . . . . Chironomidae
Olive stone . . . . *Isogenus elongatus*
Olive stone . . . . *Isogenus* species
Olive/brown stone . . . . *Isogenus tostonus*
Pale morning dun . . . . *Ephemerella inermis*
Plain brown sedge . . . . *Lepidostoma pluviale*
Salmon fly . . . . *Pteronarcys californica*
Scuds . . . . *Hyallela azteca*
Shrimp/scuds . . . . *Gammarus lacustris*

Small western green drake . . . . *Drunella flavilinea*
Small golden stone . . . . *Hesperoperla pacifica*
Small western dark hendrickson   *E. tibialis*
Small western red quill. . . . . *Rhithrogena undulata*
Small western salmon fly . . . . *Pteronacella badia*
Snails . . . . Gastropoda
Sowbug . . . . *Asellus communis*
Speckled peter caddis . . . . *Helicopsyche borealis*
Speckled wing dun . . . . *Callibaetis nigritus*
Spotted sedge. . . . . *Hydropsyche cockerelli*
Spotted sedge . . . . *Hydropsyche occidentalis*
Tan short horn sedge (little) . . . . *Glossosoma velona*
Trico . . . . *Tricorythodes minutus*
Water beetles . . . . Heteroptera
Western green drake. . . . . *Drunella grandis*
Western march brown . . . . *Rhithrogena morrisoni*
Western yellow drake . . . . *Heptagenia elegantula*
Western black quill . . . . *Rhithrogena undulata*
White fly. . . . . *Ephoron album*
Yellow sally . . . . *Isoperla* species
Yellow sally . . . . *Isoperla mormona*

APPENDIX B
List of Insects by Latin (Taxonomic) Name

Acrididae . . . . Grasshoppers
Alloperla signata . . . . Little olive stone
Alloperla species . . . . Little olive stones
Amiocentrus aspilus. . . . . Little western weedy-water sedge
Annelida. . . . . Aquatic worms
Asellus communis . . . . Sowbug
Baetis tricaudatus . . . . Blue-winged olive
Brachycentrus americanus. . . . . American grannom
Brachycentrus occidentalis. . . . . Early grannom

Calineuria californica . . . . Golden stone
Callibaetis nigritus . . . . Speckled wing dun
Cheumatopsyche campyla . . . . Little sister sedge
Chironomidae . . . . Midge
Claassenia sabulosa . . . . Giant western golden stone
Coleoptera . . . . Black beetle
Drunella flavilinea . . . . Small western green drake
Drunella grandis . . . . Western green drake
E. tibialis . . . . Small western dark hendrickson
Ephemerella hecuba . . . . Giant western red quill
Ephemerella inermis . . . . Pale morning dun
Ephoron album . . . . White fly
Formicidae . . . . Ants (black, cinnamon)
Gammarus lacustris . . . . Shrimp/scuds
Gastropoda . . . . Snails
Glossosoma velona . . . . Tan short horn sedge (little)
Gryllidae . . . . Crickets
Helicopsyche borealis . . . . Speckled peter caddis
Heptagenia elegantula . . . . Western yellow drake
Hesperoperla pacifica . . . . Small golden stone
Heteroptera . . . . Water beetles
Hirudinea . . . . Leeches
Hyallela azteca . . . . Scuds
Hydropsyche cockerelli . . . . Spotted sedge
Hydropsyche occidentalis . . . . Spotted sedge
Isogenus elongatus . . . . Olive stone
Isogenus species . . . . Olive stone
Isogenus tostonus . . . . Olive/brown stone
Isoperla mormona . . . . Yellow sally
Isoperla species . . . . Yellow sally
Lepidostoma pluviale . . . . Plain brown sedge
Lepidostoma veleda . . . . Little brown sedge
Odonata . . . . Dragonflies
Oecetis avara . . . . Long horn sedge
Paraleptophlebia bicornuta . . . . Mahogany dun
Pteronacella badia . . . . Small western salmon fly

Pteronarcys californica . . . . Salmon fly
Rhithrogena morrisoni . . . . Western march brown
Rhithrogena undulata . . . . Western black quill
Rhithrogena undulata. . . . . Small western red quill
Rhyacophila bifila . . . . Green sedge
Siphlonurus occidentalis. . . . . Gray drake
Tipulidae . . . . Cranefly larva
Traverella albertana . . . . Ghost fly
Tricorythodes minutus . . . . Trico
Zygoptera . . . . Damselfly

Index

311